Wolverhamp

Great War

1914 - 1921

Edited by
Quintin Watt

First published in Great Britain in 2019
by The Wolverhampton Society

A CIP catalogue record for this book is available from the British Library.

PROUDLY
PROMOTING
WOLVERHAMPTON

ISBN 978-1-9162901-0-5 Paperback

Printed by Wombourne Printers Ltd,
Smestow Bridge, Bridgnorth Road, Wombourne
Wolverhampton, WV5 8AY

This book is dedicated to the people of Wolverhampton whose lives were touched by the Great War and to the generations that followed; preserving their legacy.

Cover Illustrations

Front cover image: *First Aid Tent*, c.1915 – lithograph by Sir Frank Brangwyn (1867-1956). Brangwyn was an Anglo-Welsh artist born in Belgium. Self-taught, he produced more than 12,000 works during his lifetime ranging from murals, oil paintings, water colours and etchings to designs for furniture, ceramics and jewellery. He was also an accomplished illustrator, creating book plates and posters. Brangwyn was made an official war artist during the Great War, gaining repute through his propaganda posters. Working in his London studio he relied on photographs from news agencies and illustrations from newspapers and periodicals for reference material. *First Aid Tent* is one of a set of six lithographic prints from Brangwyn's series titled *At the Front*, which was printed as a set of charity stamps for the *Daily Mail* and *Evening News* in 1915. Brangwyn was particularly recognised for his war art. He became a Royal Academician in 1919 and was awarded a knighthood in 1941. *First Aid Tent* probably came into the possession of Wolverhampton Art Gallery when the artist donated many of his pictures to galleries in industrial cities across the UK.

This illustration is used courtesy of Wolverhampton Art Gallery and with the kind permission of David Brangwyn.

Text by Carol Thompson.

Frontispiece and back cover image: *Competition drawing for Wolverhampton War Memorial*, c.1922 – sketch by Robert Jackson Emerson (1878-1944). Born in Leicestershire, Emerson was appointed Second Master at Wolverhampton Municipal School of Art in 1910 – at that time located on Wulfruna Street, at the rear of the Art Gallery. Alongside his teaching, Emerson maintained a professional artistic practice and accepted commissions for public sculptures, most notably the memorial for Able Seaman Douglas Morris Harris in St. Peter's Gardens. He also created the marble sculpture *War Memorial (He Is Risen)* which originally stood in the main entrance of Queen Street Congregational Church. This image, from Emerson's unsuccessful submission for Wolverhampton's main war memorial, depicts a young girl handing an offering to a marching soldier. The sketch is a plan for a bronze plaque that would have decorated the south side of the monument. A corresponding frieze, depicting a group of soldiers standing over a fallen comrade, was intended for the north side. The Wolverhampton Coat of Arms was to feature on the east face, with a wreath on the west.

This illustration is used courtesy of Wolverhampton Art Gallery.

Text by Andrew Yarnold.

Wolverhampton's Great War, 1914 - 1921

Contents

Wolverhampton's Great War, 1914 - 1921

Foreword
Dr John Bourne

A knowledge of history breeds familiarity and familiarity stales the mind. Because we know what happened during the Great War we have lost the sense of how astonishing it all was.

The first thing to be astonished about is that the war happened at all. There have always been people, then and since, prepared to argue that the war was somehow 'inevitable', even expected. This was not how it felt in the summer of 1914. The British government was concerned about war alright, but it was a civil war in Ireland not a great European war. Only during the last week in July did the situation on the continent become alarming following the publication of the Austrian ultimatum to Serbia. From that moment, despite the best efforts of the British Foreign Secretary, Sir Edward Grey, the descent into war proved unstoppable. The descent was regarded with dismay in many circles in Britain, but the German violation of Belgian neutrality virtually removed dissent overnight and gave the war the character of one of 'liberation', 'the holy war of English liberalism', as one American observer called it.

If the fact of war was a surprise, the enemy was not. Since 1900 British foreign policy had been successfully focused on 'squaring off' a series of potential threats to the British Empire, from Japan, France and Russia. No one thought a war against the United States was a good idea. That really left only Germany as a possible enemy. Except it didn't. The second surprising thing is how quickly the war expanded beyond that of an Anglo-German conflict, largely as a result of British actions. Within weeks of the outbreak of war, Britain also found itself at war with Austria-Hungary (certainly no threat to the British Empire), seemingly on the basis of my 'enemy's friend is my enemy', and, even more amazingly, with the Ottoman Empire, the upholding of which had been a cardinal element of British diplomacy for much of the nineteenth century. This rapid extension of the war greatly complicated it politically, strategically and logistically at a time when British ability to cope with a one-front war was strictly limited. A war that had been entered as one of 'liberation' would result in one of the greatest expansions of British imperial territory in history.

But it was the nature of the war on which Britain had embarked that was the most astonishing. In the decade before the outbreak of the Great War there had been huge improvements in British military capability. The Royal Navy had pioneered the 'Dreadnought revolution' and was, by 1914, one of the most powerful instruments for 'force projection' in the world, possibly in history. The army, although a poor relation, had also undergone significant reforms in doctrine, training, weaponry and kit, though its numbers remained small. The Territorial Force had been established for home defence, allowing an expeditionary force of six infantry divisions and a cavalry division (the BEF) to be made available for possible continental operations. Arrangements for the mobilisation of the expeditionary force were co-ordinated across government departments and with the privately owned and run railways, and practised annually. A Defence of the Realm Act (DORA) had been placed on the statute book, giving the government significant powers of compulsion in a 'national emergency'. It is arguable, therefore, that Britain was 'ready for war' by 1914. But the war for which the country was ready was not the war in which it soon found itself. The war for which Britain was prepared was based on naval power. The Royal Navy would sweep the seas of hostile shipping, render the nation impregnable to invasion, guarantee British food supplies and establish a crushing economic blockade of the enemy. The British military contribution would be confined to the despatch of the expeditionary force, which was seen principally as a gesture of allied political solidarity. No one (except possibly the deluded Major-General Henry Wilson) expected the BEF to 'win the war'. These comfortable assumptions proved equally delusional, however, following the appointment of Field-Marshal Lord Kitchener as Secretary of State for War on 5 August 1914.

Kitchener's impact was immediate, decisive and fundamental. He declared that Britain must raise a mass army and keep it in the field for at least three years. His declaration was met with very little Cabinet scrutiny, no parliamentary scrutiny and almost no public debate. It was acted on within days. This changed everything and gave us the war we know, a war of huge armies, huge casualties and huge cost that required the full mobilisation of the nation's financial, economic, industrial, manpower and 'moral' resources. Virtually every part of the country, all social classes and most families would experience the consequences of this mobilisation, not least in the industrial town of Wolverhampton and its environs. As Lady Cynthia Asquith, daughter-in-law of the prime minister, put it, 'history had rudely intruded into personal life'.

The Great War was to be a war of the masses and of the classes. This lent importance to it in the eyes of social historians. Arthur Marwick's seminal account of 1965, *The Deluge: British Society and the First World War*, which is still in print, popularised a view of mass war as an agent of social change, weakening traditional values and institutions, effecting changes within and between classes, rationalising industrial structures and processes, increasing the power and influence of trades unions, widening the scope of taxation, greatly augmenting the power and ambition of the state, making central the issue of child health and welfare, and improving opportunities for women. This was an entrancing account, which chimed with many social changes in post-1960s Britain but, as I have grown older, I have become increasingly dubious about it. Traditional values – Christian belief, concepts of duty, honour and sacrifice, patriotism and stoicism - proved stubbornly resilient and were central to British ability to endure the challenge of war. Some women may have seen employment in war-related industries or transport as an escape from drudgery and

2

poverty, but the main role of women during the war was as mothers and wives and their main employment remained domestic service. The lives of women in the domestic sphere were sometimes eased by the payment of 'separation allowances' from the pay of their soldier husbands. This came direct to them and gave them greater economic control of the family budget, but the full emotional impact of the war's human costs fell principally on women and must be weighed in the balance. Working-class women had also to fend off the increasingly intrusive interference of middle-class 'do-gooders' who thought they knew best how to bring up children and keep house. The lack of a national system of rationing until the summer of 1918 also put the queue at the heart of the war experience of women. Whatever this was, it was not 'liberating'.

These reservations are not to diminish the impact of the conflict, which is apparent on virtually every page of this account of Wolverhampton's war. Wolverhampton's contribution was immense both on the war fronts and the Home Front. Staffordshire was the greatest supporter of the Territorial Force before 1914. Staffordshire's Territorial battalions, which were sorely used in 1915 and 1916, endured to play a key role in breaking the German 'Hindenburg Line' in September 1918. The South Staffordshire Regiment also had two Regular battalions, one of which (the 2nd) was immediately in action on the Western Front and was soon joined by the other. Three New Army battalions followed, seeing service at Gallipoli, on the Western Front and in Italy. Wolverhampton was also one of the first places in British history to experience the impact, more psychological than physical, of aerial bombardment. The town was a major centre for the manufacture of munitions. Its traditional 'metal bashing' industries quickly adapted to the demands of war. Sankeys alone produced some 5.5 million steel helmets, as well as aircraft parts, mortars, rifle grenades and field kitchens. Nearby Wednesbury manufactured 75 per cent of the tanks first used in war on 15 September 1916. Much of this industrial effort rested on the mining of coal, which not only fuelled British industry, but also the industry of Britain's allies, as well as powering domestic heating and transport. Wolverhampton was a major transport hub and the vital role of the railways is vividly illustrated in Quintin Watt's chapter. The willingness of Wolverhampton's population to support the war effort is also apparent, not least in Richard Pursehouse's account of 'Tank Week'. Given the view of the war that emerged in the 1930s and was reinforced in the 1960s, it is now often difficult to understand the level of popular support that the war received at the time. This was not the result of propaganda. The local Press, so much more important then than now, was barely subject to censorship and no one reading the pages of the *Express & Star* could be in any doubt about the true nature of the war. This is, perhaps, the final and most astonishing thing about the war.

The recent centenaries of the Great War have once again placed it in the mainstream of British consciousness. One of the most impressive aspects of British culture is the widespread and tenacious survival of the 'voluntary principle', despite huge increases in the power and intrusiveness of the state. 'Volunteering' is at the heart of what political scientists call 'civil society', the world of clubs, associations and more informal groups, encompassing a multitude of human endeavours, free of government control and unmoved by the 'profit motive'. The most impressive aspect of British remembrance and commemoration of the Great War in the past five or so years has been the involvement of local people working to their own agendas. Britain is a much more impressive country when it is viewed bottom-up rather than top-down. This book is firmly located in this tradition. Its editors should be congratulated in not seeking to impose a list of topics to be covered or insisting on a uniform length for contributions. This means that the book truly reflects the way in which the war resonates among 'ordinary people'. The First World War was a global event with global consequences, many of which are still with us today, but the impact of the war on the lives of individuals, families and local communities should not be lost among the geo-politics. This book is a welcome contribution to that survival. I salute the editors and their contributors.

John Bourne
University of Wolverhampton
September 2019

New recruits marching down Lichfield Street towards Wolverhampton Station, 2 September 1914.
Photograph courtesy of Wolverhampton Archives & Local Studies.

Wolverhampton's Great War, 1914 - 1921

Introduction

Quintin Watt

When the Great War began Ronald Towers Minors was a twenty-one-year-old accountant living at 56 Tettenhall Road, Wolverhampton. Like many of his pals, this eager young man enlisted into the 7th Battalion of the Worcestershire Regiment and by August 1915 had been promoted to the rank of Second Lieutenant. Possibly in pursuit of more adventure Minors transferred to the Royal Flying Corps and by the end of the war was a Captain with 18 Squadron, Royal Air Force. After the Armistice his duties included carrying the Post between Great Britain and its victorious army, now deployed as an army of occupation in western Germany. For this purpose an airmail corridor was established between Folkestone and Cologne. However, on Thursday, 27 March 1919 Captain Minors' DH9A aeroplane was caught in a sudden snowstorm while flying over Belgium. In an open cockpit the young pilot struggled to keep control of his aircraft and was forced to make an emergency landing at Profondeville, south-east of Brussels. He successfully managed to crash-land but was so badly injured in the process that he died later the same day. Although Captain Minors had no connection with the scene of this tragic accident he was buried, as was the custom, in the nearest British cemetery – Belgrade Military Cemetery at Namur. It is not known whether any of the family attended his funeral or visited his grave but when Minors' headstone was being prepared, his grieving mother chose a single word to be added as the personal inscription on its base. That word was:

"WOLVERHAMPTON."

This book was conceived in the autumn of 2017 during discussions about marking the centenary of the end of the Great War in Captain Minors' home town. At that time members of the Wolverhampton Civic and Historical Society (WC&HS) were considering projects to commemorate the centenary of the Armistice.[1] It was decided to open out these discussions to members of the wider public and an initial meeting was held at the City Archives in February 2018. Unfortunately this event coincided with the arrival of the *'Beast from the East'* arctic weather phenomenon and was not well-attended. However, a second meeting at Wolverhampton Civic Centre produced a number of ideas for discussion. These included: a Wolverhampton digital street map pinpointing the homes of military personnel who died in the war, local information/noticeboards showing names (and pictures) of people from specific districts who died, creating individual poppies to display in relatives' windows, arranging guided tours of war graves in local cemeteries – also producing leaflets to help people carry out their own self-guided tours of these sites - and holding dramatic

---

[1] The WC&HS is now part of The Wolverhampton Society.

re-creations of some of the actual events in Wolverhampton on Armistice Day 1918. Finally, there was a proposal to write a book on Wolverhampton in the Great War – probably articles or essays by local authors based on their particular interests and specialisms. Wolverhampton Council officers also outlined their commemorative plans and agreed to set up an online 'noticeboard' – to publicise all First World War-related events and help prevent repetition or clashes. By June 2018 the WC&HS 'long list' of suggested projects was whittled down to three firm proposals: the production of household Blue Plaques incorporating a poppy design, arranging visits to local war graves and memorials along with printing a leaflet/map to help visitors carry out self-guided tours of these sites and writing a book about Wolverhampton in the Great War. The war memorial map was duly completed, three guided city-centre war memorial walks took place - between June and November 2018 - and the mini Blue Plaque finally emerged as a fridge magnet - available from the Wolverhampton Society. In summer 2018 authors known to have an interest in the Great War were contacted to ask if they would like to contribute to the book, along with others who responded to media coverage of the project. In this way the writing team was recruited and the process of writing the book began.

'What you leave behind is not what is engraved on stone monuments, but what is woven into the lives of others.' Pericles.

It is hoped the book that has now been produced will serve as an educational 'war memorial' – to prompt and support future research into the Great War locally, keeping alive its memory in the collective consciousness of succeeding generations of Wulfrunians. This volume is meant to inspire others to write their own histories and to be the first of many words on the subject, not the last. This aspiration fulfils a key aim of the Wolverhampton Society - to encourage local people to become actively engaged in researching and recording their history. As it appears there is no other general history of Wolverhampton in the Great War, this volume also attempts to fill a significant gap in our knowledge. By including a bibliography listing all known existing sources it also aims to provide a starting point for future writers.

As the story of Captain Ronald Minors has already illustrated, the Great War did not end on 11 November 1918 and Wulfrunians continued to fight and die long after hostilities ceased on the Western Front. Corporal Samuel Hill from Heath Town was killed in action on 10 August 1919. This twenty-two-year-old lost his life with the 45th Battalion Royal Fusiliers, North Russia Relief Force, fighting Trotsky's Red Army. His name is recorded on the Archangel Memorial. A tour of Wolverhampton's Municipal Cemetery in Jeffcock Road also reveals that forty-eight (42%) of its 115 military graves from the Great War period are of people who died *after* 11 November 1918. This includes John Wilkinson of the South Staffordshire Regiment who died of pulmonary tuberculosis on 21 July 1921. His interment appears to have been the final Great War burial in the Wolverhampton area - a month before the official end of the *'war service'* period stipulated by the Commonwealth War Graves Commission – 31 August 1921. For this reason, as well as having several chapters deal with significant events in the three years after the Armistice, an end date of 1921 has been identified as this book's official conclusion.

A thorny issue was deciding the book's exact geographical parameters - what constitutes Wolverhampton? Restricting chapters to the 1918 city limits might have resulted in just a leaflet, not a book. So the broadest possible definition of Wolverhampton was accepted – including everywhere with a modern WV postcode and beyond! Consequently, it would be more accurate, but far too clumsy, to call this book 'Wolverhampton, and anywhere within a ten mile radius of the modern city's, Great War'. As a result some chapters contain material from across south Staffordshire and the Black Country, including towns such as Dudley and Walsall, where locals baulk at being linked to Wolverhampton. Much heat and passion is generated in this region by arguments about historical geography.[2] The authors appreciate that a century ago Tiptonians and Bilstonians would have felt an even stronger sense of local identity than they do now, so we apologise in advance for trespassing on long-held geographical sensibilities. We genuinely hope our work will encourage much greater scrutiny of the microhistory of communities across the area.

Historians trying to write a comprehensive history of Wolverhampton in the Great War are also faced by the problem of a lack of accessible sources. What they really need is the discovery of a yet undisclosed cache of documents to help create a structure around which to build such a narrative. For example, there appear to be few contemporary memoirs of town life during the war – at least none yet uncovered or published. Why did local luminaries like Sir Charles Wheeler (1892-1974), Albert Bantock (1862-1938) or Emma Sproson (1867-1936) not keep a detailed record of their lives during this momentous period? Notable exceptions include Roy C. Evans' excellent *Wolverhampton Warriors* – focusing on men of the South Staffordshire Regiment - and the superb online history, *Wolverhampton's War – Lost voices from the Great War* by Heidi McIntosh - one of our authors. What follows here is an eclectic mix of chapters, rather than an all-embracing account of the war in Wolverhampton. It balances detailed chapters based on extensive knowledge of a specific topic with shorter more personal contributions linked to family history research. Historical investigations of all kind have flourished in the past twenty years thanks to the internet and websites such as Ancestry, Findmypast and the British Newspaper Archive. The authors have selected their own way to identify their sources; including direct reference in the text, footnotes or a brief bibliography at the end of their chapter.

As editor I would like to thank everyone involved in writing the book and the core team of authors who also assisted with proof-reading and correcting. In particular, Jim Barrow - 'The Butcher of Burslem' - deployed his outstanding editorial skills to improve readability of the text and track down additional information for almost every chapter. While we have tried to ensure the content is as accurate as possible, we know some errors will have slipped through unnoticed. For those unintended mistakes, we humbly apologise.

---

[2] For instance, is Wolverhampton in the Black Country?

Authors' Details

Jim Barrow was born and grew up in Burslem, Stoke-on-Trent, but has lived and worked in Wolverhampton for the past forty years. His education began in the Potteries but only semi-ended at Keele University, because he believes you never stop learning. He retired from being a newspaper sub-editor but employs his *'Butcher of Burslem'* skills on history of all kinds. His interest in Great War memorial trees was sparked by entries about them in the logbook of Wolverhampton Higher Grade School, Dunkley Street, Whitmore Reans - now Newhampton Arts Centre (NAC). Jim is vice-chair of the NAC board as well as a board member at Central Youth Theatre (CYT) - also based there. CYT have made many theatre, film, videos and workshop productions about Wolverhampton and Black Country history. He is a member, friend and/or supporter of local groups, including: Wolverhampton Archives, the Art Gallery & Museum, Bantock House & Park, Tettenhall Transport Heritage Centre, the Light House Media Centre & Cinema, and the Wolverhampton Society.

Gornal's John Hale has had a life-long interest in military aviation which prompted his chapter about some of the many Black Country lads, like Ronald Minors, who found adventure in the skies. The internet helped him carry out research that would have only been dreamt of twenty years ago and uncover the stories of local airmen in the Great War.

Heidi McIntosh was born in Berlin and lived in the United States, as well as various UK locations before settling in Wolverhampton. She studied History at the University of Edinburgh and completed her Masters in Archives and Records Management at University College, London. Heidi has worked in the field of archives and records management for nearly twenty years and has been Wolverhampton City Archivist since 2010. As well as articles in the *Black Country Bugle* and *ARC* magazine (published by the Archives & Records Association) her book, *Wolverhampton in Old Photographs*, was published in 2013. She is interested in all kinds of history but particularly likes individual and personal stories touching on everyday lives. The subject of her chapter followed the deposit of a unique white feather letter to the archives, and her subsequent research to uncover its historical context.

Mick Powis has always lived in Wolverhampton. Educated as a mature student at Coleg Harlech, Aberystwyth University, Warwick University and Wolverhampton University, he worked as an engineer, social worker and Open University lecturer. Mick first heard about the Zeppelin air raids as a small boy when his grandmother told him, *"you know you are lucky to be here."* She then recounted sheltering in a doorway with his mother – then a baby - as bombs dropped around them. After many years wanting to find out more Mick wrote an article about these events for the Wolverhampton *Express & Star* on the eightieth anniversary of the Zeppelin raids. Since then he has written several newspaper and magazine articles on subjects relating to both world wars, as well as two books on the Zeppelin raids:

Zeppelins over the Midlands, 2016, and *Defeat of the Zeppelins*, 2018, both published by Pen and Sword.

Richard Pursehouse grew up in Cannock, Staffordshire, and obtained a degree at Middlesex University. He is a regular contributor to the Staffordshire Newsletter, Sunday Mercury, Black Country Bugle and Western Front Association journals. Richard has written articles on a variety of topics but most have a military theme. His particular interest is the New Zealand Rifle Brigade and its Brocton depot on Cannock Chase and he was involved in the installation of a new information panel at the Great War Hut at the visitors centre, in May 2019. Richard has written a forthcoming book about the Great War German Prisoner of War camp on Cannock Chase, and at the time of writing was working on one about the Messines Ridge model and another about local Victoria Cross recipients.

Beverley Reynolds grew up in Smethwick but is now based in Halesowen. After graduating she became a secondary school History teacher. Her chapter was prompted by old family photographs which sparked an interest in genealogy that has kept her busy researching her own family history for more than ten years. Beverley is particularly interested in her ancestors who served during the Great War and has made several visits to France and Belgium to further her research.

Roy Stallard was born and grew up in Springfield, Wolverhampton, where he attended St. Stephen's Primary and Springfield Road Secondary Schools. Before National Service in 1952 he worked at Baker's Nursery Landscape Department. After leaving the Royal Army Medical Corps (RAMC) in 1954 Roy trained to become a State Registered Nurse at Wolverhampton's Royal Hospital. After working as Staff Nurse he transferred to the town's Eye Infirmary to train in Ophthalmic Nursing but eventually returned to the Royal where he helped train many new recruits to the nursing profession. Roy was President of Wolverhampton's Nurses League, has written extensively about the city's hospital heritage and appeared in the BBC 2 documentary, Nursing Today. He also served in a Territorial Army medical unit of the RAMC for thirty-five years - for which he was decorated. Roy is still passionate about hospital issues and frequently writes letters commenting about these to local and national newspapers.

David Taylor is mainly interested in economic and social history - particularly relating to the West Midlands in the nineteenth and early twentieth centuries – and was awarded an MA in Local History by the Open University. He has had articles published in the journal, *The Local Historian*, and written two books about the history of South Staffordshire: *The Impact of World War One on the Smestow Vale Villages*, 2017, and *The 1926 General Strike in Wolverhampton and the Black Country*, 2017. David was the award winner at the Wolverhampton City Archives Local History Symposium in 2017.

John Thomas was born in Wolverhampton and developed an academic interest in historic buildings, particularly church architecture, whilst at the Royal

School. He enjoys writing fiction and his novel, *Aubrey Annesley's Lucky Day,* 2016, is in Wolverhampton Libraries. He still lives in Merridale, but only really 'discovered' his grandfather, John Vincent, as the centenary of the Great War approached.

Chris Twiggs was born and grew up in Exeter where he attended Hele's School. He studied at the University of Kent at Canterbury and later at Keele University. After moving to Wolverhampton in 1978, he taught at Dartmouth High School, Great Barr, and Colton Hills Community School, Wolverhampton. He retired in 2009 but has since been a Workers' Educational Association (WEA) tutor - teaching courses on the Great War. He has written for WEA publications, the Black Country Society and Western Front Association. He is an occasional guide, leading parties of school pupils and adults around the French and Belgian battlefields of the Western Front. Chris' interest in the Sankey family and the Great War developed after meeting the late James Sankey about ten years ago.

Quintin Watt is a Londoner who attended Hackney Downs School, studied History at St. David's College - University of Wales, and completed his MA in West Midlands History at the University of Wolverhampton in 1993. Living in the West Midlands since 1979, and Wolverhampton for the past three years, Quintin taught History at South Bromsgrove High School for thirty-nine years. He was editor of *The Bromsgrove Guild – An Illustrated History,* 1999, and held various positions in the Bromsgrove Society's Local History Group. Having retired in 2018 he now helps to run the Wolverhampton Society and is editor of *The Lamp* magazine. He cannot remember a time when he was not interested in the Great War and still has a copy of the school project he produced when it was the fiftieth anniversary of the Armistice! Quintin's mission is to finally discover exactly where his grandfather saw action whilst serving with the Royal Horse Artillery (RHA) and Royal Field Artillery (RFA) between 1915 and 1919.

Ettingshall Park
June 2019.

Chapter 1

Sankeys at War – The Firm and the Family, 1914-18

Chris Twiggs

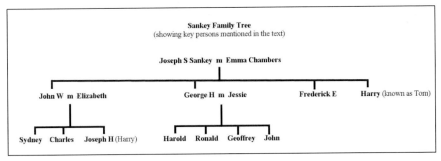

Sankey Family Tree
(showing key persons mentioned in the text)

Joseph S Sankey m Emma Chambers

John W m Elizabeth   George H m Jessie   Frederick E   Harry (known as Tom)

Sydney   Charles   Joseph H (Harry)   Harold   Ronald   Geoffrey   John

The Sankey Family Tree

Part One: The Sankey family and their business before 1914

In the early 1900s the Sankey family was well-established in Wolverhampton and the surrounding area. The family's prosperity was built on the success of their business - *Joseph Sankey and Sons Ltd* - primarily based at Bilston in the Black Country. The company, founded by Joseph in 1854, was simply known as *'Sankeys'* in the local area. Three of his four sons: John, George and Fred went on to work in the business whilst Harry pursued a career in farming. The eldest son, John William Sankey, became company chairman following his father's death in 1886. In the early 1900s John and his wife, Elizabeth, lived at *Claremont*, 43 Penn Road, Wolverhampton with their three sons and three daughters. Their house still stands and at the time of writing was owned by the Royal Wolverhampton School. A few years later the family moved to a new home at the *Foxhills*, near Wombourne, South Staffordshire. John Sankey died suddenly while visiting brother Harry at Manor Farm, Luddington near Stratford-upon-Avon. He was succeeded as company chairman by brother George Herbert Sankey. George regarded this as a temporary measure and fully expected that his nephew Sydney, would eventually take on that role. George was married to Jessie Marie Bantock, a member of another prominent Wolverhampton family. They lived at Finchfield House with their four sons. Brother Fred Sankey also lived locally with his wife and two daughters at *Waterdale,* in the Compton area of Wolverhampton. In the early 1890s John had been joined by George and Fred as directors of the company.

The family business steadily expanded and prospered during the fifty years preceding the outbreak of the Great War and its Albert Street Works (currently the site of Wm. Morrisons supermarket) and Bankfield Works (in Greenway Road, Bradley) employed many people in the Bilston area. In 1904 *Sankeys* acquired the Manor Rolling Mills at Ettingshall from Steven Thompson Ltd and also took over the

Hadley Castle works at Wellington in Shropshire in 1910. The company specialised in making a wide range of metal products from domestic hollow-ware to wheels for motor vehicles. In the years before 1914, *Sankeys'* willingness to take risks and expand into newly emerging markets helped the company embark on a period of *"general expansion and steady profits."* In fact profits only dipped in years of general economic depression or during the coal and railway strikes of 1912 and 1913.

Workers at the Bankfield Works of Joseph Sankey & Sons Ltd. This photograph was probably taken at the end of the Great War. *Photograph courtesy of James Sankey.*

Part Two: The Impact of the Great War on the Business

The initial impact of the outbreak of war in August 1914 was twofold, when two family members quickly became involved in the military campaign. Company director Sydney, son of the late John Sankey, was a junior officer in the 1/6th Battalion of the South Staffordshire Regiment. Harold, George Sankey's eldest son, also enlisted in the same regiment as soon as he completed his education at Wolverhampton Grammar School. A further 342 workers, many of whom were members of the Territorial Force like Sydney Sankey, enlisted immediately or were eventually called up. *Sankeys*, along with fellow local employer Mander Brothers, in Wolverhampton, had encouraged their men to join the Territorials. At first the business suffered as Britain went through the process of shifting to a wartime economy and an increasing number of women were recruited to replace men who enlisted. However, matters improved when the company took on a number of government contracts and produced a wide range of war-related products. After the Ministry of Munitions made *Sankeys* a controlled establishment in 1915 a wide range of items were manufactured for all three branches of the armed services. These included anti-submarine devices, parts for Handley-Page and Vickers aircraft, mortar bombs, rifle grenades and field kitchens for the army. One estimate suggested that by 1918 some 95 per cent of all company production was war-related. Of all the items produced possibly the most important was the Brodie steel helmet for the army. The Brodie became the standard issue helmet for British soldiers from the spring of 1916 and it is estimated that some 5.5 million were produced by the company by the end of the war. Production actually began in 1915 and steadily increased as the war progressed. Many soldiers were saved from serious injury or indeed owed their lives to the helmet.

Although the order books were full it might be expected the war would have boosted *Sankeys* financial fortunes. This did not prove to be the case and Edgar Jones has argued that on balance the Great War was of no commercial benefit to the business. Like much of British industry, machinery and factories were run flat-out during wartime without adequate maintenance or future investment, and there was a price to pay. Also, whilst £95,000 had been set aside to pay an anticipated tax bill, after the war a tax demand for £110,000 was actually received. Edgar Jones believed the tax issue and *"reduced level of profit,"* as the economy reverted to peacetime requirements, probably influenced the Sankey family's decision to sell the business. George and Fred Sankey were mentally and physically exhausted as a result of running the company throughout the war and the human cost to the family and the firm was also significant. Along with the thirty-six employees known to have died whilst serving in the Forces, the firm also lost Sydney John Sankey – the young man being groomed to become the future chief executive. Harold Sankey, who did return from the trenches, was also expected to play a major role in the company. However, he was keen to take up his delayed place at Cambridge before settling into a career with the family business. Consequently, the directors came to the conclusion that the best course of action was to sell the company. Although some of its hollow-ware products might be expected to be less in demand in the 1920s, *Sankeys* pre-war move into manufacturing items for the motor and electrical industries still made it an attractive proposition for potential buyers. In 1919 the company was merged with John Lysaght Ltd and shortly after it became part of the Guest, Keen and Nettlefolds (GKN) group. *Sankeys* company war memorials, originally sited at the Bankfield and other works, are currently housed in St Leonard's Church, Bilston. These record the names of thirty-six employees who died in the Great War, but it is believed the real figure could well be twice that many. Harold, Ron, Geoffrey and Charles Sankey would all go on to work for the company at some point in the 1920s.

Part Three: The Impact of the War - the Sankey Family at Home

A collection of wartime letters have survived in the Sankey family for more than a century and now provide a fascinating insight into life in the household at Finchfield House as well as the increasing demands of war work on George and Fred Sankey. This correspondence, between Second Lieutenant Harold Sankey and other members of his family, mainly covers the period from November 1915 to February 1916 and includes letters written by Harold, his mother and father, but also brother Ron and the younger twins. Several letters detail George Sankey's visits to London for meetings at the Ministry of Munitions, or to Hadfields in Sheffield, regarding supplies of sheet metal for steel helmet production. One refers to demands from the Ministry to increase the production of helmets and giving the go-ahead for the company to manufacture field kitchens for the army. On the domestic front, with Christmas 1915 looming, George had organised the purchase of Christmas trees for the families of employees now serving at the front. Jessie Sankey was also busy running the household, sending an apparently endless supply of parcels to Harold, involving herself with the Red Cross and buying lots of toys for workers' children. She explained in one letter that husband Fred Sankey was very tired and ill and had been told to rest. On 19 December 1915, George wrote to Harold describing yet another visit to Sheffield and commenting that helmet production at Bilston was steadily improving. It was no wonder George was feeling tired as his frequent journeys often involved travelling back to Wolverhampton late in the evening and setting out again early the following day. A letter dated 20 December 1915 included the news that George had hit a pedestrian while driving through Wolverhampton. He proceeded to check the twelve-year-old boy was not badly injured before taking him back to Finchfield House for a wash and meal, before driving him home to explain the situation to the boy's mother.

As Christmas got closer Jessie continued to organise the family celebrations and parcels for Harold. She wrote that steel helmet production at Bilston had reached 6,000 on Christmas Eve, which she believed was a record at that point. Correspondence continued over the Christmas period giving details of events at Finchfield and at the Christmas party organised for the workers' children. George announced that he had sold the family car (a *Nazarro*) and was intent on buying a new and more powerful replacement. He asked for Harold's thoughts about this and whether it would be a good idea to send 1cwt of coal out to him as he had heard fuel supplies to front line troops were being reduced. George subsequently organised the dispatch of a weekly supply of coal to Harold. One can only speculate how this must have increased young Harold's popularity with his fellow officers as it seemed he was the source of no end of home comforts and treats. According to George's letter of 10 January, he had now purchased a new car - a *Dodge* - and was suitably impressed with his purchase. He also expressed hopes that the telephone exchange Ron had sent out to France would be a great success and enquired whether the bottles of *Salutaris* Water were arriving on a regular basis. Mrs Sankey wrote that the cook was leaving - *"so no more cakes"* – and was also concerned that they might lose the gardener in the near future. These concerns were probably prompted by the Military Service Act which introduced conscription in Britain in 1916. Early January saw some of the family travel to the family's property at *Sych Nant* in North Wales. Ron had been unwell and it was hoped that the break would speed his recovery. George joined them for a few days but pressure of work meant he returned to Wolverhampton soon after. Fred Sankey remained unable to work as he was suffering from bronchitis. George was on his travels again; this time to Sheffield for more discussions with Hadfields about the supply of sheet metal for steel helmet production.

Although *Sankeys* were making about 5,000 helmets per day, the Ministry of Munitions continued to press for increased production as it was determined to equip every soldier at the front with this protective headgear. In a letter dated 1 February 1916 George reported to Harold that helmet production reached 6,000 on 27 January and believed *"the whole Army should soon benefit from Albert Street"*. He also commented on the death and destruction in the Black Country resulting from the recent Zeppelin raid. Fortunately *Sankeys* had not been hit. Jessie Sankey was hoping Harold might be granted a period of leave to celebrate his 21st birthday in February, but this was unlikely as he had only recently enjoyed a week's leave in November. Meanwhile he received further updates about developments at Bilston where steel helmet production had increased to 11,000 per day in mid-February. However, the hectic pace of life was having consequences for both Fred and George. Jessie noted in her letters that Fred's recovery was making slow progress and his father had been ordered to rest by the family doctor. There was some concern that he may have contracted diphtheria and because of this Ron was kept off school until the matter was cleared up. It was these health concerns about George and Fred Sankey that eventually led the family to try and get Harold released from military service in 1917. It was felt he could take on part of the burden of leading the firm during the most demanding time in its existence.

In February 1916 Harold received many letters from family and friends on his 21st birthday. George gave his son £1,000 worth of company shares and Ron wrote that he was planning to build a model of an 18 pounder field gun or an electric clock as a present. Fewer letters from Wolverhampton exist after February 1916. Apart from family and business news a few local events are mentioned: details about the introduction of lighting restrictions, rumours from Wolverhampton Grammar School that a master was to be interned, reports of a spy in Wolverhampton, a car in Codsall being shot at by a Voluntary Constable for displaying its headlights and a small earthquake in the area. The twins were disappointed that building work on the new railway at Castlecroft had been suspended for the duration of the war. This was the Great Western line between Brettell Lane, near Brierley Hill, and Oxley Junction, north-west of Wolverhampton. The railway, which passed through Wombourne, was eventually opened in 1925 but a proposed extension to Bridgnorth never materialised. Mrs Sankey also took Ron to see *The Scarlet Pimpernel* at the Grand Theatre in Wolverhampton and reported that it *"was packed, but mostly with the artisan class and scarcely any in evening dress."* Meanwhile George had purchased a new piano for Finchfield House but was quick to reassure Harold that it was definitely not German!

Part Four: The War and Sydney John Sankey

Sydney John Sankey, the eldest son of John and Elizabeth, was born in Wolverhampton on 28 October 1889. He was brought up in the family home in Goldthorn Road and later at Claremont on the Penn Road. In the early 1900s he was a boarder, along with younger brother Charles, at Rydal Penrhos School, Colwyn Bay. As the Sankeys were committed Methodists this explains why their children were sent to the only Methodist boarding school in Britain, rather than Wolverhampton Grammar School. No evidence of Sydney's academic progress survives but it is safe to assume he did well before leaving in 1906. Between 1907 and 1908 he studied Applied Science at McGill University in Canada. On his return he began work at the company's premises in Bilston and by 1914 had already been appointed a director of Joseph Sankey and Sons Ltd. Sydney was at the start of a career that was planned to lead to the most senior position in the firm. The outbreak of the war changed everything, as it did for so many young men and their families.

In May 1911 Sydney had been commissioned as a Second Lieutenant in the 1/6th Battalion of the South Staffordshire Regiment (1/6 South Staffords) - the Wolverhampton Territorials. Just as with his civilian career he enjoyed success in his military role and was promoted to Lieutenant in March 1914. When the war began, like most Territorials, Sydney committed himself to overseas service in defence of his country. His feelings at the time can be gleaned from letters he wrote in August 1914, including one sent to his uncle George, who had taken on the role of company chairman following the death of his father the previous year. In this he commented about the likely impact of the war on the company's orders and acknowledged that by serving abroad with the army he was unable to *"take more of the burden off the shoulders of yourself and Uncle Fred."* It is clear from this letter that Sydney was well aware that George had only reluctantly taken on the chairman's role and needed to explain why he was serving in the army rather than working for the family business at such a difficult time. He also mentioned he was aware that Harold had also joined up and they were looking forward to him joining their battalion. The other issue that concerned Sydney was whether it was appropriate for him to draw a director's salary while his primary occupation was clearly going to be his service in the army. George's reply has not survived but, judging from Sydney's reply to him, he clearly believed that at such an early stage in hostilities no clear decision on Sydney's salary needed to be made. Perhaps, like many others, George was hoping that the war really would be over by Christmas. Sydney's letter to George, dated 23 August 1914, also sheds some light on why Harold eventually served in the Royal Field Artillery instead of the 1/6 South Staffords. Harold had received a commission as a junior officer but the army was experiencing considerable difficulty in *"transferring a private in one branch of the Army to an officer in another."* In fact it took several weeks for Harold's commission as an officer in the RFA to be confirmed.

The period from August 1914 to March 1915 saw the 1/6 South Staffords undergo training in the south of England before being deemed ready for active service on the Western Front. At this stage of the war Territorial units were a vital part of the British Army's commitment in France and Belgium. The original British Expeditionary Force (BEF), dispatched to the continent in August 1914, had been severely depleted by the battles during the retreat from Mons and at the Marne and First Ypres. Along with troops from India, Territorials provided invaluable reinforcements who held the line whilst Kitchener's volunteers were being trained to fight. Whilst that was taking place it was down to the Territorials to shoulder much of the burden on the Western Front.

16

Sydney's battalion arrived in France on the 2/3 March 1915. They had completed their final training at Saffron Walden and travelled to Southampton for embarkation to Le Havre - one of the main routes used by the army to get troops and supplies to the continent. The next few weeks saw them make their way to Armentieres where they had their first brief experience of the trenches. An officer in the regiment took a series of photographs which provided a visual record of the route taken by Sydney and his men as they made their way by train from Le Havre to Noordpeene. The journey depicted was fairly typical of that experienced by many other units, with the officers enjoying the "luxury" of an antique railway coach whilst other ranks travelled in cattle trucks. Progress was slow with frequent stops to allow more urgent rail traffic to pass before their destination was finally reached. After two days at Noordpeene, Sydney and the battalion were on the march along the roads and through the villages of northern France and eventually into Belgium. Many of the photos show marching soldiers, some depict the buildings used as billets along the way, but most are of gatherings of officers. This is no surprise, given that only officers could usually afford to buy a camera. For instance, one picture shows a group of them relaxing and shopping in Armentieres. On 2 April 1915 Sydney and his men were at Bulford Camp, a military base close to the Franco-Belgian border, near the Belgian village of Neuve Eglise. This was a relatively safe spot a few miles behind the front line trenches, south of the Ypres Salient. Another photograph taken here shows men boiling shirts, an activity undertaken in the vain hope it might eradicate the inevitable lice problem - a feature of life in the trenches for men of all ranks. After a few days of preparation Sydney's battalion took over the trenches just beyond the village of Wulverghem, about two miles from their base at Bulford Camp. Newly arrived units to the Western Front were usually sent to relatively quiet areas to help acclimatise to the nature of trench warfare and Wulverghem very much fitted the bill. The Germans had captured the high ground of the nearby Wijtschate-Messines ridge in the autumn of 1914 and enjoyed a commanding view of the British lines until June 1917. Fortunately for the 1/6 South Staffs the heaviest fighting in the area was to the north-east of Ypres, where on 22 April the Germans launched the opening phase of the Second Battle of Ypres. This offensive was notorious because it involved the first use of chlorine gas, but fortunately for Sydney the southern sector of the Salient was spared such horrors.

One of Sydney's fellow soldiers described the village of Wulverghem in a letter home which was subsequently published in the *Wolverhampton Express & Star* newspaper. At the time censorship regulations meant the village could not be named but sources now available allow the precise location to be identified. Lance Corporal Duddell wrote the following: *"Passed through a village which 8 months ago might have looked like Codsall. Now every house and barn is in ruins and the old church looks like a relic of some centuries back. Not a soul lives in the place. Away on one side of the road, a deserted farm set on fire by the German shells was blazing away and every now and then the roadway was broken up by huge shell holes"*. Another soldier, Lance Corporal Fred Rice, wrote: *"The village in front of our trenches is a monument to German 'Kultur'. There is not a roof that is not gaping, there is not a wall that is not riven and tottering, there is not a beam or door post that is not pitted* with bullets. *The church is a shattered despoliation and in the churchyard are the last resting places of several of our old comrades.*" Today Wulverghem churchyard is still the resting place of those men.

Sydney and his men followed a routine of spending a few days in the frontline trenches and then a few days in reserve positions. The men of the 1/6 South Staffords were often engaged in improving and maintaining the trenches at Wulverghem - at this stage of the war these were quite rudimentary. Casualty figures were generally quite low and usually resulted from artillery fire or occasional German sniping. Many soldiers of the battalion who were killed in this period were buried in what became St Quentin Cabaret Cemetery, just south of Wulverghem. Whilst in the frontline Sydney's routine duties included allocating men to work and sentry duties and carrying out foot inspections to check for signs of trench foot. Once behind the lines life was a little more relaxed, but the men were still busily occupied cleaning clothes and equipment, undertaking route marches, PT exercises and firearms drill. The officers found themselves faced with the task of reading and censoring their men's letters home. The 1/6 South Staffords remained at Wulverghem until 25 June when they marched to a fresh billeting area at Ouderdom, near the village of Reningelst, west of Ypres. This was a very busy area and home to many units in several hutted camps, located out of range of German artillery. At Ouderdom the pattern of activity while out of the front line continued much as it had when the battalion was at Bulford Camp.

On 19 June Sydney was promoted to the rank of Captain and few days later, on Monday 5 July, his battalion moved to Zillebeke, south-east of Ypres. These were reserve positions built around the partially destroyed village and several hundred yards from the British frontline below the notorious Hill 60. This was an artificial hill created by spoil dug from a cutting when the Ypres-Comines railway line was built. It was also one of the highest points in the Ypres salient, with commanding views towards the city. In 1915 it was in German hands and had witnessed some of the bloodiest fighting on the Western Front. It had been captured by the British in April but quickly regained by the Germans a few weeks later. Hill 60 may well have been the most heavily fought over location on the whole front line - other areas around Ypres looked almost untouched in comparison. Sydney's first experience of the trenches came on Sunday 18 July when 1/6 South Staffords moved into the frontline for five days. Although the battalion war diary described each day as *"Situation quiet except for artillery duels,"* life at Hill 60 would have been very tense for frontline troops. The enemy positions were very close, dead bodies and shattered equipment lay everywhere, the stench was awful and in addition, there was always the prospect of an underground mine being detonated. Soldiers lived on their nerves. Lieutenant J.A.C. Pennycuick, 59 Field Company Royal Engineers, wrote a graphic account of conditions at Hill 60; a description which summed up much that Sydney probably witnessed and experienced during his time at this dreaded location. Pennycuick wrote: *"When we got to the cutting we found it full of the most awful fumes from the bursting shells which made our eyes water and smart and which were most unpleasant. As we were going up the cutting, which is about 20 yards broad with a single line, the Germans began putting great big crumps into the bank almost abreast of us. We waited in some dugouts for about a quarter of an hour being nearly blinded besides being deafened and suffocated. We eventually made our way via 39 trench through a communication trench to Hill 60 where the scene was too awful for words. There were hundreds of dead lying thickly all over the place and in every conceivable attitude. Among them were also many wounded and craters about 40 feet across packed with dead and wounded. They moaned and cried out to us all the time for help, few of the officers or men having even a first field dressing on their wounds. The stretcher bearers were being ordered up but it appeared impossible for them to deal with such numbers, and there was no doctor to help them."*

During the rest of July and August the 1/6 South Staffords' duties followed the regular pattern of a few days in the frontline, some in reserve at Zillebeke and then a return to Ouderdom before the whole cycle started all over again. On Saturday 18 September the battalion resumed their positions at Hill 60 and the situation remained relatively quiet, punctuated only by routine artillery exchanges and the detonation of a small British mine on 21 September. British casualties had been comparatively light when, on the night of 24/25 September, Sydney found himself in charge of the company as the usual commander was on leave. An order was received that a patrol should be sent out into no man's land under the cover of darkness. This was a standard procedure undertaken by both sides for scouting purposes, prisoner capture or to carry out repairs and improve defences. The task of commanding the patrol was given to Second Lieutenant Walter Nelson. This forty-five-year-old officer from Warwick joined the battalion in July 1915 having spent time serving with the French Foreign Legion. For some reason Nelson's patrol was late returning and Sydney became rather anxious about his men. He stood on the fire step and looked over the parapet to see if he could locate them. It was a decision that cost him his life as he was instantly shot in the head by a sniper and collapsed back into the trench. Although quickly taken to a nearby dugout for emergency first aid nothing could be done for him and he died at 4.30 am. A report of the incident in the Colonel's diary gives a clear idea of the sort of officer Sydney was: *"Sydney John, as he was affectionately called by the other officers, was a sound quiet boy, with plenty of ability which did not at once appear on the surface; extremely zealous and dependable, always anxious to be working. Had seen much of him last week in (trench) 37, and he was full of good ideas."* If he had survived the war Sydney would undoubtedly have gone on to enjoy a successful career with Joseph Sankey and Sons Ltd, probably becoming the chairman. The tragedy of his story was that he had already applied for special leave to get married at the time of his death, so he was also denied the happiness of future family life. Sydney's death came as a great blow to those who knew him especially his mother, Elizabeth Sankey, who had lost her husband in 1913. George Sankey and Fred Sankey were also well aware that the issue of the leadership of the company had been thrown into doubt for the foreseeable future.

At 8 pm every night the Last Post Ceremony takes place at the Menin Gate Memorial to the Missing in the Belgian city of Ypres. The traffic is halted and buglers sound the Last Post in memory of British and Empire soldiers who gave their lives defending their town during the Great War. Over the past twenty years numbers attending this ceremony have grown considerably and during a twelve month period after the 25,000[th] playing of the Last Post, on 31 October 2001, an individual soldier who fell in the Ypres Salient was specifically mentioned and remembered. On 25 September 2002 the soldier chosen was Captain Sydney John Sankey. Today he lies at rest in Larch Wood cemetery - a short distance from trench 39 at Hill 60 where he met his fate - alongside six other men from Wolverhampton who saw service in the 1/6 South Staffords. Sydney is also commemorated on a number of war memorials in the Wolverhampton area which reflect the places where he lived and his family's religious affiliations.

Left: Sydney John Sankey. *Right:* Sydney's grave in Larch Wood Cemetery, near Ypres.

Part Five: Harold Bantock Sankey's Great War

Harold Bantock Sankey was born on 18 February 1895, the eldest son of George Herbert Sankey and Jessie Marie née Bantock. The family home was at Finchfield House, in an area to the west of Wolverhampton where a number of well-off families lived. It was a large imposing house which, according to the 1911 census, Mr and Mrs Sankey shared with their four sons; Harold Bantock, George Ronald, Geoffrey Baldwin, John Malcolm as well as a number of servants. Harold's father, George, was one of the sons of Joseph Sankey who established the company in Bilston in 1854. Harold attended Wolverhampton Grammar School from 1903 until 1914 and was involved in many aspects of life there. The Wolverhampton Grammar School Register records that he was a prefect, editor of the school magazine, *The Wulfrunian,* a team member of the first XI for football and captain of the cricket team in 1914. In addition he won a number of academic prizes, was an enthusiastic contributor to the school debating society and committed member of the school's fledgling Officers' Training Corps (OTC). Harold made steady progress in shooting and signalling and regular promotions were a feature of his time in the OTC - in 1912 he was made a Colour Sergeant. Although the OTC was popular with some boys it experienced difficulty in expanding its numbers and in April 1914 *The Wulfrunian* magazine tried to encourage junior pupils *"not to be put off by grumbles about uniform parades and rifle inspections."* Had the Great War not broken out in August 1914 Harold would have progressed to university and then a career with the family business in Bilston.

In 1914 the Sankey family business was under the leadership of Harold's father, who took over when his cousin, John, died in 1913. Harold's civilian career plans were put on hold as he initially enlisted as a junior officer with the 1/6 South Staffords alongside his cousin Sydney. However, at some point in late 1914 or early 1915 Harold was transferred to the 2nd South Midland Brigade Royal Field Artillery (RFA) but whether this was at his own request is unknown. When Harold joined the brigade it was undergoing training in the Chelmsford area and making preparations for eventual transfer to the Western Front. Harold was one of three Second Lieutenants serving with the brigade's ammunition column, along with A. C. Williams - who went on to write the history of the brigade in the 1920s - and J. K. Turpin, who was killed during the Third Battle of Ypres. Harold's commanding officer in the ammunition column was Captain M. C. H. Smith-Carrington. Apart from shooting practice on Salisbury Plain the brigade was based near Ingatestone during the early months of 1915. In late February Harold wrote a letter to brother Ron, in which he mentioned that all leave had been cancelled until further notice. The reason soon became clear as final preparations for the long awaited move to the Western Front were nearing completion. On 29 March the brigade began the leisurely process of travelling by train to Southampton. Harold believed his tortuous journey was due to a derailed horsebox and a locomotive that lacked sufficient motive power. It was more likely it was delayed by the sheer amount of railway traffic at a time when tons of war materials and thousands of troops were being transported across the country. The brigade embarked for Le Havre on 31 March and Harold's parents and brother Ron came down to Southampton to see him off. Three ships were involved in the transfer of the 2nd South Midland Brigade: SS *Munich*, a Great Eastern Railway passenger ferry and two cargo vessels; SS *City of Dunkirk* and SS *Archimedes*. Harold seemed to have had a pleasant journey and, as befitted an officer, a cabin for the duration of the crossing.

In early 1915 the British Army was engaged in a rebuilding process whilst also holding the line against the much larger German Army on the Western Front. The original BEF of August 1914, which had been composed of professional volunteer soldiers, had suffered heavy casualties in the autumn and winter of that year and was increasingly dependent on Territorial and Indian troops. Kitchener's volunteers would not be ready for many months as they underwent basic training back in Britain. Harold's unit, the 2nd South Midland Brigade RFA, was a Territorial artillery unit composed of three batteries from Kidderminster, Worcester and Redditch. The usual procedure with any new unit on the Western Front was to send it to a quiet sector to gain experience and adapt to the rigours of modern warfare. Harold's brigade was first sent to the area around Ploegsteert - or Plugstreet, as it was known to the British

Tommy – a Belgian village just north of Armentieres. Whilst serving here Harold wrote home regularly to his parents and several letters from 1915 have survived. This correspondence can now be used to help build a picture of the life of a junior artillery officer during a period when his unit experienced action in a relatively quiet sector near Ypres before moving south to the Somme.

After its arrival in France the brigade set off towards its first destination and Harold described the journey as being so slow he could have got off the train and walked faster. It took the train twenty hours to travel as far as Hazebrouck in uncomfortable carriages which were neither lit nor heated. A. C. Williams, writing in the brigade's history, mentions that the highlight of the journey was the provision of hot drinks and cigarettes by the YMCA at one of the stops. However, Harold's disagreeable journey was fairly typical of rail transport to the frontline during the war. In his first letters home to his mother, father, brother Ron and Auntie Evelyn he described how the brigade made its way from the railhead at Hazebrouck to Plugstreet Wood by road. At this time he was attached to the ammunition column. They arrived at Hazebrouck at 3 am in the morning of 2 April and then marched to Caestre arriving at 7.30 am. Their stay here was short and they soon moved to Armentieres and the brigade HQ, ammunition column and three batteries were each dispersed to different locations around the town. On 16 April the brigade received orders to move up to Plugstreet Wood, a quiet sector south of Ypres often referred to as "The Nursery." During his first few weeks in Belgium one of Harold's main tasks was finding billets for the men, something he saw as a full-time job. It must have been quite a challenge for the young officer because, although his French was quite good, most of the locals spoke Flemish. He soon discovered many Flemish speakers were less than welcoming and declared they would be quite happy if the Germans came back! Despite this, Harold found a family of farmers who were well disposed towards the British and arranged comfortable billets for himself and his fellow officers. Doubtless his immediate Commanding Officer, Captain Carrington Smith, and fellow junior officers were grateful for his efforts even though not everyone had the luxury of a bed with blankets.

Life was very quiet in the first few weeks and Harold's letters reveal his unit was rationed to firing only three rounds of ammunition per gun per day. This reflects the struggle of Britain's munitions industry to supply the frontline and the famous shell scandal erupted after the Battle of Aubers Ridge the following month. Harold's main concerns were with creature comforts and he asked his parents to send out foodstuffs, razor blades and other technical equipment. Pre-occupied with water supplies and the smells of being in an agricultural area, on 12 April he told his mother that the stench was awful and the *only safe drinks are wine and beer,"* adding "*If some of the temperance societies and anti-smoking leagues were dumped down here they would either die of thirst or smells, or have to retract their vows."* In a letter to his mother, dated 20 April, Harold revealed he was being transferred from the ammunition column to Number 2 Battery and the following day he wrote again to explain how his responsibilities would be changing. Instead of arranging billets he was to be a Forward Observation Officer (FOO), one of the most dangerous tasks for an artillery officer. In his first visit to the frontline trenches he found it all *"quite exciting,"* but little did he know just how exciting his new role would become in the months and years ahead.

In a letter to his Aunt Kittie Harold described his unit's position as being about 3,000 yards from the German trenches and below the crest of a hill. Although they were out of direct sight of the enemy guns, planes of the Royal Flying Corps (RFC) had to keep German spotters away. At this time there were occasional exchanges of artillery fire and some German shells hit farm buildings nearby without causing any casualties. Up until this point the brigade's only casualty had been an officer who suffered a broken leg during disembarkation at Le Havre. In his early letters home Harold often referred to acquiring a decent collapsible periscope and another matter of practical concern that often cropped up in letters to his younger brother Ron was telephone communications. The younger Sankey spent many hours constructing a portable telephone exchange with the assistance of staff at Wolverhampton Grammar School and the company workshops. Good communications were vital to Harold in his role as FOO and he often referred to poor or disrupted telephone lines or too many voices caused by crossed wires. In these early days of telephone communications there was much to be desired and problems relating to battlefield communications affected all units during the Great War.

Another regular topic in the correspondence between Harold and his family in Wolverhampton was the subject of food parcels and cosmetic items such as razor blades. The steady stream of cakes and other confectionery dispatched to the frontline were doubtless much appreciated by Harold and his fellow officers, along with regular deliveries of coal and *Salutaris* mineral water. His fears about the dubious quality of local drinking water prompted the request for bottled supplies. In a letter to his mother dated 10 June 1915 he wrote: *"It is very nice to have some water to drink. We mix it with lemonade and it makes top-hole stuff for this hot weather. It is so hot that we have to do as much as possible before breakfast and after tea."*

Harold was aware that cousin Sydney was serving nearby, with the 1/6 South Staffords, and hoped that they might be able to meet up in either Armentieres or Bailleul. These places provided opportunities for relaxation and shopping and on one visit Harold met Captain Strange and Major Stidson – two doctors at Wolverhampton General Hospital. He wrote in a letter to Ron, *"I found out from Strange the exact position of Sydney's billets when they are out of the trenches* (at this time the 1/6 South Staffs were in the front line east of Wulverghem) *so if I have another half day I will try to look him up."* Unfortunately this meeting never took place as, towards the end of June, Harold's brigade was moved to a new location on the Western Front. In this same letter to his brother, he told Ron about changes to his FOO role and how he was now only doing one day in ten in the trenches - *"Quite an agreeable change. Only majors and captains observe so we spend our time in the battery or wagon line. This isn't nice but we don't have so much to do."* By this time Harold had been reunited with his favourite horse, which he described as being in better condition than when back in England, and he often went for rides behind the lines when the opportunity arose.

Part Six: A Forward Observation Officer

Harold's new role as the brigade's No2 Battery Forward Observation Officer (FOO) was arguably one of the most dangerous tasks for anyone serving with the artillery. The FOO was very much the eyes of the artillery and he required both considerable skill and personal bravery. Harold had to go forward from his own gun positions and find a place from where he could observe and report back on the work of his own unit and the activities of the Germans. Such locations were invariably dangerous - close to the British front line trenches and sometimes beyond them in no man's land. Once a suitable position was found the job involved patient observation of the enemy; making careful note of every detail and subtle changes made by the Germans made to confuse the British artillery. During an attack the FOO reported back on the accuracy of British gunfire. This task required absolute precision as mistakes could result in bringing down fire on one's own men, especially during a creeping barrage. Communications were maintained by telephone and a FOO worked with a team of telephonists and assistants. The nature of the job clearly explains why Harold's early letters expressed a desire for a decent periscope and a mobile telephone exchange – he obviously felt the equipment supplied to the RFA was not up to the job. In a letter to his father, dated 8 May 1915, he asked for a *"Lifeguard patent collapsible pocket Periscope with spare mirror in khaki waterproof case. 15s from : F.Duerr & Sons, Manchester. The one mentioned is advertised in Punch nearly every week and is the best I've seen so far."* George Sankey went all the way to London to find such an item, whilst Harold resorted to drawing up blueprints for a trench periscope of his own design – even acquiring a patent for the device. However, his plans were never realised and, according to his own son James, he somehow obtained a German one which he regarded as far superior to those of British design. Apparently this periscope ended up back in German hands in 1940 having been lent to a friend of Harold's who lost it during the chaos of the Dunkirk evacuation.

Part Seven: The Somme – 1915

When the 2nd South Midland Brigade RFA were sent to the Somme in 1915 it was still regarded as a relatively quiet backwater on the Western Front. However, moving away from an area where a unit had been based for some time was rarely popular, especially if it meant leaving familiar surroundings and comfortable billets. The order to move from Plugstreet was implemented on 24 June and the journey south took several weeks. The brigade made its way through various towns and villages in northern France and at one point found itself at the mining settlement of Marles-les-Mines, where Harold's battery was based for a fortnight in a field inside a colliery. Whilst this might have made gunners from the Black Country feel homesick, Harold and his fellow officers found superior accommodation in a local chateau. The brigade's journey south eventually brought them to Doullens and from there they marched to their new location in the area around Authie. On 24 June Harold received the new trench periscope obtained by his father. A few days later his letter home made clear it had arrived but explained he would not be using it until his unit was established at their new location. Harold also mentioned that Adshead, a fellow officer, had contracted measles and that meant he was now in charge of the telephones. In his role as FOO, he was always keen to improve telephone communication and Harold asked if his father could enquire if *Efandem*, a local manufacturer of batteries, could help in the construction of improved switchboards. Harold also mentioned that the chateau at Marles-les-Mines, which had recently served as a temporary billet, was owned by an officer in the French Army. It was being looked after by a caretaker who had put some furnishings into storage, to protect them during hostilities, but the library was well stocked. One can only imagine how much of a contrast a few days spent in such an opulent location must have been with time spent on the battlefield. The brigade history makes reference to a swimming competition held at this time and although Harold did not mention it in any of his letters it is difficult to imagine that, with his sporting prowess, he was not involved in some capacity. During the two weeks spent at the chateau at Marles-les-Mines a few more packages arrived for Harold including a large food parcel. As he received a regular supply of such items from Finchfield he was doubtless very popular with his fellow officers. Harold informed his father that an order had been issued *"against sending fuses and shells home."* Quite clearly the nature of some wartime souvenirs being sent back to Blighty was causing alarm!

POSTED MAY 7th.

Dear Uncle Alfred,
                    Thanks so much for your letter. We have been out now just over a month and so far we have not had at all a bad time. Where we are an artillery officer has to be down in the firing trenches all the time, so we take spells of two days each—three of us—so we have two days in and four days out. There is'nt much for us to do in the trenches we are ther in case of an attack so as to be able to direct the artillery fire and I am not specially keen for it to be my turn in the trenches when an attack does come off! Nor are the others as far as I can make out. If we are'nt in the trenches we split up the day between us to go to one observing station and watch for any movement behind the German lines. It's quite an interesting though rather a tiring job as it means one has to have an eye glued to telescope for four hours on end. There is very little to see

Left: Harold Bantock Sankey MC. *Right:* One of his early letters home.
Courtesy of James Sankey.

On 21 July Harold's brigade received several 18 pounder field guns to replace their obsolete 15 pounders - the standard field gun used by Territorial artillery units. These old guns only fired shrapnel shells and were of little use against targets requiring high explosives. Acquiring 18 pounders meant the brigade became a more effective fighting unit and Harold was one of the officers involved in handing over the old and receiving the new guns. In a letter written shortly afterwards he commented,

"We are the first Territorial Division to get them (18 pdrs) although at least two other divisions came out before us. So we are rather bucked about it." The brigade spent the following week undergoing training to use the new guns and preparing new firing positions at their location on the Somme. Harold noted that these guns were far superior to the old 15 pounders and the men soon learnt the new firing procedures - so the rate of fire was much quicker. However, he also reflected that, *"Of course the French 75 is in quite a different class and there seems nothing to touch them for speed or accuracy"*. Early August was spent on further training and registering of guns and the brigade took over a number of former French artillery positions around Sailly-au-Bois. This possibly explains Harold's positive comments about the French 75mm gun – a highly respected weapon at that time. His own battery - B Battery - was located near the Chateau de la Haie with the brigade ammunition column nearby at Authie, the wagon lines at Couin and headquarters at Bayencourt. In his letters home Harold gave plenty of hints to his whereabouts when he said the countryside was *"like Salisbury Plain, flat and undulating, with no cover or houses for miles"* – a perfect description of the Somme landscape. He also made it clear he believed his unit would be in the area for at least the duration of the forthcoming winter. The sense of settling in was confirmed when he received news that his transfer from the Divisional Ammunition Column had been made permanent.

The brigade spent most of August training with their new guns and B Battery actually found itself in action on the 14th, although Harold missed this event as he was unwell. In a letter to his mother he speculated if the poor weather was responsible for the chill that meant he was sidelined when the battery engaged the enemy. The wet conditions also prompted Harold to request fresh stocks of envelopes as all his existing ones had stuck together in the damp atmosphere. Even today, amongst all the wartime letters in the Sankey family's possession, there are a large number of sealed but empty envelopes - presumably the ones Harold referred to in 1915. August was such a quiet month for the brigade that the war diary referred to its men being sent to help local farmers bring in the harvest. Harold's letters refer to having time to go riding and meeting up with his friend John Thompson, a fellow artillery officer and member of the famous engineering family from Wolverhampton. Clearly, in the summer of 1915 the Somme was still a quiet sector of the Western Front, far removed from the hotbed of action it would become twelve months later. September proved similar to August and the gunners of the brigade's batteries spent their time consolidating and improving their positions. Whilst Harold focused on artillery matters and making the brigade, particularly B Battery, as effective as possible, his letters home continued to request helpful items to be sent out to France. Some of these needed to be made in the company's workshops, for instance metal brackets on which to hang small lamps that would be an aid when firing the guns at night. Harold was very pleased when he received a new periscope and wrote that it was *"quite simple and much better than mine."* By then he had acquired a patent for one of his own design but decided this was no longer worth pursuing as this latest model finally did the job. His mind was also busy with another priority – improving telephone communications – having spent time working with a line-laying detail. Harold Sankey was obviously a creative young FOO – constantly thinking of more efficient means to observe the enemy and relay vital information back to the guns. Although he undoubtedly believed the British Army were making progress in some ways, other aspects of military life were less satisfactory in his eyes. He thought the morning exchange of artillery fire, known as the daily *"hate"*, served no real purpose. Whilst the High Command wanted to pursue a doctrine of being "offensive," Harold felt it simply resulted in the unnecessary and random deaths of many frontline soldiers. His other frustrations were clear in a comment to his mother, *"We are of course always on a ration of ammunition, and it isn't enough to really do any damage to them."* In late September the brigade was given instructions not to fire and this embargo continued into October, which saw little action apart from occasional retaliatory shelling. By then the brigade's priority was preparing reserve positions and ensuring the existing ones were ready to survive the rigours of the coming winter.

A couple of Harold's letters at the time give a good reflection of events and his own concerns. In response to his parents' questions regarding the possibility of leave he told his mother *"I went out last night to see John (Thompson) about leave. As you know, all leave is at present stopped. John said he has written to Daddy to say that it is of course no use putting forward any sentimental reasons for leave and that the only thing is to urge business reasons. To say that I had been out here 6 months without leave is of course no reason as leave is only a privilege and not a right. And also there are very many who have been quite as long out here as I have been and who have not yet been home."* The *"sentimental reasons"* to which he referred may well have been the news of Sydney's death. In a letter of 4 October Harold gave more details about the brigade's activities. *"We haven't fired a shot for just a week. There's nothing to do in the battery except keep a few men on each gun in case of emergency. The rest are out most of the day digging a reserve position about a mile and a half in the rear."* It is worth reflecting that the apparent lack of firing at this time was probably because Britain was still struggling to produce enough shells – the munitions crisis had surfaced after military failures at the battles of Neuve Chapelle and Aubers Ridge in the Spring of that year. In addition the Battle of Loos was the key focus of the British Army's activities in late September and October. While Harold's brigade was busy preparing rear positions the Germans were busily engaged in doing the same thing along their side of the Western Front.

Harold gave an account of his FOO role when he wrote *"Every third day I go down to the trenches on a horse. We get down to within 200 yards of the trenches on a horse in broad daylight. We tie up the horse to a post and leave him for the officer we are relieving. In the trenches there is quite a comfortable mess room with a stove, and in our dugout, which is about 10 feet underground, we have a spring bed. One of the folding kind. It has, I expect, been looted from a chateau. We go to bed about 9.30 pm and get up at 8 am, have a wash and shave and then breakfast. Between breakfast and lunch perhaps a telephone line needs relaying or the infantry have spotted a machine gun emplacement and want us to go and have a look at it and take note of its position. All this time there is practically no firing at all. In the evening and early morning there is generally a 'five minutes hate' which means that the infantry put ten or twenty rounds each into the German lines".*

Meanwhile many of Harold's letters home commented on the continuing flow of parcels and their contents, although not everything went to plan. A letter dated 12 October mentioned that his waders had arrived but unfortunately the manufacturers had *"sent two right boots instead of a left and right".* One particularly poignant letter was sent to his aunt Elizabeth in which Harold explained the reasons why she had not received his letter of condolence since Sydney's death. One wonders how much he regretted not meeting up with his cousin when they were both serving near Ypres earlier in the year. As the weather worsened during November the brigade's batteries saw only occasional action in retaliation to German fire. B Battery was now firmly established in position and its officers billeted in dugouts around Chateau de la Haie. Harold finally started a period of leave on 17 November and in a letter home set out the travel plans for his return to Finchfield House. He expected to arrive home at 8 am on the 19th and sent his mother a list of items he wished to obtain while he was back in "Blighty". These included a number of personal items but also *"a football and a few games for the men,"* which gives a hint as to why Harold was a popular and respected officer with all ranks. His time back in Wolverhampton was spent catching up with family and friends and was over all too soon. Some family members travelled with him as far as London on the return journey before saying their farewells. His mother wrote of the pleasure in seeing him once again and added a thought that must have been in the mind of many at such a time, *"It is for a noble cause that you are giving up some of the best days of your life."* The same letter contained the bad news that Tom Bantock had been seriously wounded while serving in Gallipoli. He was to die from his wounds shortly after Harold received this report about him.

In the weeks leading up to Christmas the routine for Harold and the men of his battery was dominated by persistent bad weather and retaliation against occasional German bombardments. The war diary noted that most of the trouble came from Minenwerfers – trench mortars. Harold and his colleagues had some good news when he took delivery of his Dulcitone piano - an instrument where the sound is produced when a range of tuning forks are struck by felt-covered hammers activated by the keyboard. The instrument was designed by Thomas Machell of Glasgow and manufactured by his firm during the late nineteenth and early twentieth centuries. The Dulcitone arrived in a specially manufactured, waterproofed case - constructed at the Albert Street works in Bilston - and doubtless helped to provide some much appreciated Christmas cheer. The brigade war diary entry for Christmas 1915 warned of *"attempts likely to be made by the Germans to fraternise on Christmas Day."* The military authorities were anxious to prevent a repetition of the famous Christmas Truce of 1914, when troops from both sides met in no man's land at several points along the Western Front. Such fraternisation would undermine the need to perceive the Germans as a brutal enemy and also present them with an opportunity to assess the state of British defences. As it turned out the German attempt to show some Christmas spirit amounted to heavy shelling of the British positions at Sailly.

Part Eight: The Battle of the Somme

When the almost daily exchange of letters between Harold and his family was occasionally interrupted it caused great concern back in Wolverhampton. Relatives often worried if bad news from the front coincided with a sudden dearth of letters from a loved one. This happened in late February 1916 when both George and Jessie noted in their letters to Harold that they had not heard from him for a few days and quite naturally feared he might have been wounded or worse. Mrs Sankey was particularly anxious as she referred in one of her letters to a newspaper report of a *"machine gun incident at Fonquevillers."* George tried to discover what had happened as the family were well aware that this was the area in which Harold was based. Just as their concerns were mounting they received good news from their boy on the Somme which put their minds at rest.

The opening months of 1916 saw a continuation of the brigade's relatively peaceful experience of life at the front and the war diary painted its familiar picture of poor weather and desultory artillery exchanges with the Germans. There were a few instances when one or more of the batteries supported trench raids by the infantry or responded to similar raids by the enemy on British positions. Inevitably there was a steady stream of casualties and on 11 February Gunner Frank Bernard Brookes of Callow End, Worcester was killed. Harold wrote to express his sympathies to the twenty-one-year-old gunner's parents, George and Emma - a task that must have been one of the most difficult for any officer to carry out. Their reply, thanking Harold, is included in the cache of letters which he brought home with him in 1918. The brigade remained in the same location on the Somme during the first months of the year and the brigade history refers to the excellent food enjoyed at this time: *"Breakfast of oatmeal porridge with fresh cream, brown trout caught in the adjoining stream, besides bacon and fresh eggs; a plentiful supply of all sorts of vegetables was always at hand and many little luxuries that were unobtainable in England."* This is a clear reminder that life at the front was not always one of horrific carnage. A description of the B Battery mess at La Haie Chateau at this time stated that it was in a *"somewhat exposed position, but the dugouts were excellent. The officers' mess in particular was especially well built (by the French) and fitted up with every modern improvement."* It went on; *"it is perhaps worth recording that a certain subaltern of this Battery (who must have been an acquisition to any mess) had a supply of coal and also a supply of soda water sent out from England every week. The same gentleman was also responsible for an elaborate water pump and a portable piano."* That gentleman was obviously Harold Sankey and these comments show how much he was appreciated by his fellow officers.

The end of March 1916 saw a significant development in terms of the brigade's structure when its three batteries of four 18 pounder guns were replaced by four batteries of four 18 pounders. The new battery was designated as D Battery and its addition meant an influx of new men joining the brigade. Harold's letters home from this period give an insight into a variety of matters, such as his disappointment at not getting leave. On one occasion this was cancelled as he was just about to depart for Wolverhampton, due to a *"German offensive down south."* This was a reference to the German attack at Verdun which had serious repercussions for the Allied offensive on the Somme planned for that summer. Harold also responded to his mother's concerns that his role as a FOO might put him at serious risk of being captured by the Germans. Evidence showing Harold was becoming quite busy can be seen in comments he made about the possibility of sending more postcards rather than letters. In one letter to his father, dated 16 March, he mentioned the fact that they were well fed and described in detail a dinner they recently enjoyed in the officer's mess. In another letter to George he wrote, *"I expect you saw the paragraph in The Times, 8th March re: helmets at Ypres. A helmet down this way was hit by a bullet and badly dented but didn't hurt the man."* The man involved was clearly lucky for although the steel helmets made by *Sankeys* gave some protection against flying debris they would not stop a well-aimed bullet at normal range.

According to the brigade war diary Harold was granted a week's leave from 28 March to 4 April 1916. His return to France coincided with the start of several weeks' preparation for the brigade's first major engagement - namely its involvement in the forthcoming Somme offensive. On 8 May the brigade began the process by vacating their well-established positions and moving their headquarters to Couin. Just over a week later another restructuring of the unit took place when the recently arrived 18 pounder guns of the new D Battery were exchanged for a battery of 4.5" howitzers from 243 Brigade RFA. The brigade was now re-designated as the 241st (South Midland) Brigade RFA and the individual batteries were also re-designated as A/241, B/241 (Harold's battery), C/241 and D/241. Harold also acquired a new officer in charge of his battery: Major Meacher, who replaced Major Taylor who returned to Britain due to ill-health. June 1916 was a hectic period for all concerned along the Somme sector as preparations for the great Allied offensive were stepped up. It was nigh on impossible to hide from the Germans the fact that a major attack was coming soon - it was a case of when, not if. In the first week of June all four batteries prepared their firing positions ready for the huge artillery bombardment which was to precede and support the infantry advance. B Battery was given a position north-west of the village of Beaumont Hamel at a location known as *'The White City'*. As part of their preparations batteries had to bring forward some 5,000 shells as an initial supply for use in the bombardment. Whether Harold wrote many letters during this period is unknown and even if he did it is difficult to believe he would have had the time, or the energy, to write as extensively as before. On the evening of 23 June A, B and C batteries were ordered to move into their new positions and the bombardment of German positions along the Somme front began the following day. The original intention was for a five day bombardment that would destroy the enemy defences of barbed wire and trenches, demoralise the German soldiers and ensure minimum resistance when the infantry finally went 'over the top' at zero hour. However, the German artillery retaliated and all British batteries suffered casualties and a steady flow of wounded men were sent to hospital facilities away from the front. On 29 June - Z Day - the original date for the infantry assault; the attack was delayed due to poor weather and a further two days of Allied bombardment took place. This was the first time Harold's brigade had been involved in a major operation in the Great War and the experience must have been shattering.

The Battle of the Somme began on the morning of Saturday 1 July 1916 and the gun batteries of the RFA were in action throughout. Harold's battery position at *'The White City'* meant he was perfectly placed to witness one of the most famous events of the whole Great War - the detonation of the mine dug under the German strongpoint on Hawthorn Ridge. This moment, immortalised thanks to the film made at the time by Geoffrey Malins, has since been shown in many television documentaries about the Western Front. The British public also saw it when Malins' film, *The Battle of the Somme,* was shown to an audience of millions in cinemas across Britain in the next few weeks. The Hawthorn mine was blown at 7.20 am and a number of others were also detonated under key German defensive positions in the minutes before zero hour: 7.30 am. These huge explosions gave the Germans warning of the impending infantry assault and all along the line they emerged from deep shelters and concrete dugouts to set up their machine guns. During the course of the next two hours these guns cut down the British infantry assault in swathes and forged this battle's infamous reputation. In the artillery lines Harold's battery opened fire at 7.30 am and continued firing non-stop until 10.30 am. As a FOO in an advanced position he would have had a clear view the devastation visited on advancing troops by German machine guns. According to its official history some 7,000 casualties were suffered in the area covered by the brigade near Beaumont Hamel – a location well-known to modern visitors to Newfoundland Park. It was here that the Newfoundland Regiment suffered more than 700 casualties from an attacking force of 800 men. At 9.30 pm the batteries were ordered to be prepared to move by 11.45 pm – the infantry attack had failed. At 2 am on 2 July B Battery eventually came out of action and returned to their bivouacs at Beaussart. The Battle of the Somme dragged on until mid-November by which time the British Army had pushed forward some five or six miles at considerable cost. 241 Brigade was in action throughout this time and moved location on a number of occasions in response to operational decisions made by the High Command. It was a period of intense activity, with few opportunities for rest, as a comment in the brigade history hints: *"The amount of ammunition expended was terrific, and the Brigade on more than one occasion fired in a single night, as many rounds as it fired during the whole of the first year in Flanders."*

The work of the gunners included covering local trench raids on German positions, wire cutting operations and full-scale support for major assaults on key positions. It was for his actions during one of the latter that Harold was awarded the Military Cross (MC). In the early weeks of the Somme campaign the brigade was based in the area around the Ancre marshes and provided fire towards heavily fortified German positions at Thiepval and along the ridge at Leipzig Salient.

Capturing Thiepval had been a first day target for the British but the attack had failed. As a consequence of intense artillery bombardments both the village of Thiepval - formerly the largest in the area - and its prominent chateau had been utterly destroyed. On 26 September, at 12.35 pm, the British launched another assault on Thiepval and 241 Brigade provided part of the artillery support. As FOO for B Battery, Harold Sankey was in the thick of the battle – moving forward with two telephones and a small team of men to report back to the battery on the effectiveness on their firing, noting targets destroyed and identifying new ones. This was an extremely dangerous task which required Harold to give a running commentary from Thiepval as the British assault progressed. His MC citation mentioned that at one point he was the only source of information emanating from Thiepval and as his team made their way forward they witnessed another party, just a few yards ahead of them, blown to bits by shellfire. Over the next few days the Germans were cleared from their strongpoints on the Thiepval Ridge and the steady advance of British units on the Somme battlefield continued.

At the start of October Harold's brigade was relieved from its position in the Ancre valley. It moved for a short time to Warlincourt before moving again to the northern edge of the Somme battlefield in the Hebuturne/Fonquevillers area - not far from where it had spent much of the earlier part of 1916. On 18 October more structural changes were made to the brigade when two additional 18 pounder field guns were added to A, B and C Batteries along with additional manpower. The brigade was called into action again during the final days of the Somme campaign when it supported the attack on Beaumont Hamel on 13 November. This assault saw the 51st Highland Division finally capture a village which had been a first day objective. Beaumont Hamel had been totally destroyed by artillery bombardments during the campaign and there was little for Harold and his colleagues to see apart from the shattered foundations of various buildings. The brigade was then briefly withdrawn for a few days rest before being sent to new positions near the village of Martinpuich. This was probably the worst position the brigade ever experienced. A combination of endless artillery fire and the steady onset of bad weather meant the location became a muddy morass; typical of the images conjured up by the fighting on the Western Front. The gun pits and dugouts inherited by the brigade were constantly under several inches of water, despite constant pumping out. The movement of men, equipment and supplies to the location became a Herculean struggle against the elements. The brigade history painted a vivid picture of the situation: *"Around the Batteries the land had been blasted away and ploughed up in the most terrible manner. Along the parapets of crumbling and abandoned trenches lay hundreds of machine gun belts, still full of cartridges. Little wooden crosses or inverted rifles depicting the graves of unknown warriors, a number of abandoned German Batteries, many thousands of used and unused shells, half a dozen derelict tanks, a wrecked aeroplane and an occasional German skeleton in uniform - all bore testimony to the severity of the fighting."*

Christmas 1916 brought another brief respite as the officers and men enjoyed the festive period away from the front line. The brigade was withdrawn from the battlezone and made its way to the village of Behencourt, near Amiens. The officers enjoyed Christmas dinner in D/241's officers' mess. Arrangements were under the direction of Captain Reginald George Pridmore MC who provided a menu consisting of oysters, roast turkey, plum pudding and ample supplies of wine, liqueurs and crackers. Harold's regular supply of *Salutaris* mineral water and his trench piano probably featured in proceedings. Reggie Pridmore was a sportsman of some note, being a Warwickshire county cricketer, England hockey international and gold medal winner in the 1908 Olympics. He was killed during the Italian campaign on 13 March 1918.

Part Nine: The Third Battle of Ypres

The New Year saw Harold's brigade continue its time on the Somme sector and there was little action until March, when the Germans unexpectedly withdrew to a formidable new defensive position known to the British as the Hindenburg Line. This created a surreal situation where it was possible to wander unhindered around no man's land and former German trenches. It also produced some rather disturbing moments when bodies that had lain dead for months were discovered and had to be retrieved for burial. In addition the Germans left booby traps in many of their old positions so exceptional care was required when entering dugouts or picking up food or equipment. It was probably at this time that Harold acquired a pair of German binoculars he prized greatly. The brigade continued to move to a number of locations at the front and took part in actions at Epehy in late March and early April. During the latter stages of this event Harold's B/241 Battery was shelled heavily and suffered considerable damage. Following this all batteries were withdrawn for a short period to recover. Given his frequent proximity to danger, it is remarkable that Harold escaped death or serious injury. All batteries were withdrawn to Montauban on 23/24 June 1917. This was one of the Somme villages that saw British success in the opening phase of the battle the previous year. The accommodation for the men and officers was poor but during this time the officers were granted permission to visit Paris and home leave to Britain was also speeded up. All ranks were allowed to visit Amiens, where an exclusive club for officers operated at the Hotel de Rhin and the Gobert Restaurant also benefitted from their patronage. However, this brief period of well-deserved rest was not destined to last and rumours circulated that 241 Brigade, as part of the 48th Division, would soon be heading back to Belgium to re-acquaint itself with the Ypres Salient.

On 6 July 1917 Harold and 241 Brigade left the Somme sector and moved northwards to Ypres. The 48th Division was to take part in the planned summer offensive in Flanders, the aim of which was to throw the Germans back off the high ground east of Ypres and then push northwards towards the Channel coast. This would allow the British to capture key railway lines and also deprive the enemy of access to Belgian ports, used as U-boat bases. Destroying the German communications network would force the Germans to withdraw from that part of

Flanders. Although 241 Brigade morale was high - their time on the Somme had turned them into an experienced and battle-hardened unit - the brigade history described the ensuing period as the *"most terrible and disastrous of the war for the 241 Brigade, and let it be said also, the most glorious."* On 13 July they arrived at Steenvorde, near the Franco-Belgian border and the following morning travelled to Poperinghe where they would have soon realised what was about to happen. This small West Flanders town had a pre-war population of about 25,000 but this swelled to more than 250,000 as a consequence of preparations for the imminent British offensive. On either side of the road into Poperinghe army camps, ammunition dumps and supply depots had been built and the original single line railway from Poperinghe to Hazebrouck in France was converted to double track by the Royal Engineers. At Remi Siding a place where hospital trains could be loaded with wounded from four nearby Casualty Clearing Stations - and evacuated to Base Hospitals - was built. In addition many narrow gauge light railway lines criss-crossed the area moving men and supplies around the immediate vicinity. It was a tremendous hive of activity and scenes of such meticulous preparation probably boosted the morale of men like Harold. The recent British attack on the Messines Ridge, south of Ypres, had also been remarkably successful. Here, the detonation of nineteen underground mines led to the capture of high ground held by the enemy since the start of the war and thousands of Germans were taken prisoner. Everything bode well for the planned offensive towards another ridge of high ground, at Passchendaele. Having finished breakfast in Poperinghe on 14 July they moved to occupy their new positions later that day, with brigade headquarters in dugouts around Reigersburg Chateau. D/241 Battery was based near the Yser Canal and the other batteries in positions in the hedgerows behind. They all went into action that very evening, firing at German positions.

During the two weeks preceding the Third Battle of Ypres all batteries were engaged in extensive counter-battery work which aimed to destroy the German artillery – a key feature of artillery operations by this stage of the war. However, at various times all batteries suffered casualties and gas was an ever-present danger. On 22 July Captain Woods, Lieutenant Crane, Sergeant Blick and other men in B/241 were all gassed. Harold possibly escaped because his work as a FOO meant he was much further forward and not caught up in the bombardment which hit B battery. The infantry attack began on 31 July 1917 and 241 Brigade's guns helped lay down a creeping barrage to support an assault on Pilkem Ridge. All batteries went into action at zero hour - 3.50 am - and after two hours of firing the order came to move forward across the Yser Canal. By then this waterway had been reduced to a stinking ditch in the centre of the muddy canal bed. It was a scene Harold witnessed as he had crossed it on one of the bridges constructed for both infantry and heavier traffic by the Royal Engineers. In the summer of 1917 the Yser Canal was not a pleasant sight and provided an unwelcome assault on the olfactory senses. The batteries moved forward to positions east of the canal in the vicinity of locations known as Admiral's Road and Hill Top Farm - which became the new brigade HQ. Although the advance was very successful some casualties occurred due to German shelling and poison gas. One of Harold's fellow officers in B/241,

Lieutenant Bonham-Edwards was shot through the lung during the advance. However, their guns were soon in action once again providing support as the British infantry pushed on to reach their objectives. Until then progress had been good, but that all changed when it began to rain during the night. During the following weeks the consequences of this unseasonal weather became the major factor in hampering British advances to the east of Ypres.

There were few days in the following weeks when it did not rain. The precipitation was often considerable and its effect on an environment where three years of warfare had taken place was significant. This was an area where the natural watercourses and man-made drainage systems had already been destroyed by artillery fire. Now, vast areas of the Ypres salient became a muddy swamp. The movement of men, supplies and artillery units across this morass became either difficult or downright impossible. Harold's brigade was forced to remain in an extremely exposed position for the next few weeks, with no proper gunpits. However, the Medical Officer, Captain Manley O'Farrell, still believed a soldier's health was better served by remaining on the surface rather than venturing underground. One man who endured time in a dugout offered this description: *"We are in a mine 80 feet deep. It has six entrances, two main passages with rooms leading off, and is illuminated by electric light. Water pours in all the time, and in parts the passages are two feet deep in green liquid. One walks on upturned biscuit boxes used as stepping stones. Two pumps are kept going day and night to keep the water down. The whole place is vilely foul, and one can scarcely breathe. The prevailing odour is that of ammonia from the decaying matter - food and rubbish - left by the troops who have been here before."*

The stresses and strains of this time took their toll on the brigade's men as did the impact of German artillery and gas shells. A steady flow of men required medical treatment and by early August every battery commander had been put out of action. As a result junior officers were often elevated on a temporary basis and Harold found himself promoted to the rank of Captain. On 16 August the brigade provided artillery support for an attack on Langemarck, but this made little headway against both German resistance and further rain. Another assault was made here during the last week of August and 241's batteries were once more involved. However, the Germans had built a series of formidable concrete bunkers and it was not until 20 September that enemy defences in this area were finally overcome. The steady flow of British casualties continued during this period with nearly all batteries being badly affected at some point. A/241 suffered what was probably the worst incident on 11 September when a gas attack killed eleven men from the battery. Further evidence of the scale of casualties was indicated by another set of temporary promotions as a number of officers took over from those already killed, wounded or sick - on 10 September Harold was given the rank of Temporary Major. This was the most difficult period faced by the brigade during the whole war and at the end of the month it was withdrawn from the frontline. After a brief at the brigade wagon lines at Vlamertinghe, they moved to Noordpeene on 28 September. Here they enjoyed some decent billets and a brief period of rest.

On 5 October Harold's brigade was summoned back into action and its guns sent to a location north of the Ypres - Zonnebeke road, about one and half miles east of the town. The next phase of fighting - the Battle of Poelcapelle - commenced on 9 October and the brigade's guns were ordered to move forward from their location to take part. This extremely difficult task was attempted during the night of 10/11 October but every battery had guns it simply could not shift. The result was that the four batteries had to combine the guns moved forward to create two effective batteries. These fired in support of an Australian assault on the Passchendaele Ridge on 12 October. Once again the brigade took casualties, their position being exposed, and their involvement in the Third Battle of Ypres ended when they were relieved the following day. In terms of losses to manpower, horses and equipment the brigade had suffered considerably during this battle. Harold was extremely lucky as he was one of the few officers that had not been killed, wounded or sent out of the lines due to sickness during the course of the whole campaign.

Part Ten: The Italian Campaign, 1918

After their departure from Ypres, 241 Brigade were sent to the Vimy sector, travelling via the town of Bethune. The journey south took a number of days and gave the men a chance to recover from the turmoil they had experienced during their time in action around the Ypres Salient. After taking over some Canadian positions in front of Vimy Ridge they were moved to other locations nearby as required. Although this was a relatively quiet time it was not without its moments and in early November Harold's battery was badly affected when a shell burst at their position, resulting in a number of casualties including two men who were entombed. On 18 November the brigade handed back its positions at Vimy to the Canadians and prepared for a move to the Italian front, as part of a large British contingent being sent to support the ally. The Italians had suffered a serious defeat at Caporetto in November 1917 and the battle front had to be stabilised in case the Germans and Austro-Hungarians decided to exploit their victory. The brigade enjoyed a period of relative calm as it travelled to and then established itself in Italy - life was much less demanding than on the Western Front. At the start of January 1918 the brigade moved to Piave but it was not until March that they actually went into action. Generally the situation remained relatively quiet and, as the brigade history recorded: *"Conditions were very different from what the Brigade had been accustomed to in France."* The greatest contrast with the Western Front was in the weather which was far more extreme and on some occasions getting food and ammunition to the batteries could involve a whole day's journey as men struggled through the snow. The distance between the batteries and the wagon lines could also be a problem. Throughout the period from April to October 1918, 241 Brigade was engaged supporting operations on the Asiago Plateau. During the periods of rest and inactivity Harold took the opportunity to relax by making use of his artistic skills. A couple of his paintings are still in the possession of his son James. A few letters from family members back in Wolverhampton have survived and indicate Harold's mother was beginning to feel more positive about the chances of the war ending favourably in the not too distant future. As always, she was also looking forward to the prospect of him getting leave. Harold was told about his brother Ron's preparations to join the RFA, now that he had completed his education at Wolverhampton Grammar School. Unfortunately, the more positive tone of the letters ended when news arrived that his cousin, Joseph Henry - Elizabeth Sankey's youngest son - had died suddenly and preparations were being made for his funeral.

Part Eleven: Coming Home and Life after the War

The war ended for 241 Brigade when an Armistice was arranged between the Allies and the Austro-Hungarian Empire on 4 November 1918 - a week before the cessation of hostilities on the Western Front. However, by that time Harold was already back in England having been given a temporary respite from the army, for a period of six months. It appears the possibility of getting Harold released from military service was first discussed in September 1917. *Sankeys* was working flatout manufacturing items for all branches of the armed forces and the company's directors were under sustained pressure to meet production targets and quotas. Fred Sankey continued to be under considerable strain and his health was the subject of great concern. It was felt that a younger person was now needed to run the company - ideally someone with knowledge and understanding of the workings of Joseph Sankey and Sons Ltd - and that person was Harold. On 20 September 1917 George H Sankey, on behalf of the board of directors, wrote a letter to local Liberal MP George Thorne, raising the issue of getting Harold released from military service. The two men met in November 1917 and Thorne agreed to make enquiries. His response was contained in a letter dated 8 December 1917 in which he explained that the army was reluctant to release men from service, especially officers of Harold's quality. He pointed out that men like Harold were valued for the knowledge and experience they had built up through service on a number of battlefronts and that replacing them with fresh men meant that those valued characteristics would be lost. The available evidence suggests that the company decided not to pursue the matter for the next few months but by the summer of 1918 the issue had resurfaced.

By then the directors were clearly feeling the strain of both physical and mental exhaustion which had first reared its head in late 1915 and early 1916. Since then the full impact of Britain's preparations for the Somme and Third Ypres offensives had also taken a heavy toll on the management at *Sankeys*. The company again enlisted the support of George Thorne and also got in touch with Lieutenant Colonel John Colville, the officer commanding 241 Brigade RFA. However, when Thorne wrote to George Sankey on 23 August 1918 he admitted that his efforts to get Harold released on a temporary basis had failed. His letter *stated: "the whole question has been under review and it is definitely laid down by the Minister of Munitions that no such application must be made by the Ministry to the War Office on behalf of an officer under 25 years of age and in General Service".* Thorne went on to suggest that Harold could approach the War Office directly; *"in view of his long overseas service."* A letter to George Sankey on 9 September confirmed the Ministry of Munitions' position but the following month brought an apparent volte-face when another letter arrived completely reversing the original judgement, giving permission for Harold to be released from military service for six months. There is no evidence to indicate whether Harold ever wrote a personal appeal to the War Office, as Thorne suggested but a letter, dated September 1918, outlining the case for Harold's release does exist:

"Major Harold Bantock Sankey MC was trained with a view to occupying a responsible position in this business for which he has shown a particular aptitude. His services are most urgently required. He could render invaluable service and would immediately be given a very responsible position which in the opinion of the Directors would greatly aid the production of munitions of war. The important developments contemplated through the installation of a large plant for the production of oxygen and nitrogen makes it extremely desirable that the talents of the younger man should not be lost.
Signed for and on behalf of the Board
George H Sankey"

The letter then detailed the extent of munitions production at each of the company's four sites. Notes also exist for the type of information Harold might include in any personal letter to the Ministry of Munitions. This included reference to the death just before the war of John Sankey, the former chairman, the death in action of another director, Sydney and the poor health of Fred Sankey. It also detailed the extent of Harold's service, emphasising the fact that he joined up in August 1914 and had served throughout the conflict. Perhaps Harold did write such a letter and this, along with one from the directors finally swung matters in their favour. Ironically, by the time George acknowledged receipt of the correspondence from the Ministry of National Service Harold had already returned home and within a matter of weeks the war was over.

Three of George Sankey's sons went on to have long careers with the company after the war. Harold and Ron both went to Trinity College Cambridge and progressed into a variety of management roles, but it was Harold who eventually became chairman of *Sankeys* in 1951. He remained in the Territorial Army until 1934, when he retired with the rank of Brevet Colonel, and he took over from his father as managing director of the company the following year. During the Second World War Harold was chairman of the Midland Regional Board of the Ministry of Production – an important role given the region was a key industrial area with many establishments vital to the war effort. He was based at offices in Birmingham and travelled throughout the region as part of his job. On many nights Harold remained at his office as the journey home to Wolverhampton could be hazardous due to blackout restrictions. After the war he returned to his role in the company, served as High Sheriff of Staffordshire, 1946-47 and was awarded the CBE for his services to industry. Harold Sankey died suddenly in his office at Bilston on 27 August 1954 – aged 59. In a tribute made after his death an unknown writer said of him; *"He saw and faced many dangers and it was a by-word in the Battery that 'Old Sank' (as he was affectionately called) would never give an order which he could not reasonably expect himself to do."*

Sankey employees who fought in the Great War. *Photograph courtesy of James Sankey*

The author would particularly like to thank the Sankey family for allowing him access to the letters of Harold Sankey, the staff at Wolverhampton Archives, the school library staff at Wolverhampton Grammar School and Pete Langford, John Hale and Andy Johnson of the Wolverhampton Branch of the Western Front Association for their valuable assistance.

Sources used:

Jones, E., *A History of GKN Vol 1*, 1987.
TNA WO 95/2687 *1/6 Battalion South Staffordshire Regiment War Diary*.
TNA DB 25/9 Sankey family papers (1886-1953).
Wolverhampton Express & Star
The War History of the 1/6 Battalion South Staffordshire Regiment (T.F.), by a committee of officers who served with the Battalion. 1924, Heinemann.
Wolverhampton Warriors, Roy C Evans. Bright Pen 2010.
Hill 60. N Cave. Leo Cooper 1998.
The South Staffords at War. August 1914--December 1915. 2 Volumes. Andrew Thornton. 2016.
The Staffordshire Brigade at Wulverghem April to June 1915. Andrew Thornton. 2000
241st Brigade RFA. A C Williams 1921 Privately published.
TNA WO 95/2749/4 241 Brigade War Diary (1 March 1915 - 31 October 1917)
TNA DB 25/7 Miscellaneous papers relating to company history (1901-1921).
The Private letters of Harold Bantock Sankey and other family members - MS.
The Wulfrunian, 1911-1914. Wolverhampton Grammar School.
www.denniscorbett.com/241.html
Dennis Corbett's website dedicated to the men of 241 Brigade RFA

Chapter 2

Clipped Wings - The Fallen Airmen of St. Philip's, Penn Fields

John Hale

Indulging my interest in local war memorials, I visited St Philip's in Penn a few years ago and photographed the memorial there. As it was a nice day, and I had some time on my hands, I then decided to visit the nearby churchyard. Having a lifelong interest in the Royal Air Force and its predecessor services, I was surprised to find several graves of airmen amongst the haphazard ranks of the citizens of Penn buried therein. Not only were there several airmen of the Great War, but I also found considerable numbers of airmen from the Second World War. Whilst there are many interesting stories to tell of these men; including a Battle of Britain pilot and a Czech serving on a RAF bomber squadron; they must be left untold for another day.

L-R: Ernest West, Percy Morgan and Haden Mostyn Kendrick.

Never flew the nest...

The only airman remembered on the Penn war memorial is Cadet 13774, Ernest A. West of *"Glengarry",* Coalway Road, Wolverhampton. However, he is noted on the panels of the memorial as serving with the Royal Field Artillery, which hindered identification of him somewhat. I was only able to positively identify Ernest when I discovered a Wolverhampton Grammar School website detailing *Old Wulfrunians* who died in the Great War. Whilst this website did not acknowledge his (admittedly brief) service with the RAF, finding his service papers on a popular genealogical website revealed the full story of his sad fate. After leaving school in July 1912 Ernest pursued a degree course in dentistry, entering Birmingham Dental Hospital. However, for unknown reasons, he abandoned his studies and secured employment as a motor tester at the Clyno Engineering car plant in Wolverhampton. Volunteering in November 1915, he served as a Private in No. 626 Motor Transport

Company of the Army Service Corps, which supported No. 19 Motor Ambulance Convoy. Ernest was then sent to East Africa where he was employed mostly as a driver of Ford motor lorries. He was not the perfect young soldier, as his Conduct Sheet reveals he spent six days *'Confined to Barracks'* for the heinous crime of failing to report he was in possession of two greatcoats! As the war entered its final stages Ernest decided on a change of career. He transferred to the RAF, on probation, and was struck off the strength of the East Africa Force on 23 October 1918. He then embarked on the steamer *Palamcotta*, at Dar es Salaam, for the journey to Egypt to commence his flying training. However, the rigours of the climate in East Africa had already taken their toll on the young man, as he had been hospitalised four times with Malaria, since February 1918. Three days into his journey to Egypt, the steamer docked at Mombasa, and Ernest was struck down with Malaria once more and hospitalised. Although he was released after thirteen days, he then contracted Influenza and Blackwater Fever and on 20 November was hospitalised again. Sadly, he was too weak to resist this final illness and died of cardiac failure at No. 1 Base Hospital, Mombasa on 18 December 1918, aged 23. Ernest's body lies in the CWGC plot in the civil cemetery in Mbaraki, Mombasa. He never made it to Egypt, and he never learned to fly.

Be careful who you fly with…

Air Mechanic 1st Class 45361, Percy James Morgan was killed in a mid-air collision whilst flying in a DH6 of 124 Squadron RAF. He was another old boy of Wolverhampton Grammar School, and lived in Jeffcock Road. After leaving school he worked for the Sunbeam Motor Company as a toolmaker. Percy volunteered to serve in the army on 12 August 1914 and joined the 7th Battalion of the South Staffordshire Regiment. Sent to Gallipoli, he was wounded in the face by a sniper's bullet. After recovery, he transferred to the Royal Flying Corps on 21 July 1916, where his mechanical skills and knowledge were undoubtedly of more use. At the time of his death Percy was on the strength of No. 124 Squadron, RAF; a training unit based at Fowlmere in Cambridgeshire. The life of the groundcrew in the airforce was a pretty safe one; the only dangers came if your aerodrome was bombed by the Germans, or if you were sent to retrieve valuable spare parts from a machine that had crashed in no man's land. On the other hand, you could be invited to go up for a spin in a machine you had just serviced: a measure often taken by experienced pilots as a form of quality control to check the work carried out by the mechanics! On his Casualty Card, held at the RAF Museum, Percy Morgan is described as an *'engine tester'*, so it was presumably for this purpose that he was invited by the Canadian Second Lieutenant, Osbert Leveson Calverley, to go up for a spin on 12 July 1918. The flight of their DH6 trainer did not go well, as the aircraft was involved in a mid-air collision with another machine at 700 feet, with fatal results for all concerned. This accident may have occurred during formation flying or a practice dogfight. When Percy Morgan died his sister, in Handsworth, was his next-of-kin; both of their parents already being dead. This may explain why nobody from the local area put his name forward to be included on the Penn war memorial.

The second groundcrew member buried in St Philips's to perish in a flying accident was Air Mechanic, 3rd Class, 191885, Frederick George Ryder. He lived in Sidney Street, near the Penn Road, and died on 5 November 1918. When Frederick joined the RAF, on 3 June 1918, his civilian trade was given as a *'fitter & turner'*. His RAF trade was Rigger (Airframes) and he served at 52 Training Depot Station at Cramlington, near Newcastle upon Tyne. A rigger was responsible for making sure the airframe was 'straight' and tight, because Great War-era biplanes were braced with wires, like a birdcage. These needed to be constantly tensioned after every flight as the stresses of flying caused them to stretch. If the flying surfaces were out of alignment, the performance of the aircraft would be impaired; a potentially disastrous scenario in a dogfight. In circumstances presumably similar to those of Percy Morgan, Frederick was the passenger in a DH9 bomber which went into a flat turn after takeoff, on Tuesday 5 November 1918. The plane stalled and nosedived into the ground, where it burst into flames. Neither Frederick nor the pilot survived the crash. The young rigger was not only just a fortnight away from his eighteenth birthday, but it was also less than a week away from the Armistice. It was a tragic end to a young life and Frederick's name is also absent from the Penn war memorial.

The fledgling pilot

Also buried in St Philip's churchyard and not named on the Penn war memorial is Second Lieutenant Haden Mostyn Kendrick. He came from York Avenue, near Bantock Park, and was another *Old Wulfrunian*, like Ernest West and Percy Morgan. Haden was the son of a prominent local solicitor and worked in the family business before the war. On the outbreak of hostilities he joined the 5th South Staffords, along with a group of chums from school. He was commissioned in March 1915, but wounded on active service and invalided home. Field Marshal Haig was appreciative of the work conducted by the RFC on the Western front, and authorised a great expansion of the service. Volunteers were called for - Kendrick put his name forward - and joined the corps in July 1916. Powered flight was still in its infancy, but proved an irresistible attraction for young men with a spirit of adventure. However, not all officers were inspired by such noble motives. For some, the attractions of going into battle sitting down and returning to their own bed every night, dinner in the Mess, a town or village a short drive away, let alone the excitement of flying, were all too good to resist. It was arguably no more dangerous an occupation than that of an infantry subaltern on the Western Front – so why be cold, wet and uncomfortable in the trenches, where the Germans were shooting at you all the time? If they failed the flying training and returned to their infantry unit, at least they'd had six months away from the trenches! This is not idle speculation on my part – many of the pilots, whose memoirs I have read, were motivated by the desire to escape the drudgery of the trenches as one of the principal reasons why they wanted to transfer to the RFC. Unfortunately, Haden's career as an airman was cut short when his Maurice-Farman Shorthorn training aircraft *"struck the top of a large oak tree"* on the evening of 18 September 1916.[3] The Court of Inquiry reports: *"Accident due to flying too low and hitting a tree. No fault of the machine."* An escort of officers and men brought

---

[3] *The Berwick Advertiser*, 22 September 1916

Haden's body home from the RFC station at Thetford, in Norfolk, where the accident happened and stayed to attend the funeral. He was twenty-five years of age and added his name to the long list of trainee pilots who failed to survive flying training - never getting the chance to serve operationally at the front.

Influenza

Two of the airmen buried at St. Philip's were victims of the great influenza pandemic that spread throughout the world in 1918. These include Clerk 3rd Class 307351 Algernon William Moore, the husband of Flora Louisa Moore, of *"Netherleigh"*, Birches Barn Road, Wolverhampton. At forty-years-of-age, Algernon is the oldest airman to be buried in the cemetery. He was employed at No. 3 Stores Depot at Woking, when admitted to the camp hospital at Steventon, Berkshire. It was here that he succumbed to his illness on 28 October 1918. Similarly, Air Mechanic 3rd Class 140813 William Bladen, the son of Alfred and Grace Bladen, of 12 Horseman Street, Wolverhampton also died as a result of the illness. Whilst serving at the seaplane station at Felixstowe he contracted influenza and died on 3 July 1918, in the hospital at Shotley, aged 24. William had only joined the RAF on 25 March, when his civilian occupation was given as clerk. Neither of these victims of 'Spanish flu' are named on the Penn war memorial.

Gone West...

Although Second Lieutenant Charles Henry Harriman is not buried at St. Philip's, nor is his name inscribed on the Penn war memorial, he is recorded on his parent's gravestone. The family home address given on his service file was *'The Drive'*, Wrottesley Road, Tettenhall. When war broke out Charles was an apprentice at Cammell Laird's shipyard in Birkenhead. Did he and Haden Kendrick know each other? He volunteered in March 1915 and joined the 5th South Staffordshire Regiment. Subsequently commissioned (being an old boy of Queen Mary's Grammar School, Walsall) he transferred to the RFC in 1916 and won his wings on 14 March 1917. Charles was posted to No. 43 Squadron at Auchel on 5 May 1917. This squadron were equipped with the Sopwith 1½ Strutter two-seater and were then later re-equipped with the famous Sopwith Camel. Unfortunately Charles was shot down on 29 October 1917 and buried at Lapugnoy Military Cemetery, located near Bethune. Obviously an experienced pilot, having served at the front for more than five months, he would doubtless shortly have been returned to Home Establishment for a rest had he not fallen prey to a German airman.

The attractions of life as an airman proved irresistible to many adventurous young men; alas, for some this fascination led to their early death.

Chapter 3

Conscientious Objectors, Military Tribunals and the White Feather Movement

"Our best must not be killed off to spare the slackers."[4]

Heidi McIntosh

Sir

Your Gallant + Protracted Defence Against the Brutal Attacks of the Local Tribunal has been brought to the Notice of the Supreme Council of the Most Noble Order of the Trench Dodgers. I am to inform you that the Council have therefore, as a reward for your devotion to self regardless of narrow patriotism, made you a companion of the said most noble order, the insignia of which is forwarded herewith.

I am, Sir

Your Obedient Servant

A Chicken Heart

Clerk to the Council

One August day during the latter years of the Great War, Wolverhampton-born architect William J.H. Weller received the letter above. The *"insignia"* referred to is a remarkably well-preserved white feather.[5] This white feather letter, as it is known, is one thread of an intriguing narrative concerning Weller who never fired a shot and did not even leave England during the War. However, he has become forever linked to the conflict which dominated his own life and possibly troubled his peace of mind. Before unravelling the strands of Weller's story it will be necessary to explore the history of the white feather movement, examine Great War Military Service Tribunals, and look more closely at the issue of conscientious objectors (COs).

Although white feathers are associated with cowardice and shame during the Great War, their symbolism originates in cockfighting many years before. It was said that purebred cockerels did not have white feathers, so a bird with one in its tail was probably an inferior crossbreed and likely to be a poor fighter. While white feathers were used to target supposed cowards before 1914, it was during the Great War that the movement came to prominence. Vice Admiral Charles Cooper Penrose-

---

[4] *Wolverhampton Express & Star*, 21 December 1914
[5] The letter and feather are in the William Weller collection at Wolverhampton City Archives under the reference D-WEL/1/1/3.

44

Fitzgerald founded the Order of the White Feather in Folkestone on 30 August 1914. The movement was supported by author, Mrs Mary Augusta Humphrey Ward, and enlisted women to shame men in civilian clothes by presenting them with a white feather. This implied they were cowards shirking their responsibility to fight for King and Country. It is difficult to know how widespread the practice was because of the shame attached to getting such a demeaning token. Some white feathers were handed out randomly in the street, while others were individually targeted such as the one sent to Weller, now at Wolverhampton City Archives. Many were delivered in an anonymous letter - a cowardly act in its own right - the irony of which was probably missed at the time by the person responsible for sending it.

Interestingly, the image of the white feather has alternative meanings and emphases for other groups and societies. The Quakers and Peace Pledge Union used white feathers as a symbol of peace and in Maori culture three white feathers are used to promote *"glory to God, peace on earth and goodwill toward people."* [6] There is also a superstition that if you find a white feather soon after the death of a loved one, it signifies that the angels are looking after them. However, white feathers are generally recognised as having negative connotations, linked to cowardice in wartime. White feathers have appeared in popular culture and television on numerous occasions. There is an episode of *Downton Abbey* where a group of women interrupt a benefit concert to hand out white feathers to the young men present, and an episode of *Dad's Army* in which Lance Corporal Jones is mistakenly believed to have been a coward when he fought in the Sudan. [7] Jones is sent two and a half feathers before he eventually clears his name - which is particularly interesting as *Dad's Army* is set during the Second World War. P. G. Wodehouse wrote a story called *The White Feather*, about a young boy who ran away from a street brawl and was branded a coward. The 1902 novel by A. E. W. Mason called *The Four Feathers* was later made into several film versions, the most recent of which starred Heath Ledger (2002) and was also set in the Sudan. It is about an officer called Harry Faversham who is so shamed by the four feathers he receives for refusing to fight he secretly gets involved in the war to redeem his honour and win back his fiancée.

In her 1938 essay *Three Guineas*, Virginia Woolf suggested that during the Great War the number of women who *"stuck feathers in coats must have been infinitesimal compared with those who did nothing of the kind."* [8] Although she regarded exaggerated reactions to the practice as a product of male hysteria, it appears to have been more common than Woolf believed. In 1964, to commemorate the fiftieth anniversary of the start of the Great War, the BBC and Imperial War Museum (IWM) made an appeal for members of the public to come forward with their memories. One of the topics covered in subsequent interviews was the white feather

---

[6]. Te Raukura – White Feather <https://theinvasionofparihaka.weebly.com/actions-taken-campaigns.html> [accessed April 2019]

[7] More details of this episode are available here:
https://en.wikipedia.org/wiki/The_Two_and_a_Half_Feathers [accessed January 2019]

[8] Virginia Woolf, *Three Guineas*, originally published 1938. Published online by The University of Adelaide <https://ebooks.adelaide.edu.au/w/woolf/virginia/w91tg/index.html> [accessed January 2019]

movement. Unsurprisingly, few respondents owned up to having sent white feathers although one woman apparently described herself as a *"chump"* for doing so.[9] However, the BBC and IWM received more than 200 responses from people who had been given a white feather. As many recipients would have died since the war and others would have chosen to ignore the survey request, organisers were surprised by the evidence showing how common the practice had been.

It was generally women who handed out white feathers - presumably because they could use their feminine wiles to shame and then entice vulnerable or gullible young men into joining up. Feathers were sometimes given in error to soldiers home on leave or others invalided out of the army. Frederick Broome joined up when the war broke out at the tender age of 15.[10] He caught a fever at Ypres and was sent home to England to recuperate. His father promptly ensured he was discharged for having lied about his age on enlistment. Soon afterwards Broome was accosted by a group of girls handing out white feathers. Even though he explained his circumstances, they refused to believe him. He felt so uncomfortable and embarrassed he promptly walked straight into the nearest recruiting office and re-enlisted, even though he was still under age. There is also evidence of collusion between women and recruiting officers and use of underhand tactics to dupe men into the forces. A Mr S. C. Lang was walking down Camden High Street when he was asked by two young ladies why he wasn't in the army. When he replied that he was only seventeen they scoffed and said they had heard that one before, shoving a white feather up his nose. A sergeant then came out of one of the shops further down. *"Did she call you a coward?"* he asked. *"Well, come into the drill hall and we'll soon prove that you aren't a coward."* Next thing he knew, he'd been signed up. [11]

It was these, and similar cases of mistaken identity that prompted Home Secretary, Reginald McKenna, to issue employees in state industries with lapel badges which read *"King and Country".* These indicated that these men were serving the war effort on the Home Front even though they were not in uniform. After September 1916 soldiers discharged due to wounds or sickness were given Silver War Badges. *Dad's Army* actor Arnold Ridley, who played Private Godfrey, fought in the First World War, took part in the Battle of the Somme and was wounded three times before being medically discharged. Ridley later spoke of how in 1917 he was handed a white feather by a young woman. Displaying a modesty reminiscent of Private Godfrey, Ridley explained he had not been wearing his Silver War Badge at the time as he did not want to advertise the fact he was a genuine wounded soldier.[12]

---

[9] George Simmers, *White feathers: Stories of Courage, Recruitment and gender at the start of the Great War* <https://greatwarfiction.wordpress.com/white-feathers-stories-of-courage-cowardice-and-recruitment-at-the-start-of-the-great-war/> [accessed January 2019]
[10] Max Arthur, *Forgotten Voices of the Great War* (London: Random House, 2002), p. 65
[11] Ibid, p. 62
[12] BBC News, *The real-life wars of Dad's Army actor Arnold Ridley*, 2016 <https://www.bbc.co.uk/news/uk-england-35491036> [accessed January 2019]

When war began in August 1914 the army relied on voluntary enlistment as well as recalling former Reservists and Territorials to their regiments. Patriotic zeal was strong throughout the country as many believed the war would not last long. However, towards the end of the year this optimistic outlook began to wane. A letter in the Wolverhampton *Express & Star* on 21 December 1914, from a James Saunders, bemoaned the fact he saw *"so many of our young fellows, who by this time should be ready for the trenches, still patrolling the streets, guarding a cigarette or a perambulator, or supposing they derive a little reflected glory by marching side by side with a real hero in khaki."* While he acknowledged that *"some young men are doing good service in providing munitions of war or necessary equipment,"* he said compulsory conscription was essential as *"our best must not be killed off to spare the slackers."* This critical attitude clearly contributed to rise of the white feather movement.

By spring 1915 voluntary enlistment averaged 100,000 men a month but relying on initial enthusiasm was unsustainable and the overall recruitment trend was slowing down. In May 1915 the upper age limit was raised from 38 to 40 years, but even this measure did not produce the numbers the army needed. The concept of compulsory military service was anathema to many members of the Liberal government, but steps were soon taken in that direction. The National Registration Act of July 1915 required all men aged 15 to 65 to register, giving full employment details. This was meant to highlight eligible young men who had not yet enlisted and who were not in so-called "protected" trades. The Derby Scheme - named after Edward Stanley, the seventeenth Earl - was introduced in October 1915 and gave men aged 18-40 the option of enlisting voluntarily or attesting. To attest meant deferring active service until called on later and men who did so wore a khaki armband to indicate this to any woman brandishing a white feather. While more than two million men enlisted under the Derby scheme, it was not a huge success as 38% of eligible single men and 54% of eligible married men still failed to attest. These percentages did not include those in "protected" occupations.

Conscription was introduced through the Military Service Act in January 1916, which called for compulsory enlistment of unmarried men between the ages of 18 and 41. In May 1916 this was extended to include men between those ages, regardless of marital status. As the need for more men increased, the terms of the act were extended to include re-examining those previously discharged due to disablement and expanding the age range from 17 to 55 years. This drastic step was taken in April 1918 after the great German offensive. Men in "protected" occupations or who had other reasons for being excused military service were called before local Military Service Tribunals to plead their case. Locally these were held at Wolverhampton Magistrates Court. Due to the sensitivities surrounding compulsory military service during and after the Great War, only a small proportion of the Tribunal papers survive. In 1921 the Ministry of Health ordered that all documents relating to individual cases of exemption from National Service, including those on the grounds of conscientious objection, should be destroyed, along with every Tribunal minute book. The only records kept were those of the Central Tribunal – to be used as exemplars should a similar situation occur in future. Luckily, not all local authorities obeyed the destruction instruction. Staffordshire Record Office, for example, has a collection of about 20,000 local Tribunal records. These do not relate to Wolverhampton cases – meaning that, as far as we know, there is very little surviving primary evidence of the actions of Tribunals in the town. Local newspapers, including the *Express & Star* and the *Wolverhampton Chronicle* reported on Tribunals but details of the individuals who came before them were anonymised, unlike elsewhere in the country. However, the newspaper accounts usually contained enough information for individuals to be identified. Details such as *"an 18-year-old youth who is apprenticed as a toolsetter and toolmaker"*[13] or, more specifically, *"the Bushbury Scoutmaster"*[14] were obvious clues that enabled local people to work out who was being referred to. Although there were lists of "exempted" occupations, Tribunals appear to have been quite arbitrary in their verdicts, so there was no consistency in how individual cases were treated. For example, a brewer's drayman who delivered beer to public houses was given an absolute exemption from military service,[15] whereas applications by two brothers working in the farming and agricultural industry were refused.[16] There were numerous cases where appeals from businesses were rejected because the Tribunal said women could do the jobs. Consequently, the Great War saw a huge rise in women working in factories and other local firms - filling the gaps left by men. Even those who seemed genuinely incapable of military service were not immune from being enlisted, or at least having to justify their case at the Tribunal. A coal merchant with a wooden leg was only granted a six month exemption,[17] as was another man *"who had had a foot taken off."*[18] There was also the case of a man who was blind in one eye and had defective vision in the other. The *Express & Star* rather grudgingly agreed that this *"was sufficient reason for an applicant's total exemption."*[19]

Conversely, men seen to be supporting their families were often exempted. A 40-year-old labourer was excused service on the grounds that he was the sole support for a widowed mother and invalid brother, as well as having had another brother who died while a prisoner of war.[20] The approach of claiming to be the lynchpin of the family did not always guarantee success. The son of a widowed mother who suffered with rheumatism and to whom he gave 20 shillings a week was granted a six-month exemption with the Tribunal even commenting *"he was a good son."*[21] One man, in addition to looking after his parents and so-called *"imbecile"* brother also claimed to have *"missed a good offer of marriage in fulfilment of a promise to his parents."*[22] However, his great personal sacrifice failed to impress the Tribunal and he was granted only one month's exemption. One young coal

---

[13] *Wolverhampton Express & Star,* 2 March 1916
[14] *Ibid,* 20 March 1916
[15] *Ibid,* 16 March 1916
[16] *Ibid,* 4 March 1916
[17] *Ibid,* 28 March 1916
[18] *Ibid,* 30 March 1916
[19] *Ibid, 21 March 1916*
[20] *Ibid,* 30 March 1916
[21] *Ibid,* 9 March 1916
[22] *Ibid,* 20 March 1916

merchant, who claimed he single-handedly kept the home solvent, was caught out. Following enquiries by the Tribunal, it was discovered his father received a pension of £120 a year so his application was refused.[23]

Tribunals also dealt with conscientious objectors (COs) - individuals refusing military service on moral or ethical grounds. These men were usually offered non-combatant service but even this was not always acceptable to the most ardent objectors. In April 1916 local authorities were asked whether they would be willing to employ them in areas which would help the war effort, such as fire brigades, civil hospitals and asylums. Bilston Urban District Council was not alone in refusing to employ such men, claiming that *"friction would result amongst their employees."* [24] Probably a quarter of all Tribunal cases cited conscientious objection as the reason for refusing to enlist. Some of these were simply thrown out of court such as the example of a man who claimed exemption on religious grounds but who was not a member of any church.[25] Many COs refused to do military service, even when verdicts went against them. In such cases the individuals were taken to court and reporting restrictions against naming them were lifted. This means historians can track their stories.

For example, we have the case of *"two assistant masters at a well-known College"* who declared their conscientious objection to war. They first appear in an *Express & Star* report of the Tettenhall Tribunal on 24 March 1916. Both joined the Non-Conscription League, and one wrote that he believed *"hate can be overcome by love."* The College Head wrote in support of their plea for exemption, but not on moral grounds as: *"he did not agree with the attitude of the men as pacifists."* He argued instead that due to the war *"he was shorthanded, and the absence of the masters would be detrimental to the boys in their examination."* Their appeal was refused at the Tribunal. Subsequently, on 17 April 1916, an article appeared which named the two individuals concerned: William Arthur Cooper (aged thirty-three) and Ronald Edward Pond (twenty-five). Both were assistant masters at Tettenhall College and they appeared before the Wolverhampton County Police Court, charged with *"having failed to report themselves for service in the army under the Military Service Act."* The article said they were offered non-combatant service, but declined. Cooper declared they could *"not serve the army in any way, believing they were serving the best interest of the country in their present profession."* Each was fined 40 shillings and remanded to await a military escort.

Twin brothers, Garnett Round Aston and Gordon Osborne Aston, appeared at Wolverhampton County Magistrates Court on Monday 3 April 1916 charged with having failed to present themselves under the terms of the Military Service Act. The *Wolverhampton Chronicle* the following Wednesday said they defended themselves by claiming *"they could not have deserted from something they had not joined."* The

---

[23] *Wolverhampton Express & Star*, 14 March 1916
[24] Minutes of Bilston Urban District Council, available at Wolverhampton City Archives at reference C-UD-BIL/1/2/6
[25] *Wolverhampton Express & Star*, 21 March 1916

court clerk said they were not being accused of desertion but being *"absentees from the Army,"* having received notice to join on 30 March and failed to do so. Despite appearing before the Tribunal and an appeal, they insisted their case was not properly heard. Both were fined forty shillings and remanded to await a military escort. This might have been the point at which the trail of this particular story went cold but a further article about the twins appeared in the *Express & Star,* on 9 February 1917. Entitled: *"Wolverhampton Conscientious Objectors Sentenced,"* it referred to Privates J. O. And J. R. Aston of the South Staffordshire Regiment. Despite the slight anomaly in their initials, it was the same set of brothers. On this occasion, they were court-martialled at Whittington Barracks *"on charges of desertion and of losing their clothing and regimental necessaries by neglect."* They were each sentenced to 84 days imprisonment without hard labour. The article noted they had already been sentenced to imprisonment by court martial for refusing to obey orders on two previous occasions. Although imprisonment was unpleasant, the brothers' continued resistance meant they successfully delayed being sent to the Front, so their punishment appeared light in comparison with what might have faced them 'over there'. But the way COs' cases were reported was meant to discourage dissent and boost morale with those objecting on high moral principles being depicted as trouble-makers.

In some cases the Tribunal hearings appeared slightly farcical. On 16 March 1916, the *Express & Star* reported that a 24-year-old man urged absolute exemption on grounds of conscientious objection as well as being a pharmacist - a certified occupation. He said: *"As a follower of the Lord Jesus Christ he felt it his duty to obey His precepts and love his enemy."* The Tribunal Chairman responded, *"Why don't you go to Germany and love them there?"* The man was asked what he would do if he saw his mother being attacked in the street? He refused to answer saying: *"That is a hypothetical case...Jesus Christ is my Master and His attitude was one of non-resistance."* The Tribunal Chairman replied, *"I suggest He goes to the Front,"* and after lengthy discourse this application for exemption was refused. In another case several minutes were spent discussing a man's grounds for conscientious objection before he happened to mention he had already been rejected five times as being medically unfit. He was dismissed from the Tribunal and criticised for wasting their time.

Finally, there is the case of a Leonard Benjamin Lamb. On 3 August 1916 he was charged with having failed to report for military service. When asked to enter his plea he replied: *"I plead technically guilty, but morally innocent."* He had applied to the Tribunal as a CO, but they failed to grant him an exemption from military service. Lamb waxed lyrical about how he *"admired greatly the courage and sincerity of the men – British or German".* He was ordered to pay 40 shillings, deducted from his Army pay, and handed over to the military authorities. Lamb pointed out that as *"a conscientious objector he should not perform any Army duties and consequently he should not draw any pay."* This CO resurfaced in an article on 20 June 1917, which said he was a Private in the South Staffordshire Regiment. The report mentioned he had been tried for a fourth time by court martial at Whittington Barracks *"on a charge of refusing to obey the order of a superior officer."* This time Lamb declined to parade for a medical inspection, saying he refused *"to sell his body and soul to a committee."* Because of continued resistance he was sentenced to two years' imprisonment with hard labour - the longest sentence passed on any CO at Whittington Barracks. It meant the war was over before Lamb completed his term of incarceration and he avoided the potentially worse fate of fighting on the Western Front or elsewhere.

Alongside COs, Tribunals also dealt with men trying to hoodwink the system - an early form of benefit fraud. Auctioneer John Harold Whitfield Baker made several false statements to the Tribunal claiming he single-handedly managed an office in London as well as one in Wolverhampton. In reality he had no office in London and this emerged when questioned about its location and he failed to remember the address he had previously given. Baker pleaded *"Not guilty"* when brought before the court on 7 September 1917, but was persuaded to change his plea to "Guilty" when presented with the overwhelming evidence against him. Further details from the prosecution case revealed he was not even an auctioneer but earned £2 a week in a local munitions factory. The court fined him £100. Baker appeared before the court again on 31 December 1917 charged with being an absentee, having failed to report for military service. However, the case was dismissed as he had lodged an appeal to be heard before the Tribunal. When Walter Edwin Cox received his callup papers he appeared before the Medical Board *"as a cripple, with bent shoulders...utterly incapable of doing useful work in civil life or in the army."* He apparently told doctors he was involved in a carriage accident six years earlier, and had been in a disabled state ever since. The Board rejected him as being *"unfit for service".* However, information was subsequently passed to the military authorities that contradicted Cox's story. He apparently earned his living as a carter - lifting heavy sacks of corn and flour - walked two miles to work each day, and had been seen digging and planting in his garden. When visited at work by the authorities, he was said to have made a *"miraculous recovery,"* was perfectly upright and engaged in heavy manual work. Cox was charged with being a fraud and a malingerer and sent to gaol for two months with hard labour.

At this point it is worth returning to William Weller - recipient of the white feather letter held at Wolverhampton City Archives. He was born in Tettenhall in 1877, son of local architect John Weller II, and died at his home in Codsall on 12 July 1960. Following in the family architectural business, his first major project was completing the vicarage of St Jude's Church, Tettenhall Road, in 1897. Strongly influenced by the Arts and Crafts movement, Weller was responsible for designing other buildings in the area. These include the Burnhill Green Memorial Village Hall, on the Earl of Dartmouth's estate at Patshull, near Wolverhampton, and a Penn Road property currently used as the headquarters of the local chapter of the Hell's Angels. Weller's own home, *Longfield*, was at 152 Penn Road, and he also designed the nearby Barons Court Hotel, 142 Goldthorn Hill. In addition to larger properties for major local families, Weller also specialised in designing homes for working people, such as local authority cottages in Willenhall, built after the Great War. Weller married Mary Cooper in 1904 and they had two children - Joan Harrison in 1905 and Geoffrey Dyson Weller in 1910. His first wife died in 1919. In 1924 he married Kathleen Brown in Alnwick, and they had two children – Ruth, born in 1926 and John, 1930.

Left: Photograph of the young William Weller. *Right:* The original white feather and letter.
Courtesy of Wolverhampton Archives & Local Studies.

It might seem strange to mark the Great War's centenary by focusing on a man who did not see active service, but it is important to remember the war thrust many ordinary people into extraordinary situations – Weller included. It is unclear from the postmark whether the white feather letter was sent in 1916 or 1918 as he appeared before the Tribunal in both years. It was not sent to his Penn Road home, but to the Conservative Club in Lichfield Street - presumably for maximum effect, if opened in the presence of others. It is possible the writer did not know his home address but this is unlikely, given Weller's many contacts in Wolverhampton. In fact, he was not a conscientious objector and never shirked his wartime duties. He contributed to the war effort by serving as a Sergeant with the Special Constables in the Wolverhampton Borough Police Force.[26] Before the Great War, Special Constables were only deployed in times of civil unrest, but the war saw them urgently needed to fill gaps left by serving officers who enlisted in the forces. As well as monitoring the civilian population they tried to prevent any German infiltrators interfering with the nation's water supplies. As well as men like Weller, deemed unfit or ineligible to serve, many Specials were former police officers brought out of retirement. Due to worsening staff shortages the Chief Constable in desperation

[26] His name is included on the illuminated manuscript at Wolverhampton City Archives, listing all men and women who served as Special Constables 1916 – 1919 (reference DX-1008/1).

asked the Watch Committee on 2 July 1917 *"for power to employ women patrols on the streets, or to do any other duty such as visiting Public Parks, Theatres, and particularly work among their own sex and juveniles."*[27] Unfortunately there is little information about the extent to which women were employed as Wolverhampton Specials.

Along with the white feather letter the City Archives has an associated file of correspondence and notes giving more detailed background information about the case.[28] There is evidence Weller approached various firms and individuals to try and secure employment in "protected occupations". The file also includes draft copies of Weller's statement to the Military Service Tribunal in which he gave three main reasons for his exemption. These were being unfit for service, contributing towards the war effort through his work, and being the main support for his family. Depending on the actual date of the letter, Weller was between 39 and 41 years of age – towards the upper end of the conscription age range. Several documents in the file also indicate he had difficulty marching long distances and experienced impaired vision and night blindness. He was directly involved in the war effort designing homes for workers at the Wednesfield Weldless Steel Tube Company Ltd, which made ships' boilers for military use. He was also an architect for Holly Bank Coal Company and said the company had a Ministry of Munitions licence to produce coal for the war effort which they would be unable to fulfil without his building work. As well as his wife and children he was solely responsible for looking after his elderly mother and disabled sister and argued that in his absence they would be left destitute and forced to enter the workhouse. His supporting statements convinced the Tribunal and Weller was given a temporary, rather than absolute, exemption until 30 June 1918. Although the Tribunal accepted his justifications, someone clearly believed he was shirking his duties and at this point decided to send him the white feather letter. Nothing is known for sure about the writer as it is anonymous and written in capital letters - in a presumed attempt to disguise the handwriting. Although there is no signature, it is believed to be by a woman as they were most frequent authors of such notes. The phrasing of the text infers it was written by someone representing a wider group and reference to the Tribunal itself suggests the author may have witnessed Weller's appearance there. Therefore, this was no random poison-pen letter, but a targeted attack on a well-known individual who had successfully defended himself in a public forum. To mobilise public opinion against those seeking to avoid military service, people were actively encouraged to attend Tribunals. Thus, someone planning to send white feather letters may have been present to take note of potential recipients. Alternatively, a Tribunal panel member may have borne a grudge against Weller and passed the details of his case to the letter's author.

---

[27] Watch Committee Minute Book 1917 – 1918, held at Wolverhampton City Archives (reference WOL-C-WAT/41)
[28] Reference D-WEL/1/1/2 at Wolverhampton City Archives

It is very unusual for such an item to have survived for more than a hundred years. As they were meant to bring shame to the recipient - accusing them of cowardice – most were probably disposed of immediately. In 2009, a white feather letter sent to a Quaker and pacifist surfaced on BBC's *Antiques Roadshow*, and was donated to the IWM. This letter was extremely curt and simply stated: *"Noble Sir, If you are too proud or frightened to fight, wear this."*[29] In comparison, the Weller letter is more extensive, sarcastic and nastier in tone. The IWM has several similar examples, including one apparently sent by the Bath Girl Scouts. This invited the recipient to join their group as a washer-up, as: *"you cannot be a man."*[30] But it would be fair to say that very few of these letters survive, and fewer still contain the original feather.

We can only speculate why Weller chose to keep the letter as he never made any public comment about it. Perhaps he thought his positive contribution to the war effort more important and he dismissed the stigma associated with it? Brian Weller, depositor of the Weller Collection and last surviving family member, was extremely proud of his family's history and heritage. He was comfortable with allowing public access to every part of the archive and would not have wanted to tamper with, remove or hide any part of the complete historical record. The Collection mainly consists of architectural plans and drawings of buildings in and around Wolverhampton, but the white feather letter adds another dimension - giving a stark and chilling alternative view of life in Britain during the Great War. We rightly remember it for the total loss of nearly forty million dead and wounded and its profound and lasting effect on Europe and the wider world. However, the white feather letter serves as a reminder of the deeper effects of the war, and its psychological impact on the Home Front. Whilst never losing sight of the bigger picture of national struggle, it is important to recall how the war caused struggles and dilemmas of an intensely personal kind. When William Weller received his white feather letter at the Wolverhampton Conservative Club, little did he realise the significance of its contents. He may have been even more flabbergasted to know it was still generating discussion today.

---

[29] *Antiques Roadshow* clip available here: < https://www.bbc.co.uk/programmes/p00dt7kp> [accessed April 2019]
[30] Imperial War Museum catalogue entry:
<https://www.iwm.org.uk/collections/item/object/1030005025> [accessed January 2019

Chapter 4

Three Cousins Against the Kaiser, 1914-17

Beverley Reynolds

Part One: Private 2685 George Alfred Gobourn, 1/6th Battalion (TF) South Staffordshire Regiment

George Alfred Gobourn, my grandmother's brother, was born in Wolverhampton on 24 July 1892, at Inkerman Street, Heath Town. He was the son of William and Sarah and the fourth of eleven children, having six sisters and four brothers. He was nine-years-old when his father died and also lost a sister and brother whilst still infants. By 1911 the family had moved to Railway Street, Heath Town, and George was listed in the census as working for the London and North Western Railway (LNWR) as a porter at Albion depot. This was located on the current main line between Dudley Port and Sandwell and Dudley stations. When the war broke out George joined the local 1st/6th Battalion of the South Staffordshire Regiment. According to family reminiscences, he had already been a member of the local Territorial Force, and George's low regimental number suggests he was in the 3rd Volunteer Battalion, which had been formed in 1908. Their headquarters were in Stafford Street, near to George's home.

The 1/6 South Staffords were at their annual training camp when war was declared and immediately returned to Wolverhampton and mobilised for action. Although members of the Territorial Force were recruited for home defence only the vast majority volunteered for overseas service. The 5 August 1914 was warm and sunny as the men of the 1/6 South Staffords paraded in Market Square, Wolverhampton. On 11 August they left the town and began their march to Burton upon Trent, covering eighteen miles the first day and the remaining thirteen, after an overnight stop. On arrival in Burton they were billeted in buildings at Allsop's brewery. Here, the battalion was reorganised into four companies A, B, C, and D, with each containing 227 Other Ranks. After only three days in Burton they were taken by train to Luton where they were billeted at nearby Chiltern Green. Several weeks of training took place here, before the battalion embarked on a two day march to Bishop's Stortford, Hertfordshire, on 10 November. Following another three weeks at Bishop's Stortford they marched on to Saffron Walden, Essex where they completed their training. This was probably quite an exciting period for these young soldiers, with the anticipation of travelling to foreign parts combined with patriotic emotions and enthusiasm for the prospect of fighting for their country. They had a particularly good Christmas dinner in 1914 because the turkeys ordered from Wolverhampton arrived late. In the meantime, replacements were obtained which meant the men had a double-ration of turkey dinner!

In January 1915 George Gobourn and his comrades continued with the final stages of their military training, before being assembled at Great Hallingbury Park, Hertfordshire, for a final inspection by King George V. On 25 February the men of 1/6 South Staffords, now part of the 46th Division, were issued with new equipment and on 1 March they marched to Audley End railway station before travelling to Southampton. At 3.30 pm, on Tuesday 2 March half the battalion boarded the *S.S. Jupiter* to sail to Le Havre, and, two days later, the rest joined them in France. On arrival they were issued with warm clothing which in most cases meant a rather smelly goatskin coat. At 5 am the following morning they boarded railway cattle trucks bound for Noordpeene, via Rouen and Calais. As there were thirty-seven men in each truck and only two bales of hay for a seat, this must have been a very uncomfortable journey. After two days, they marched fifteen miles to reach Sailly on the 11 March, despite experiencing delays en route caused by the volume of bus and lorry traffic on the roads. Here they were billeted in houses in Rue de la Lys. The battalion moved next to Armentières, on 20 March, and then to Flêtre, where they spent more time practising digging trenches and trench combat. The battalion then marched to Bailleul and reached Bulford Camp, one mile south-west of Neuve Eglise, on Good Friday, 2 April. It rained heavily over Easter 1915 but the weather had improved when the men marched to Wulverghem, in Belgium, to take over the trenches there, on Tuesday 6 April. It was here that the battalion suffered its first casualties before returning to Bulford Camp the following Saturday. Thus began a period of regular rotation in-and-out of the frontline trenches until Friday 25 June, when they marched to Ouderdom. Here they practised running drill, bayonet fighting and went on route marches as well as having a daily inspection of smoke helmets and respirators. On Monday 5 July they went in the trenches at Zillebeke, near Ypres, and returned to Ouderdom on Monday 12 July, to spend even more time cleaning their arms and clothing. Between Sunday 18 and Friday 23 July the Battalion was based at Hill 60, before going back into reserve at Zillebeke. It was here that George Gobourn spent his last birthday - resting behind the frontline trenches.

For two months the 1/6 South Staffords remained in the vicinity of Hill 60; one of the grimmest, most dangerous places on the Western Front and scene of fierce fighting above and below ground. Then, on 2 October, the battalion moved south to positions at Loos in France. After practising bayonet fighting, hand grenade throwing and other drills they tested their machine guns and marched to the assembly trenches near Vermelles on 12 October. According to the records, the following day was fine and sunny and, at noon, the action began. It was a final attempt to take ground the 7th and 9th Divisions failed to gain on the 25 September 1915 - the opening day of the Battle of Loos. The preliminary bombardment was of the area around the Hohenzollern Redoubt, a well-fortified strongpoint that protruded about 500 yards into no man's land between the La Bassee Canal and the slope of Grenny, near Lens. The barrage, between Hohenzollern and the Vermelles-Auchy road, was due to begin at noon and last for two hours, accompanied by the release of gas and smoke clouds between 1.00 and 1.50 pm. The gas was to stop ten minutes before zero hour: 2 pm. However, at noon the wind was blowing from the south-west and when the gas was released it rose from the cylinders to form a white cloud between six and eight feet above the ground; some even drifted back towards the British trenches. The Hohenzollern Redoubt was a honeycomb of trenches and machine gun emplacements, supported from behind by Fosse 8, a great black slag heap about sixty feet high. This also included a network of trenches and machine gun emplacements that gave excellent shelter for their crews. As the men of the 46th Division waited to go over the top the Germans rained down a very effective counter-barrage on their trenches. At zero hour, when the troops advanced into no man's land, they came under sustained heavy gunfire and suffered serious losses. The attack of the 137th Brigade ended virtually where it began because the Germans were able to direct a terrific enfilade of flanking fire from close range. The battalion war diary records thirty-five Other Ranks killed, 105 men missing and five men dying later of wounds. Most of the 'missing' had in fact been killed, including Private George Gobourn. The total casualties for 1/6 South Staffords on 13 October were 389 men and 18 officers, with most losses occurring during the first few minutes of the attack. Two days afterwards, the scene of the failed attack was described as one of complete devastation with obliterated trenches and unburied bodies lying in a confused mess with equipment and debris all jumbled together. The Hohenzollern Redoubt had justified its formidable reputation as one of the strongest positions on the whole of the Western Front. On 20 October 1915 an account of the battle appeared in the Wolverhampton Chronicle, under the headline: *"Covered With Glory, Staffordshire Territorials in Action, Local heroes have fallen in action."* Although the newspaper report listed Private Gobourn as one of the wounded men, he was dead.

Left: George Gobourn. *Right:* His name on the LNWR memorial at Wolverhampton station.

George Gobourn is remembered on the war memorial in Heath Town Park, opposite the main gates on Church Street. The memorial – with a bronze figure of a soldier mounted on a granite base – was created by G.A. Walker c.1920. As George has no known grave, he is commemorated on the Loos Memorial at Dud Corner Cemetery, near Lens, northern France. His name is also inscribed on the London and North Western Railway (LNWR) memorial at Wolverhampton station along with sixty-seven other local men from the Goods department of that company who died in the Great War. For the rest of her life my grandmother was always very superstitious about the number thirteen because her brother George was killed on the 13 October 1915.

Part Two; Lance Corporal S/21662 Sidney Gobourn 5th Battalion The Queen's Own Cameron Highlanders

Sidney Gobourn was a cousin of George Alfred Gobourn. He was born on 5 August 1896 in Wolverhampton and baptised on 6 September 1896 at Mount Zion Chapel, Horseley Fields. His father was also called George and his mother, Edith née Hawkins, died two years later in childbirth. In the 1901 census Sidney was living with an aunt and uncle in Lancashire, suggesting his father was unable to look after him. However, after his father remarried in 1903 he returned to Wolverhampton and was brought up with his step-brothers and sister in Inkerman Street. When Sidney left school he became a warehouse assistant, but on 11 December 1911 he started work as an engine cleaner on the Great Western Railway (GWR) at Wolverhampton Low Level station. As his career developed as a railwayman he transferred to Chester as a fireman on 21 April 1915.

Sidney enlisted as a Private in the 5th Battalion, The Queen's Own Cameron Highlanders, on 29 November 1915 and, by the end of January 1916, had been sent to France. For more than a year he fought on the Western Front, during which time he was promoted to the rank of Lance Corporal. In the Spring of 1917 the Cameron Highlanders were engaged in the Battle of Arras (9 April - 16 May), and Sidney's battalion were due to launch a joint attack with the Black Watch. The night of 2 May was still and clear and there was no hint of dawn when the British artillery began to fire at zero hour - 3.45 am. This was the start of a creeping barrage which was how artillery supported an infantry attack by this stage of the war. When the Highlanders went over the top and advanced towards the German front line the British shells, landing just ahead of them, hit the dry earth and threw up a thick curtain of smoke and dust which blew back towards them. As a result, the attacking troops became disorientated almost straight away, with the Cameron Highlanders veering to their right, across the path of the 2nd Battalion Essex Regiment, who inadvertently fired on them in the confusion. The failure of this chaotic and costly attack was largely due to the fateful decision to launch it before dawn without making adequate arrangements to help the soldiers reach their objectives in the dark. One of the many wounded casualties was Sidney Gobourn who was shot in the head near the temple, permanently losing the sight in both his eyes. He lay in no man's land for two days before making contact with an injured comrade who could see but was unable to walk. Miraculously, the two soldiers worked together to reach their own lines, with Sidney carrying that other unknown casualty whilst he guided his blinded pal. Having been treated for his injuries, on 21 July 1917 Sidney was sent to St Dunstan's Hostel for Blind and Wounded Soldiers, Regent's Park, London to convalesce. He was also discharged from the army on 6 August 1917 and awarded the Silver War Badge.

Sidney's rehabilitation from his devastating injuries included training to become a professional masseur or physiotherapist. Still only a young man, he was now a disabled ex-soldier who needed to survive in the harsh post-war world. He eventually passed the examination of the Incorporated Society of Trained Masseurs and came fifth in the national Medical Electrical Examination. Sidney's recovery was also helped by meeting his future wife at St Dunstan's. She was a nurse named Kathleen Esther Maitland-Makgill-Crichton, whose titled family lived at Breamore House, near Salisbury. Despite her family's concerns that she was ten years older than Sidney and that he was a working class man, they were married on 17 September 1919. It was to be a long and happy marriage. After the war Sidney successfully set up in practice as a physiotherapist in Cheltenham and he and Kathleen raised a family of three sons. They both died in 1976.

Left: Sidney Gobourn in a post-war photograph. *Right:* Kathleen Maitland-Makgill-Crichton

Part Three: Corporal 562 Frederick Constable 4th (Staffs) Bty RFA

Frederick Constable, another cousin of George Alfred Gobourn, was also born in Wolverhampton, in 1892. In 1911, aged eighteen, Frederick was living with his parents and siblings in Walsall Street and working as a pattern maker's fitter in a hollow-ware foundry. Frederick, like George, may have been a pre-war Territorial, and they appear to have enlisted around the same time, as both cousins began their overseas service on 5 March 1915, at Ypres. He was to reach the rank of Corporal in the 4th Staffordshire Battery, Royal Field Artillery, before being killed on 2 September 1915. His death was recorded in the war diary as taking place at Dickebusch, at 7.30 pm, during a German bombardment that blew up an ammunition dump, as well as killing the unfortunate NCO. Frederick Constable was buried in Railway Dugouts Cemetery which is located 2 km south-east of Ypres. The following notice appeared in the Wolverhampton Express & Star: *"Died for his country, Constable. In loving memory of Corporal Frederick Constable Staffordshire Battery R.F.A. (T.A.) Killed in Action – Ypres, September 2nd 1915, age 23. Dearly beloved eldest son of Alfred and Emma Constable, 54 Walsall Street, Wolverhampton. Sadly missed by father, mother, brothers and sisters. A sad day recalled."*

Chapter 5

Zeppelins over Wolverhampton
The German Air Raid of 31 January 1916

Mick Powis

Part One: A Noise like Thunder and Lightning - Zeppelins bomb the Black Country

The canal towpath near the old pumping station in Bradley is now a peaceful place and totally evocative of the Black Country. The building - part of John Wilkinson's famous ironworks - housed a steam beam engine that once pumped waste water into the Bradley Arm of the Birmingham Mainline Canal. Walking here it's easy to imagine a time when the spot was surrounded by glowing blast furnaces and an important location in Britain's industrial revolution. However, on the wall of the pumping station is another reminder of the nation's past - a reminder of war. In 1994 a plaque was erected to commemorate Maud and William Fellows - two innocent civilians killed by a bomb dropped from a Zeppelin airship on 31 January 1916. This was one of the heaviest German air raids of the Great War - remembered by many Black Country families - including my own. That night my grandmother was travelling home to Wolverhampton having just visited her mother in Wednesbury. She was holding my mother - then just a babe in arms. As they waited for their tram, my grandmother later told me, she clearly saw the Zeppelin and she and my mother were completely covered in dust by the exploding bombs. Trams stopped running immediately after the bombings and she and my mother returned to stay the night at her mother's. As ordinary people had no access to telephones in those days my grandfather spent an anxious night waiting for news that they were safe. Although tens of thousands of Black Country folk saw the Zeppelins, and even more heard their bombs, it is surprising how little is actually known about the events of that frosty foggy Monday night - 31 January 1916.

Nine Zeppelin airships of the *Reichskreigsmarine*, the Imperial German Navy, were involved in this attack. They had set out from bases on the north-west coast of Germany to bomb Liverpool – their primary target - but none of the Zeppelin's bombs landed there. It was the Midlands that bore the brunt of the raid which killed seventy people: thirty-five in the Black Country, fifteen in Burton upon Trent, ten in Loughborough, five in Derby, three in Scunthorpe and two in Ilkeston. About 113 people were injured, twenty of them in the Black Country. The casualties also included two British night fighter pilots, sixteen Zeppelin crew and four German airmen from two sea planes sent to locate a missing airship. Two Zeppelins bombed the Black Country on 31 January-1 February 1916: the L.21, between 8.00 pm and 8.30 pm, and the L.19 at about midnight. The raids led to considerable political pressure for adequate blackout and air-raid precautions as well as ferocious anti-German atrocity propaganda. Several coroners' juries returned verdicts of 'murder' by German Kaiser Wilhelm II and his son, the Crown Prince. This chapter examines the events of that infamous evening and brings together military and civilian research. It is perhaps surprising that far more is known about the military aspects of the raid than what happened to civilians on the ground. Much of the information used is from secret documents produced by GHQ (Home Forces) as well as other sources including: statements given by captured Zeppelin crews, anti-aircraft spotters' reports and police records. These all help piece together the routes taken by the various airships and the ultimate destination of their bombs. Modern historians are also assisted by the original German Zeppelin codebook, which was top secret at the time. The British War Office had acquired a copy of this and knew when air raids were imminent thanks to decoding intercepted Zeppelin radio messages. However, although warned whenever German airships left their bases for raids on Britain, their precise targets were unknown to the defenders. This meant ground forces had to stay alert and carefully monitor each Zeppelin's progress whilst it flew over the country – creating high quality records of routes taken by each enemy airship.[31]

Maud and William Fellows - unrelated despite sharing the same surname – were sweethearts from the Coseley/Bradley area. Maud, aged twenty-four, lived at 45 Daisy Street, Bradley and worked in a butcher's shop in Bilston. As a single parent she had a difficult life and was forced to supplement her income by working most evenings as a barmaid in the Old Bush Inn, Bradley Lane. William, aged twenty-three, and known locally as Fred, lived at 33 Castle St, Coseley. He was employed as a stoker and had previously been a deliveryman for Wardells Mineral Waters. Like thousands of courting couples they went for a stroll along the canal towpath at about 8 pm on that fateful Monday evening. They may have chatted about the war on the Western Front where almost a thousand men of the South Staffordshire Regiment had recently perished in the Battle of Loos. Or, perhaps talked about events on the Home Front and how London and places along the east coast had been attacked by Zeppelins on several occasions during 1915. London was surrounded by a ring of protective aerodromes, searchlights and anti-aircraft guns, whilst the rest of the country was largely undefended. Only the previous night the Wolverhampton *Express and Star* reported that German Zeppelins had attacked Paris, but hastened to reassure readers that: *"in spite of this, the morale of the citizens remained unshaken."* Closer to home there was news that the Government was planning to introduce conscription and perhaps Maud and William discussed how before long their lives would be changed by the war. However, the inconsequential chatter of lovers was ended abruptly by the harsh reality of total war at about 8.10 pm. Maud's deathbed statement recorded what happened next. She told her brother she heard a sound like *"thunder and lightning"* as she and her *"young man"* ran to seek shelter from the bombs that began to fall. They may have heard the detonation of those dropped by the Zeppelin on Tipton a few minutes earlier or, more likely, one of the five reported to have fallen on Bradley. As they sheltered by the wall of the pumping station a high explosive bomb landed on the towpath just a few feet away. It killed William outright and fatally injured Maud. The first people on

---

[31] Intelligence Section GHQ Home Forces, Secret Document, Air Raids 31 Jan.-1 Feb. 1916. Probably written by Lt. Col. H G de Watterville.

the scene saw two bodies. Arnold Wolverson, from the nearby Britannia Iron and Steel works, told the Coroner's Inquest he had dashed for safety to the canalside. He then heard someone crying for help and found Maud lying injured across the breast of William - who was quite dead; his head almost severed. About eight feet away from the couple was a five foot deep crater, now rapidly filling with water. Maud was taken to the nearby Old Bush Inn, where she was given basic first aid on a pub table whilst repeatedly asking after her *"young man."* She had sustained a broken arm, wounds on her right side, her loins and all over her back. A local GP, Dr Waddell, rushed to the scene and arranged for her to be taken to the Wolverhampton General Hospital. However, Maud never recovered from her injuries and died from septicaemia on 12 February 1916. It is unlikely Maud or William saw the airship that killed them as it was flying at a height of nearly 10,000 feet. Likewise, the Zeppelin crew were oblivious to the carnage they caused in Bradley and elsewhere. From his combat report we know that her commander, Kapitanleutnant Max Dietrich of the Imperial German Navy Zeppelin 'L.21', was hopelessly lost. He had been in the air for more than nine hours and believed he was bombing Liverpool docks.

 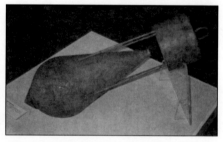

Left: Bradley Pumping Engine House. *Right:* 50kg bomb at the Aeronauticum Museum, Nordholz.

Max Dietrich was born on the 27 November 1870 at Angermunde, north of Berlin, and at forty-six was old for a combat officer. His solidly middle class background also made him different from most other Zeppelin commanders. As one of sixteen children, he left home for a life at sea when seventeen years old and did well as a merchant seaman; becoming the youngest captain in the North German Lloyd shipping line. Dietrich commanded a number of ocean liners before the war and was feted as an early German hero when he broke through the British naval blockade – successfully sailing the SS *Brandenburg* home from the USA. He was awarded the Iron Cross 2nd Class for this exploit. As an officer in the merchant marine Dietrich was also an officer in the Imperial German Navy and his exceptional navigational skills led him to the Zeppelin Service. Before taking control of the L.21 he had already commanded two Zeppelins in combat, gaining the Iron Cross 1st Class in the process. He was also the uncle of Marlene Dietrich (1901-1992), the legendary German-American film star, singer and dancer. She was just an unknown teenager when her Uncle Max set out for England on 31 January 1916.

L.21 left her base at Nordholz, near Cuxhaven, on the north German coast at about 11 am GMT. Dietrich's orders were to bomb Liverpool. The Zeppelin crossed the English coast near Mundesley, Norfolk, as dusk fell around 4.50 pm. Observers on the ground noted L.21 over Narborough at 5.20 pm and King's Lynn at 5.25 pm. Her westward course took her south of Grantham at 6.30 pm and between Nottingham and Derby just before 7.00 pm. Dietrich flew south-west thinking he was over the Irish Sea when he saw the lights of two towns separated by a river, which he mistook to be Liverpool and Birkenhead. The lights were actually those of the Black Country which was not subject to blackout regulations at that time and the river was probably one of the many canals in the district. Dietrich aimed his bombs at the fiery glow from iron foundries glimpsed through the clouds. His target, when Maud and William Fellows were hit, could have been Capponfield Foundry on the opposite side of the canal. In his report Kapitanleutnant Dietrich said he bombed docks, harbour works and factories, with thirty-five 50kg (110lb) high explosive and twenty incendiary bombs. He claimed to have seen them all explode and wrote that good results were clearly achieved.[32]

Left: Zeppelin L.21 in her shed at Nordholz. *Picture from the Wolverhampton Express and Star.*
Right: Kapitanleutnant Max Dietrich. *Picture from Tonder Zeppelin Museum Website*

The L.21 was the pride of German technology - flown for the first time only three weeks earlier on the 10 January 1916. The Black Country raid was her first military operation. A 'Q' type airship, built at the Zeppelin Works at Lowenthal, L.21 was a massive machine: 585 feet long and 61 feet in diameter. Her aluminium frame was covered by cotton fabric and she was kept in the air by some 1,264,400 cubic feet of hydrogen gas, contained in eighteen internal cells. Along with her crew of seventeen men, L.21 carried about 4,910 pounds of bombs. The four 240-horse power Maybach engines gave her a top speed of 59 miles per hour, which was slower than opposing fighter aircraft. However, L.21's service ceiling of about 13,000 feet made fighter interception very difficult for Allied aircraft in early 1916. This all changed during the course of that year, when the hydrogen in Zeppelins' gasbags made them especially vulnerable to incendiary bullets. However, in January 1916

---

[32] Robinson, D H, *The Zeppelin in Combat*, Shiffer Publishing, 1994

airships such as L.21 roamed freely over England, relatively safe from the activities of the Royal Flying Corps (RFC) or Royal Naval Air Service (RNAS).

Blue plaque commemorates the Zeppelin's victims in Union Street, Tipton.

From Derby L.21 flew south-west, passing over Rugeley before reaching Stafford at 7.25 pm. Ground observers reported she then suddenly turned due south, heading for Wolverhampton at high speed. The town was subject to a partial blackout but at 7.45 pm an eyewitness named Jack Burns watched L.21 flying over Wednesfield. Many years later he told his grandson how he had seen it over his back garden, heading towards Fibbersley Bank: *"flying so low he could have almost stuck his pitchfork in the bugger."* This was almost certainly an optical illusion and repeated by others who also claimed to have seen the airship flying very low. One even said he could almost have hit it with a brick. Though we have no precise details it is likely L.21 bombed whilst near its maximum altitude - perhaps at about 9,000 feet. People on the ground could not appreciate the Zeppelin's enormous size, especially in the dark. In 1916 they were used to watching aeroplanes fly overhead and would have used their scale to judge the height of an airship. Most aircraft were single or two-seater biplanes, about twenty feet long with a wingspan of twenty-five to thirty feet, whereas a Zeppelin was some thirty times longer at 585 feet. As people naturally underestimated the size of an airship they thought it was flying much lower than it actually was. L.21 reached Netherton at 7.55 pm and hovered there for about three minutes. It is probable Dietrich then spotted the lights and furnaces of the Black Country and turned north over Dudley, reaching Tipton just after 8.00 pm. This is where the killing started. The bomb aimer was second in command, Leutnant zur See Von Nathusius. Using a bombsight made by optical manufacturer Karl Zeiss of Jena he dropped three high explosive bombs on Waterloo Street and Union Street, quickly followed by three incendiaries on Bloomfield Road and Barnfield Road. In Waterloo Street outbuildings at the rear of properties were destroyed and one person died. In Union Street two houses were completely demolished, others damaged and the gas main under the road set alight. Another thirteen people were killed. The three incendiary bombs fell in yards and gardens and failed to ignite.

The L.21 probably followed the LNWR - now the main line between Birmingham and Wolverhampton – before dropping three incendiary bombs on Bloomfield Brickwork's. Two of these also failed to ignite and no damage was done. The Zeppelin then reached Lower Bradley and dropped five high explosive bombs. The first of these landed on Pothouse Bridge canal basin and sank two canal boats. A second landed near St Martin's Church where it destroyed a house and shattered most of the windows in the area. The third hit a pile of ash from the boiler outside the pump house, the fourth landed on the canal towpath killing William and fatally injuring Maud, and the last fell in a field where it did no damage. Dietrich then turned L.21 eastwards, bombing Wednesbury at about 8.15 pm, killing fourteen people in the Crown Tube Works and King Street areas. Other bombs landed at the rear of the Crown and Cushion Inn, High Bullen, and along Brunswick Park Road. Damage was also done to the Hickman and Pullen brewery, railway wagons and buildings in Mesty Croft goods yard - where one person was killed. Slight damage also occurred at Old Park Colliery. From Wednesbury, Dietrich flew on to Walsall which L.21 reached at about 8.25 pm. Here he dropped seven high explosive and four incendiary bombs with one landing on Wednesbury Road Congregational Church. A few hundred yards away incendiaries hit the grounds of the General Hospital whilst others landed in Mountrath Street, damaging homes and Elijah Jeffries' Saddlery Works. The last bomb L.21 dropped on the Black Country landed in Bradford Place, outside the Art and Science Institute, killing a number of people and completely demolishing the public toilets. Walsall's Cenotaph now stands on the exact spot where that last bomb landed. With the killing over Dietrich turned L.21 for home, travelling at high speed. She was reported over Sutton Coldfield at 8.35 pm and Nuneaton ten minutes later. L.21's last attack of the night occurred at about 9.15 pm when Dietrich ordered her six remaining incendiaries to be dropped on a blast furnace at the Islip Ironworks near Thrapston, Northamptonshire. They missed, landing in fields causing no further damage. L.21 was spotted over Ely at 10.00 pm, Thetford at 10.35 pm and she crossed the English coast, south of Lowestoft, between Pakefield and Kessingland, at 11.35 pm. Dietrich's crew spent another exhausting eleven hours crossing the North Sea before finally arriving back at their base at Nordholz, at about 10.45 am on 1 February 1916. L.21 was one of the last Zeppelins to return home and had covered 1,056 miles in just over twenty-three hours.[33]

The L.21's Tipton to Walsall bomb run probably lasted about twenty-five minutes as the Zeppelin flew a sweeping seven-mile course at her cruising speed of forty miles per hour. Observers reported she appeared to circle whilst looking for targets and glided slowly for a better aim before dropping her bombs. There were railways near all areas attacked by L.21 and most of its bombs landed close to lines belonging to the LNWR and GWR. This suggests Kapitanleutnant Dietrich navigated using railway lines and attacked brightly-lit areas nearby - explaining why most bombs landed close to Tipton, Wednesbury and Walsall town centres. War Office GHQ records confirm L.21 killed thirty-five people in the Black Country and injured at least twenty-nine. Dietrich's combat report shows he dropped a total of thirty-five

---

[33] Powis, M., *Zeppelins over the Black Country*, The Blackcountryman, Nos 3 and 4, Vol. 29, 1996

high explosive and twenty incendiary bombs as his Zeppelin carried out its mission in accordance with the traditions of the Imperial German Navy.

Dietrich's airship was a strange dark world of glowing dials and gauges accompanied by sounds made by throbbing engines and squeaking and creaking wires and struts. He would have felt immensely proud. Zeppelin commanders were national heroes and commanding new and vastly expensive machines such as L.21 was recognition of exceptional navigational skills and a great honour. The expertise required and danger involved in Zeppelin operations was recognised by the German High Command and national Press. It was said that every member of a Zeppelin crew would be awarded the Iron Cross after a successful mission. Coping with extreme cold was just one of the challenges faced by Zeppelin airmen. While it was almost freezing at ground level it was well below zero in the control gondola of L.21, two miles above. Zeppelin crews wore fur-lined clothing and even padded them with newspaper to try and keep warm. In the intense concentration of the bomb run it is possible Dietrich forgot his patriotic pride and the cold, but it is almost certain another emotion remained: fear. All Zeppelin crews were acutely aware of the dangers they faced in being kept aloft by more than one million cubic feet of highly inflammable hydrogen gas. Fire was their real enemy and they must have thought constantly about the possibility of a terrible death in a burning airship - for that was to be the fate of most Zeppelin crews. Dietrich was probably haunted by this prospect more than most because in November 1915 his previous airship, L.18, had blown up in its shed while being filled with hydrogen. One crew member died and many others were seriously burned.[34] On another night in 1916 this was to be the fiery fate of Kapitantleutnant Dietrich and L.21.

If the crew of L.21 felt constant dread, what of Black Country folk below? There is no doubt they felt shock and terror when the bombs started falling but most failed to realise what was happening. Tom Cope from Bilston was a schoolboy at the time and later recalled these events.[35] He was taking part in a school choir practice in the Parish Room of St Martin's, Bradley, when a terrific bang shattered all the windows. Someone shouted *"It's a boiler explosion"* and as the children dashed outside their choir-mistress fainted. Walking home, Tom saw a youth climb up a lamppost to extinguish the gaslight. Whilst looking up he caught sight of the Zeppelin: *"a huge silent cigar shape"*. Like the author's grandmother, Tom's parents were very late arriving home. They had been to the theatre in Wolverhampton and walked back to Bradley because the trams stopped running. In the 1990s a number of people described their own experiences that night in a series of letters to the *Black Country Bugle*. Mrs V. Owen, who was also in Bradley that night, said she saw what looked like a *"flash of lightning, followed by something like a thunderclap."* Several others, on the way home from Bilston Market, initially believed a boiler had exploded before the police rushed around the district telling them there had been an air raid, to black out all lights and take shelter in cellars. Mrs D. Griffith remembered a bright moonlit evening and how the canal was like a silver thread, which the Zeppelin

[34] Robinson, *The Zeppelin in Combat*, op. cit.
[35] Cope, T., *Zeppelins Over the Black Country*, The Blackcountryman, Vol.1, 1980

seemed to follow before scattering its bombs everywhere. Many other descriptions of these events come from contemporary newspapers like the daily *Wolverhampton Express and Star*. Press accounts are problematic because wartime censorship meant they were unable to name victims or identify locations. However, they did report the bombing and included stories full of human interest taken from inquest or eyewitness accounts. These descriptions are well worth quoting even though they lack personal detail. The *Express and Star* described the air raid as happening in an *"area in Staffordshire"*, but this deliberate vagueness has caused problems for historians. Whilst the bombings did occur in a number of towns and villages in Staffordshire, two distinct areas of the county were attacked by different Zeppelins - the Black Country and Burton upon Trent. Press reports from these two locations were described together and this blending has confused some researchers who inadvertently combined events from two places into one narrative.

The *Wolverhampton Express and Star* of 4 February 1916 reported that the first air raid started between eight and nine o clock, and the second at about midnight. No damage of a military nature was done: *"though twenty six innocent civilians, many of them women and children were sent to immediate and violent deaths, while a number lie on beds of pain, in the agony of wounds received from flying fragments of the bombs or the collapse of buildings."* The report goes on to tell us there was no panic - indeed the only morale result was that it engendered an even stronger resolve amongst the people to bring the war to a speedy and successful conclusion. Be that as it may, the Press reports certainly give a flavour of the time. The *Express and Star* was referring to Tipton when it wrote that at ten past eight bombs began to rain down on the poorest residential area of a Staffordshire town. The occupants were mainly coal miners or iron workers, paying rent of five to six shillings (25p-30p) for their tightly packed houses. In one street all homes were damaged, one completely demolished, two or three partially destroyed and about a hundred more had their windows broken by the force of the explosions. Thirteen people died and seven were injured. A poignant passage tells us that hanging on the wall of one wrecked house, completely open to the street, was a cage containing a canary. Its occupant *"continued to whistle exuberantly directly the smoke and dust had cleared away."*

A few hours later another Zeppelin – L.19 - bombed the Black Country. It also flew over Wolverhampton but dropped no bombs on the town. Zeppelin L.21 had now departed, leaving behind a frightened and confused Black Country population. The Press claimed there was no panic but this is almost certainly an exaggeration. Tens of thousands had heard bombs and thousands had probably seen L.21. Before long people realised there had been an air raid, though very few knew exactly what had happened. Fires caused by bombs could be seen for miles around, many of the streetlights were extinguished, and the trams had stopped running. Although police patrolled the area advising locals to take shelter in cellars, many were out in the streets - walking home or trying to make sense of what had gone on. In the aftermath, rumours spread rapidly: King Street, Wednesbury, was *'completely destroyed'* and Owen Street, Tipton, was *'running with blood.'* Tom Cope recalled that when his parents finally arrived home in Bradley everyone went to bed. The family was then woken in the middle of the night by more explosions caused by L.19, but these seemed further away. They decided to huddle together in one bed instead of going down to the cold dank cellar. Fearfully they awaited further bombs, but heard no more.[36] It is fortunate Zeppelin L.19 did not reach the Black Country until after midnight or casualties might have been much greater. By the time it dropped its first bomb on Wednesbury locals were aware one air raid had already taken place and were indoors. Most had taken simple precautions - many sheltering in cellars and others going to bed. These measures would have made little difference if a house received a direct hit. However, most injuries were caused by shrapnel or flying glass, so being in bed was relatively safe.

Zeppelin L.19 was commanded by Kapitanleutnant Odo Loewe, with Leutnant zur See Erwin Brunhof as executive officer. Loewe was an experienced commander and veteran of previous attacks on England. His was an earlier model of Zeppelin than L.21; slightly smaller at 536 feet long. She had been out of commission for the previous two months due to engine trouble and this meant Loewe was determined to complete a successful mission and go all the way to Liverpool. He was not to know that L.19's on-going engine problems would prove fatal for him and his crew of sixteen men. She left her base at Tondern, Schleswig-Holstein, at 11.15 am on 31 January to rendezvous with other Zeppelins over Borkum Island, off the north German coast. After crossing the North Sea she made landfall over Sheringham, Norfolk, at about 6.20 pm. L.19 travelled more slowly than the other airships, but it is impossible to be precise as her combat log was lost. Her meandering progress also caused problems for ground observers charting her route. L.19 was spotted over Swaffham at 7.05 pm, Stamford at 8.10 pm and Loughborough at 9.30 pm. Whilst over Loughborough Loewe probably observed fires caused by other Zeppelins at Burton upon Trent. He flew there directly and dropped a few of his own incendiaries at about 9.45 pm. It is not possible to say how many of Burton's fifteen deaths that night were caused by L.19. From Burton Loewe headed in a south-westerly direction passing over Wolverhampton. Between 10.30 pm and 11.30 pm she was reported 'wandering' about north Worcestershire and other districts south of Birmingham. She was seen or heard near Enville, Kinver, Wolverley, Bewdley, Bromsgrove, Redditch and Stourbridge. In May 1939 an unexploded 'Aerial Torpedo' was discovered by workmen rebuilding the Iron Bridge on the Worcester Road, Kidderminster. This two foot long, 50 lb bomb - complete with "tail vanes, or fins" – was "found to be still alive" and "believed to have been dropped by Zeppelin L.19" when that "airship went over Kidderminster on the night of January 31, 1916."[37] Ground observers at Wythall recorded L.19 heading towards Birmingham as she passed over that location at 11.00 pm. After Loewe failed to find the blacked-out city he may have been attracted back to the Black Country by fires started earlier by L.21. At about midnight L.19 commenced its own attack on Wednesbury, which started when a single high explosive bomb was dropped on the axle department of the Monway Works, doing slight damage to the building and machinery. From Wednesbury Loewe turned

[36] Cope, T., *The Blackcountryman*, op. cit.
[37] *Birmingham Daily Mail*, 31 July 1939

towards Dudley, dropping five high explosive bombs en route at Ocker Hill Colliery, damaging the engine house and one private dwelling. The Zeppelin reached Dudley at 00.15 am and dropped seventeen incendiaries in the grounds of Dudley Castle and fields nearby - now the site of Dudley Zoo. One landed on a grain shed at the railway station and caused five pounds worth of damage. L.19 inflicted much more destruction when it flew north to Tipton, probably attracted by the gas mains that were still ablaze. Loewe attacked almost the same area as L.21 and the *Express and Star* later commented that bombs fell *"scarcely before the dead and injured had been removed."* At about 00.20 am, according to the GHQ Home Forces report, Loewe dropped eleven high explosive bombs on the western part of the town between the LNWR station and Bloomfield - these caused considerable damage to a number of homes but no further casualties were reported. Along with the destruction of domestic properties; railway track and sleepers on the Stour Valley and Princes End branch lines were blown some distance. Two high explosive bombs fell near the Bush Inn, 127 Park Lane West, and newspapers described in graphic detail the destruction caused by one of these. It hit the roof of a house without exploding and then bounced down into the roadway, where it detonated five feet in front of the Bush Inn. The pub was completely wrecked by the explosion; every door and window smashed and the whole place rendered a ruin. We know exactly when the bomb dropped as the clock in the bar was damaged and stopped at precisely twenty past twelve am. From Tipton, Loewe seems to have followed the LNWR line to Walsall and at about 00.25 am dropped two high explosive bombs on Dora Street and Pleck Road, Pleck. The one that landed in Pleck hit a stable, killing a horse, four pigs and about a hundred fowl. In a rare display of dry humour the *Walsall Pioneer* later commented: *"With a fellow feeling for the rest of their kind, the Germans no doubt, would have spared the pigs if they had known."* L.19 then turned north and flew over Birchills, where she dropped another high explosive bomb that damaged St Andrew's Church and Vicarage, Hollyhedge Lane. Although these buildings were severely damaged, there were no more deaths or injuries. In all L.19 seems to have dropped twenty high explosive and seventeen incendiary bombs on the Black Country.

After bombing Walsall, Kapitanleutnant Loewe steered an eastward course for home. Due to technical problems, L.19 had made slow progress during her six hours over England as well as having an unpredictable flight pattern in the target areas. On her journey back to the coast she was spotted over Sutton Coldfield at 00.30 am, Coleshill at 00.40 am, between Coventry and Bedworth at 00.50 am and ten minutes later was seen flying to the north of Rugby. After this L.19 slowed down even more and did not cross the English coast at Martham, Norfolk, until 5.25 am - several hours after the other Zeppelins. It was another ten hours before Loewe radioed to report that L.19 had finally reached the German coast – at 3.05 pm on the afternoon of 1 February. His signal, decoded by British Naval Intelligence read: *"Radio equipment at times out of order, three engines out of order. Approximate position: Borkum Island. Wind is favourable"*. In fact, L.19 had not reached Borkum but was about twenty miles north of the Dutch Friesian island of Ameland. This correction was radioed to Loewe, but it is not known if he received the message. It was to be a costly navigational error. Hardly able to steer or maintain forward speed, Loewe probably gave up hope of returning to Tondern and decided to crash land the Zeppelin as soon as he reached the German coast. Though only a few miles from home luck was fast running out for him and his crew, as their crippled airship was buffeted by the wind. At 4.00 pm on the afternoon of 1 February, L.19 was spotted over Ameland Island, which belonged to neutral Holland and was heavily garrisoned. When she appeared out of the fog, Dutch soldiers shot at L.19 causing no immediate casualties but actually sealing the Zeppelin's fate. Their intense rifle fire punctured the gas cells causing serious leakage of hydrogen. It is possible that if her engines had been working properly L.19 might have reached Germany. However, the combination of engine trouble and gas leakage meant she could maintain neither speed nor height and the airship sank inexorably downwards. Her crew had long since discharged all ballast, but now threw overboard any heavy objects; even her machine guns and useless petrol tanks. Finally, anything not fixed to the structure of the Zeppelin was ditched, but all in vain. At some time during the night of 1/2 February, perhaps thirty-six hours after leaving her base, L.19 splashed down into the cold North Sea.[38]

The L.19 and British trawler *King Stephen*.

On the morning of 2 February 1916 the German Navy sent out destroyers and seaplanes to try and find her, without success. Two seaplanes were lost - their crews, a pilot and observer in each - adding four more casualties to the death toll of the raid. Nothing more was heard of L.19 until 3 February when a British fishing boat reported seeing her, and became embroiled in a war crime controversy. The trawler *King Stephen*, out of Grimsby, had been fishing in a prohibited area. At 07.00 am on Wednesday 2 February Captain William Martin spotted a large white object in the water. He sailed close to and found the Zeppelin looking *"like a great White*

---

[38] Robinson, *The Zeppelin in Combat*, op. cit.

Mountain in the sea." Some of its crew were in a roughly constructed shelter on top of the envelope and the trawlermen could see others sheltering inside the hull. Kapitanleutnant Loewe hailed the English skipper and asked to be taken abroad, but after consulting his own crew, Martin refused. The *King Stephen* had a crew of nine, whereas Martin erroneously believed the Zeppelin had a crew of thirty – it was in fact sixteen. Skipper Martin feared, probably correctly, that if he took the Germans aboard, they would take over his ship and sail her to Germany. He later told the Press that *"it went to a seaman's heart not to take them off"*, but he had to think of his own men and their families. Martin promised Loewe to report L.19's position to the first warship he saw. Unfortunately the *King Stephen* came across no other vessels until she reached the Humber on 3 February. By then it was too late and the airship had gone down with all hands.

Once the fate of L.19 became known the balance of propaganda changed. The German Press promptly accused the *King Stephen's* skipper of a war crime; by leaving the crew of the airship to perish in the North Sea. This was a predictable reaction – to counter criticisms of the recent sinking of passenger liner *Lusitania* by a German U-boat as well as other air raids on civilians. However, the British position was not helped when the Bishop of London, Arthur Winnington-Ingram, was quoted supporting skipper Martin's decision to leave the Zeppelin *'babykillers'* to drown. The German media declared the Bishop *"acted less as an apostle of Christian charity than as a jingoistic hatemonger,"* whereas the cleric claimed the skipper had no choice in the matter because the airmen would have overpowered his crew if he had taken them aboard. Opinion is still divided over whether skipper Martin had a genuine crisis of conscience or if he lied and even sent potential rescuers to the wrong location to conceal his 'illegal' fishing. As he died of a heart attack a year later the truth of his version of events was never verified. The final fate of L.19 was eventually revealed in a report written by Kapitanleutnant Odo Loewe that he then placed in a bottle and cast into the sea. This was picked up by a Swedish yacht several months later. Loewe wrote: *"With 15 men on the top platform and backbone girder of the L.19, floating without gondolas in approximately 3 degrees east longitude. I am attempting to send a last report. Engine trouble three times repeated, a light head wind on the return journey delayed our return and in the mist carried us over Holland where I received heavy rifle fire; the ship became heavy and simultaneously three engines failed. February 2nd 1916, towards 1.00 PM, will apparently be our last hour. Loewe."* In 2000 an underwater archaeology team recovered parts of Zeppelin L.19, off the coast of Holland; some of these remains are exhibited at the National Maritime Museum in Greenwich, London.

Part Two: How to shoot down a Zeppelin.

On Tuesday 1 February 1916 a German Admiralty Press statement reported an airship squadron had dropped a number of bombs in and near Liverpool and Birkenhead and that docks, harbour facilities and factories were damaged. Other targets included Manchester, Nottingham and Sheffield, as well as factories on the Humber and at Great Yarmouth. The German report said that the effect of the bombs was very heavy, and caused mighty explosions. It also stated the Zeppelins had been fired on by shore batteries, but none was hit and all returned safely. The raid of 31 January 1916 was the second heaviest air raid on England in the Great War - seventy civilians died and 113 were injured. If military casualties are added to the civilian toll, more died due to this air raid than any other on England. Unlike earlier attacks on London, where defence forces were active with searchlights and anti-aircraft guns, these Zeppelins caused considerable damage and flew unmolested over the country for up to eleven hours. This caused consternation and anger amongst the people of the Black Country, the extent of which can be seen in the advertisement columns of the Press. Local firms moved quickly to take advantage of demand created by the new fear of air raids. On 2 February Beattie's of Wolverhampton advertised blackout blinds in the *Express and Star* which pointed out that *'prudence and patriotism'* demanded people darken their windows. Beattie's could supply various dark blinds; all made to order in their own workrooms. People's anger was directed at the Germans and at the Government, but it was not easy to take revenge on the enemy. In some cases any foreigner would do and a few distasteful incidents took place. In Cradley Heath a naturalised Russian Jew called Harry Harris, a refugee from Tsarist pogroms, had set up as a draper and corset maker. On Tuesday 1 February 1916 a hostile crowd gathered in front of his business shouting *"Fetch the Germans out!"* and prepared to attack the shop. The police were called and advised Harris to close early, but he was followed home by an angry mob. The next day several hundred people gathered in the area and accused Mrs Harris of making pro-German comments. Stones were thrown and about £30 worth of damage was done to glass and clothing. The police made several arrests. A similar incident is reputed to have taken place in Bradley. The *Black Country Bugle* reported on rumours concerning an unpopular elderly lady - manager of a foundry across the canal from where William and Maud Fellows had been sheltering. There were rumours the Zeppelin had several local works on its target list and it was alleged she guided the airship to its target by shining a light in the air. Another hostile crowd gathered outside her house and when a volley of stones were thrown she and her son were rescued by the local constabulary and taken to Bilston Police Station for questioning. It seems she was later sent to Stafford Gaol, but there are no details about what happened to her.

A few days after the bombings the different coroner's inquests began their melancholy work. Newspapers were permitted to describe the events, but telegrams from the Home Office gave strict instruction that the names or addresses of victims, or anything that could identify the location of the air raids could not be published. The inquest on thirteen victims of the Tipton bombing took place on Thursday 3

February 1916. The jury determined that they had been killed by explosive bombs dropped by enemy aircraft and delivered a verdict of *"wilful murder against the Kaiser and crown prince of Germany as being accessories before and after the fact"*. The coroner tried to argue that there was no evidence the Kaiser or his son personally knew anything about the raid. He understood the jury's feelings, but they had to return a verdict on the evidence before them. A juror said *"He is the controller of Germany and as such orders these things"*. After much argument the jury refused to change their verdict and the coroner reluctantly accepted it. Normally, when a coroner's jury returns a verdict of murder against particular persons it is his duty to issue the police with warrants for their arrest. It is not recorded whether the Tipton coroner did this. In this case it was a process hardly in keeping with the dignity of the office. The jury in the case of Maud Fellows returned a similar verdict. Her inquest was held at Wolverhampton Town Hall on 15 February 1916 and the jury in this instance was made up of men mainly from the Graisley area of the town. They recorded she died of septicaemia following injuries caused by the explosion of a bomb dropped by an enemy aircraft, and were of the opinion that *"the Kaiser and Crown Prince were guilty of the murder of Maud Fellows as accessories before the fact."* Once again the coroner, George Maynard Martin, pointed out that there was no possibility of taking proceedings against the Kaiser and asked if the jury would change its verdict. They refused, saying it might carry some weight after the war. The coroner accepted this but said he did not intend to commit the German Kaiser or Crown Prince. William Fellows' inquest was adjourned until 28 February 1916 and that jury returned a verdict of *"wilful murder against some person unknown"* who in their opinion was acting on the instructions of Germans in authority. The coroner said he thought this was *"a very sound and proper verdict."* After the inquests the victims in Wednesbury and Tipton were given public funerals and large processions followed the corteges to the cemeteries. Public subscriptions were raised for victims in both towns with that in Tipton collected £1,264. Considerable public anger was directed at the Government, with people asking why no warning had been given of the impending attacks? Did the authorities know the enemy airships were approaching? Why were Zeppelins able to fly unhindered over England for so long without being confronted by British aircraft? Why was there no blackout in many target areas? To protect military secrets and avoid political embarrassment, it was hard to give effective answers at the time and it was many years before full explanations took place. By intercepting German radio signals, the British Government certainly knew about the impending air raids from about noon on 31 January 1916, but they had no way of predicting exactly where the Zeppelins would attack and neither did the Germans. As has been seen, their air raids were often hopelessly inaccurate. In the past the prime target had been London and a series of defence aerodromes were sited near the capital. Searchlights and anti-aircraft guns were also in short supply and most deployed to the Western Front or areas of Britain that had already been attacked. The Midlands was not considered being at significant risk, so its defences were minimal. In addition most fighter aircraft were ineffective against Zeppelins in early 1916. While generally faster they had great difficulty operating at the same altitude as airships which could easily outclimb aeroplanes. In addition, in the pre-radar era and with only primitive radio communication, simply finding enemy raiders was an extremely difficult task. Zeppelins were big enough to carry radio equipment, British fighters were not.

On 31 January 1916 British Defence Forces were totally ineffective and only one Zeppelin, L.17, had to drop her bombs prematurely when caught in a searchlight's beam. Most RFC aircraft were based at airfields around London while enemy raiders bombed targets at least eighty miles to the north. Fog also caused problems for British pilots looking for Zeppelins and not one was seen. When they tried to land many pilots failed to find their landing flares and crashed - six British aircraft were wrecked and two men died in such accidents. Only one aeroplane was available for defence in the Midlands – a very slow R.E.7, two-seater night fighter operating out of Castle Bromwich, near Birmingham. That night it was piloted by Major A. B. Burdett, with Second Lieutenant R. A. Cresswell as the Observer/Gunner. They had no idea Zeppelins were in the area despite taking off at about 8.20 pm, just as L.21 was bombing the Black Country. Burdett and Creswell saw nothing of this and flew instead towards Birmingham; noting how the city centre blackout was effective, but suburbs easily visible as they were not subject to lighting restrictions. In January 1916 large cities had blackout regulations but small towns and railways did not. There appears to be no logical reason for this. It was probably assumed they were not vulnerable to attack. Major Burdett wrote later that visibility over Birmingham was generally good but this did not apply to Castle Bromwich, and when he returned at 9.50 pm the flare path was hidden by mist. Although his R.E.7 was destroyed on landing, Burdett and Creswell survived unhurt.

After the air raid on 31 January the whole country became subject to blackout regulations. Statistically, this decision probably cost more lives than it saved as many civilians now died in road accidents and the like. However, civilian morale demanded something be done and blackout seemed to provide obvious protection against the raider from the sky. At the very least it showed the Government was doing something. Local councils held emergency meetings to deal with the crisis and on 2 February Bilston Urban District Council resolved that all public lighting be discontinued - except for certain lights at dangerous places, and that these should be masked. The same restrictions applied to shops and houses. Wolverhampton Council was asked to reduce the lighting on its trams. At a later meeting Bilston UDC resolved to insure civic property against air raids. Property to the value of £44,580 was insured by the Royal Insurance Company for an annual premium of £70-13 shillings and 3 pence. Most importantly a system for giving air raid warnings was introduced. After official notification by the police, warnings would be given by three local factory hooters sounding five long blasts, followed by a further five long blasts. On hearing this everyone was to take cover and extinguish all external lights. The factory hooters designated to give the warning were at: John Thompson Ltd, Ettingshall, J. Sankey & Son, Bankfield Works, and Bradley & Company, Albion Works, Mount Pleasant. Other councils passed similar by-laws establishing blackout regulations and air raid warning systems, but in the weeks following the raid there was little standardisation. Many years since that tragic night, an edict passed by

Smethwick Council seems rather amusing. A factory hooter at the local carriage works was to sound 'cock-a-doodle-doo' at the approach of any Zeppelins.

Some of the confusion of the night was reflected in the minutes of the Wolverhampton Watch Committee of 7 February 1916. *"Resolved: That this Committee are astonished to hear that the Mayor of the Borough was not advised by the Chief Constable either on Monday or Wednesday last of the visit or anticipated visit of hostile aircraft and that the Chief Constable be instructed to explain why this was not done and to give the Mayor and Committee information in the future."* It must have been of comfort to the worried citizens of Wolverhampton that even a Zeppelin raid failed to destroy bureaucracy at its best.[39] A major political initiative came on 8 February 1916 when a conference for all Midland Mayors was held at Birmingham Council House. This meeting was chaired by the Lord Mayor of Birmingham, Neville Chamberlain - a man better known for his role in another war. It is interesting to speculate whether his experience of Zeppelin raids influenced his policy of 'appeasement' – a key factor in which was the belief that *'the bomber will always get through'*, a phrase coined by another Midland politician to serve as Prime Minister in the 1930s – Stanley Baldwin. Britain's leaders in both world wars had to prevent the collapse of civilian morale after destruction caused by large scale city bombing. Those attending the Birmingham Conference in 1916 included the Earl of Dartmouth, Mayors of most West Midland boroughs, town clerks and chief constables. The meeting took place in private but a Press statement was issued. In this Chamberlain expressed in the strongest terms his opinion that the arrangements for warnings were inadequate on the night of the raid; however, it was important to improve the system rather than apportion blame. The conference agreed a uniform system of lighting regulations and discussed how telephone warnings could be given to local police forces. It also elected a committee to meet with the military authorities to discuss an effective air raid warning system. This included Chamberlain, the Earl of Dartmouth and Mayors of Coventry, Dudley and Walsall. They went to London to meet Field Marshal French and an improved air defence system was soon introduced. Meeting French was opportune. He had recently been sacked as Commander of British Forces on the Western Front, mainly because of the debacle at Loos in September 1915, and replaced by Sir Douglas Haig. As a sop to his feelings he was made a Viscount and given what seemed to be a non-job - Head of Home Defence. Determined and bitter and considering himself a scapegoat, the now Lord French was probably the only man with the background, contacts and clout to produce a workable air defence system. When he received reports on the situation on the night of 31 January he was not a happy man. It was over generous to say the system failed to work well; the truth was there was no system at all. There was just chaos, where inter- service rivalry and poor communication with the civil powers led to that night being described as: *"a disaster for the defences, producing the highest proportion of aircraft losses, casualties and accidents per sortie of any home defence operation of the entire war".* Moreover, none of these casualties were a direct result of enemy action, just poor equipment, leadership and communication. To

---

[39] Powis, M., *Zeppelins over the Midlands*, Pen and Sword, 2016.

understand these shortcomings we need to examine the British air defence system and how it operated that night.

Plans to transfer responsibility for the air defence of the United Kingdom from the Admiralty to the War Office had not come into effect at the time of the raid. At about noon on 31 January 1916 Naval Intelligence knew an enemy attack in strength was developing. Zeppelins were fitted with powerful radio transmitters and in the early days of radio their German operators were probably unaware of the range at which their communications could be intercepted. In fact, all enemy signals were monitored by Naval Intelligence through radio stations positioned along the east coast, from Lerwick in the Shetland Isles to Lowestoft. These intercepted all radio signals from the German High Seas Fleet and instantly transmitted them to the Admiralty in London by telephone cable. The Royal Naval cryptography and code breaking section - known as 'Room 40' - monitored all such radio communications. Highly sensitive British radio receivers were developed to give urgent warning if the Kaiser's navy threatened to invade - the dreaded *'Bolt from the Blue'*. Even a high flying Zeppelin on the other side of the North Sea could be located from its low powered transmissions and by a system of triangulation that measured the direction of the radio signal. Although the Admiralty knew at noon that a raid was due it did not know its precise targets. Police forces across the country were told an air raid was possible, but no public warnings were given. Ground observers were also alerted that a raid was likely and good observations and excellent records were kept. Yet there was no satisfactory system to cope with or pass on the intelligence that came into the Admiralty. It appears to have been communicated to the localities in an ad hoc way that provided no basis for decision making at local level.

At first the British defensive system worked well on 31 January 1916 - probably because of direct communication from the Admiralty to naval vessels. A number of anti-aircraft trawlers and a light cruiser were sent from Lowestoft to try and intercept the attackers, but fog in the North Sea prevented contact. The first German airships crossed the coast as dusk fell and searchlights were activated. This was when Zeppelin L.17 was caught in the beam of one at RNAS Holt, in Norfolk, and fired on by a 4.7 inch gun. She dropped her bombs to try and kill the searchlight before heading home. After this early success British defence measures proved completely ineffective. By 7.00 pm the War Office knew that seven Zeppelins had crossed the coast but mistakenly assumed London was the intended target - predicting the enemy would be over the capital by about 8.15 pm. This judgement had fatal consequences and the defensive operation that then commenced was a mixture of chaos and bravery. British night fighter aircraft were ordered to take off from airfields on the outskirts of London from about 7.15 pm. Based on previous experience this was a rational decision because the slow rate of climb of aeroplanes meant they needed this time to reach the same altitude as approaching airships. Unfortunately, the real enemy that night was not Zeppelins, but patchy, drifting fog. In momentary breaks in the murk dozens of brave young pilots were ordered to take off into the misty darkness by senior officers who should have known better. In all twenty-two sorties were flown by pilots who aimlessly circled London searching for non-existent Zeppelins. Problems started when each fighter ran out of fuel and oil and needed to land. In the cold calm weather the drifting fog had worsened, landing flares on the airfields were obscured and most aircraft crashed on landing. Six machines were totally wrecked, many more seriously damaged and two highly experienced pilots were killed. The operation on 31 January 1916 produced the highest number of casualties and accidents per sortie of any home defence mission in the entire war and was subsequently described as *'one of the biggest fiascos in British air defence history'*. It is always easy to criticise operational decisions with the benefit of hindsight, but there were a number of obvious failures. The first is summed up by the old RAF saying *'Take-offs are discretionary, landings are compulsory'*. If it was foggy at 7.15 pm it would almost certainly still be foggy at 10.15 pm, making the loss of invaluable pilots and aircraft almost inevitable. It says much about the RFC command structure that no one questioned an order to send men on a virtual suicide mission. The second problem went right to the top of British defence strategy - the total lack of organisation and any kind of 'system'. After Zeppelins crossed the coast intelligence about their positions came into the Admiralty from observers, where it was recorded and presumably sent to the War Office. However, there was no system to collate this vital information it and use it to make military decisions.[40] On 12 February 1916 the Ministry of Munitions reported a complete lack of faith in official air raid warning arrangements, and stated: *"Workmen are refusing to work at night at all unless guaranteed that warnings will be given in sufficient time for them to disperse"*. It was not merely a question of putting out the lights. A circular was issued to police forces, asking them to notify all munitions factories in their area that hostile aircraft were approaching, either by telephone or a system of public warnings such as hooters or sirens. After Lord French arrived the Government took the issue of Home Defence much more seriously. Major changes took place in February 1916 and the blackout was imposed on smaller towns and cities. A nationwide air raid warning system was introduced; sirens appeared and were tested on factory buildings all over the country. The War Office clarified responsibilities for the air defence of Britain: the RFC was ordered to protect inland cities while the RNAS concentrated on defending coastal positions. Broadly speaking the air raid warning system worked but there were several months of false alarms until the first Zeppelins were shot down. The blackout caused a temporary fall in industrial production and for a time railway companies became scapegoats whenever air raids did take place. However, it was difficult to run a railway system in the dark and they were essential for war production. Compromises were made and air raids became just another wartime hardship to be endured. The air defence system which resulted in part from the Chamberlain/French meeting was probably the finest achievement of two men whose failures now define their reputations in history. Most importantly it established a network with centralised control in the War Office - the embryo of a fighter control system which served the country so well during the Battle of Britain, twenty-five years later. The new system was based on the principle that the gathering and communication of intelligence was separated from decision making. When a Zeppelin first crossed the coast it was given a simple code name. Initially a number

---

[40] Cole, C. & Cheeseman, F. G., *The Air Defence of Great Britain, 1914-1918*, Putnam, 1984.

was used, but this became overly complex when several Zeppelins were being tracked. In a moment of pure imagination, even genius, it was decided to swap numbers for children's names - a boy's name for an army airship and a girl's name for a navy one. These were put on counters to move around a large map. Names chosen deliberately avoided anything ogreish and were simple, such as Tom, Dick or Harry for a boy and Annie, Mary or Jane for a girl. Household, even humourous names endowed each Zeppelin with a personality that reduced tension and inspired confidence rather than fear in War Office staff. As intelligence came in from ground observers the position of each Zeppelin was updated and the counters moved around the map. The officers responsible could then decide when to scramble fighters to take off from different airfields, alert searchlight and anti-aircraft batteries, as well as order civil powers to sound air raid warning sirens. On 27 November 1916 the airship L.21 was baptised 'Mary'. Having crossed the coast her progress was tracked to Stoke-on-Trent, which she bombed. As she retraced her steps over Lincolnshire, fighter defences were scrambled but the RFC failed to find her. However, her course continued to be plotted and a message relayed that: 'Mary is going home' and would cross the coast near Lowestoft. Local fighters were ordered to take off and set a trap that closed when Mary was shot down over the sea a few miles from Lowestoft - a very different outcome than the shambles ten months earlier.

The Government requisitioned land to establish more aerodromes for anti-Zeppelin operations and by the end of 1916 there were thirty-two such bases for Flights of Home Defence Squadrons. Each one's headquarters was located along the east coast between Dover and Edinburgh. In theory, Home Defence airfields were about twenty miles apart, each with its own searchlights as well as others in between, marking out patrol lines for fighters. The squadron defending the West Midlands was 38 Squadron RFC - formed on 14 July 1916 - with airfields at Stamford, Leadenham and Buckminster. Its original HQ was at Castle Bromwich and first commander was Captain Arthur Travers Harris – later Air Marshal 'Bomber' Harris, Commander-in-Chief of RAF Bomber Command in the Second World War. After a few weeks, the HQ was moved near to the airfield at Melton Mowbray, where its commander was the exotically named Major Laurence J. E. Twisleton-Wykeham-Fiennes. This squadron had an establishment of eighteen aircraft and eighteen pilots although in practice fewer were available - typically fifteen aeroplanes and eight pilots. As well as main airfields night landing grounds were established for pilots low on fuel to make emergency landings. Two of these were near Wolverhampton - at Perton and Kingswinford. The Perton airfield was not where the Second World War airfield was later sited – where Perton housing estate was built, but further west between Pattingham Road and the modern Perton Golf Course (OS 853993). Perton was never used for anti-Zeppelin operations but was busy during the day with training and communication flights and after the war hosted several Wolverhampton air displays.[41]

[41] Davis, M. The RFC in the UK – December 1916, Cross & Cockade International, Vol.47/4, 2016.

Another important factor in 1916 was the introduction of specially adapted aircraft for use as night fighters. These were mainly B.E.2c biplanes, a pre-war design by the Royal Aircraft Factory, first used in 1912. The initial B.E stands for 'Bleriot Experimental', which also explains some of their problems. To the modern eye they look like typical wire-braced biplanes of the era – fragile, fairly primitive and far from aerodynamic. However, by the standards of the day they were sturdy and reliable aircraft. The problem was they were built to a design specification which made them the world's first *'inherently stable'* aeroplane. In aeronautical terms an inherently stable aircraft would naturally fly straight and level unless the pilot moved the controls. Consequently, the B.E.2c was very difficult to manoeuvre. It was so slow and clumsy that when used in daylight in its original role as a reconnaissance aeroplane over the Western Front, it was easy prey for German fighters. It was such a death-trap that during one House of Commons debate in March 1916 an MP called the B.E.2c *'Fokker Fodder'*. He said British pilots on the Western Front sent up in such outdated and outclassed aeroplanes were being murdered rather than killed. However, the B.E.2c was reprieved when it was realised its inherent stability made it the perfect night fighter and during the rest of the war they shot down six enemy airships. It was relatively easy to fly at night - with a top speed of about 85 mph it was faster than a Zeppelin - but still took sixteen minutes to reach 6,000 feet as its rate of climb was slower. As a result its Lewis guns were angled upwards over the wings - the established method of attack being to fly under a Zeppelin and fire at a small area in the airship belly. Even though higher performance aeroplanes replaced the B.E.2c later in the war most retained upward firing Lewis guns as their main armament. In 1916 more agile fighter aircraft were regarded as unsuitable for night missions. This only changed when experienced pilots later proved they could fly high performance planes such as the Sopwith Camel in the dark. It is a tribute to the bravery of British pilots that they were able to shoot down any airships with the limited performance advantage provided by the B.E.2c.

Along with effective fighter control and air raid warnings, another important factor in defeating the Zeppelin menace was the development of incendiary and explosive ammunition for aircraft machine guns. After a long period of evolution the summer of 1916 saw the mass production of Buckingham incendiary and Pomeroy and Brock explosive bullets. These were reliable enough for use in night fighters and spelled doom for Zeppelins. Production of effective incendiary ammunition showed the strength of research and development in wartime Britain, but such bullets were not difficult to make and had been used in rifles for many years. The problem was ensuring they could be stored safely and loaded and fired from the hot breech of a machine gun without exploding prematurely. The answer to the problem of producing such ammunition was learned by a process of trial and error and experiments in firing different combinations of incendiary and explosive bullets from Lewis guns. Pure hydrogen is difficult to ignite - tracer bullets passed straight through Zeppelin gas cells without starting a fire – but it was soon discovered it became highly flammable when mixed with air. By loading a Lewis gun with the correct balance of incendiary and explosive ammunition ignition could literally be sparked. Explosive bullets caused the gas bags to tear and leaking hydrogen combined with air to produce the combustible mixture that was ignited by incendiary bullets. British airmen soon discovered a technique to defeat a Zeppelin – firing their angled Lewis guns into one area on its lower hull. It usually took dozens of bullets to cause a fire but, once ignited, airships burned like a furnace in the sky with machine and crew incinerated in minutes. Contemporary descriptions referred to the way Zeppelins would first glow like a huge Chinese lantern. Then, as fire spread an airship would fall like a stone as the hydrogen lifting gas burned away. The blaze created by a million cubic feet of hydrogen meant a burning Zeppelin was visible to other airships or aircraft as much as one hundred miles away.[42] The German navy tried to counter British incendiary ammunition by building even larger Zeppelins known as 'height climbers'. These could operate at 20,000 feet, well above the ceiling of British fighters, and had some limited success. However, the day of the Zeppelin as a terror bomber was over and by the end of the war they could be outclimbed by fixed wing fighter aircraft; their vulnerability to incendiary ammunition making them flying death traps.

Part Three: Dulce et Decorum est Pro Patria Mori.[43]

The bombing of Bradley by L.21 was part of the wider German strategic bombing campaign in the Great War. On 31 January 1916 this included eight other Zeppelins of the Imperial German navy that attacked targets in the Midlands and North of England. While the Zeppelin is best known for bombing its main function was actually aerial reconnaissance. The reason the Germany Navy was so enthusiastic about Zeppelins was they served as the eyes of the fleet. It is less well known that the United States Navy still used airships in a similar way in the Second World War. Goodyear Blimps, like Zeppelins, could stay aloft for days and were widely deployed for anti-submarine reconnaissance. However, Zeppelins will always be remembered as the first terror bombers while their original role as observation platforms will remain only a footnote in history. In 1915 Zeppelins carried out a number of raids on England. At first the Kaiser insisted bombing should be restricted to military targets such as shipyards, arsenals, docks and military installations. However, cities were soon included as the concept of total war developed and commanders realised high flying airships could not carry out precision attacks. As strategic bombing developed London became the focus for Zeppelin raids and a number of these occurred in 1915. The German army and navy operated their own fleets of airships. Zeppelins were huge – the L.21 was the length of two football pitches (585 feet) – and are still the largest combat aircraft ever to have flown. A Zeppelin such as L.21 would weigh about 53,000 pounds empty. However, once inflated, its 1,264,100 cubic feet of hydrogen would lift it, a crew of twenty, fuel, oil, ballast (used to control height) and about two tons of bombs. While they were slower than fighter aircraft they could climb much faster than any aeroplane opposing them in 1916.

---

[42] Jones, H.A., *The War in the Air*, Clarendon Press, 1931.
[43] Usually translated from the Latin of Roman poet Horace as 'It is sweet and honourable to die for one's country.' Chosen by Wilfred Owen as the ironic title of his famous war poem.

The 31 January 1916 raid was the first Zeppelin attack on England since the bombing of London in October 1915. It was part of a wider strategic plan to increase attacks on Britain's industrial capacity and ability to make war. In January command of the German High Seas Fleet was taken over by *Vizeadmiral* Reinhard Scheer and his brief was to concentrate on degrading Britain's industrial capacity. The main thrust of his campaign was the introduction of unrestricted submarine warfare, along with naval bombardments of British east coast towns and air attacks on industrial centres. Naval Airship Division commander, *Korvettenkapitain* Peter Strasser, promoted this strategic air offensive in the belief it would significantly alter the course of the war. He confronted and justified the moral dilemma of terror bombing in a letter to his mother: *"We who strike at the enemy where his heart beats have been slandered as 'baby-killers and 'murderers of women'...What we do is repugnant to us too, but necessary, very necessary. Nowadays there is no such animal as a non-combatant: modern warfare is total warfare. A soldier cannot function at the front without the factory worker, the farmer, and all the other providers behind him. You and I, Mother, have discussed this subject, and I know you understand what I say. My men are brave and honourable. Their cause is holy, so how can they sin while doing their duty? If what we do is frightful, then may frightfulness be Germany's salvation."*

In January 1916 Strasser met Admiral Scheer to agree details of this 'frightful' strategy. There were to be three attack zones: England North - From the River Tyne to Edinburgh; England Middle – from Liverpool east to the River Humber; England South - London and East Anglia. The raid of 31 January 1916 was the first conducted according to the new strategy. The plan was for nine navy Zeppelins to bomb industrial centres in 'Middle England' - Liverpool being the primary target. What happened was probably the most important air raid of the war as 205 high explosive and 113 incendiary bombs were dropped, killing seventy and injuring 113 civilians. It is also estimated to have caused £53,832 worth of damage. The Zeppelin raid on London, 13/14 October 1915, is generally considered the most serious airship attack of the war. On that occasion seventy-one people were killed, 128 injured and about £80,000 worth of damage caused. However, by adding on the two British pilots killed on 31 January 1916, a total of seventy-two fatalities is reached, making this the most costly raid. It was also followed by much greater public outrage and demands for action. Zeppelin commanders claimed they bombed Liverpool and other cities of military importance and Germany boasted it was a huge success. In fact, it was a failure in terms of military damage and the country was not destroyed by fire. For most of the night the enemy airships that roamed above England were hopelessly lost. The effect of the raid on civilian morale was more difficult to assess. There was some initial panic, and for a few months' afterwards air raid false alarms affected industrial production in a few places. Perhaps the most important consequence of the raid was to force the Government take national air defence seriously, not just the London area. The raid also cost the Germans dearly, especially the loss of Loewe's L.19 and the four airmen who died in the futile search for it off the Friesian coast. In the wider context of strategic bombing throughout the twentieth century, or the contemporary carnage taking place on the Western Front, the final 'butchers bill' for the raid was small – ninety-two people had died (British: seventy civilians, two airmen. German: sixteen crewmen from the L.19 and four airmen sent to find them.) However, the fact that terror bombing had reached the heart of British industry was a portent for the future – the grim new reality that war was no longer just a matter for soldiers and sailors. This was graphically illustrated by the fact that fifteen of the dead British civilians were children. The 31 January 1916 raid was carried out by nine Zeppelins and their 154 crewmen. By the end of 1916 half of these men were also dead.

The reorganisation of Home Defence began to show results within a few weeks. On 1 April Zeppelin 1916 L.15 was damaged by anti-aircraft fire and landed in the sea near Margate due to loss of gas. Her commander *Kapitanleutnant* Breithaupt and most of her crew were captured. The real prize came later with the shooting down of the first airship over British soil on Sunday 3 September. This was not a Zeppelin, but a wooden framed Schutte-Lanz, SL.11, of the German army, commanded by *Hauptmann* Wilhelm Schramm. Lieutenant William Leefe Robinson of 39 Squadron RFC saw SL.11 caught in a searchlight beam while flying over north-east London. He flew between 500 and 800 feet below and fired three magazines loaded with Brock and Pomeroy ammunition into her belly. He reported her hull started to glow and seconds later her whole rear was blazing. The spectacle of SL.11 falling to earth near Cuffley in Hertfordshire was witnessed by hundreds of thousands of people all over London. All sixteen crew members died in the inferno and the airship wreckage became a major attraction, with thousands visiting the crash site over the next few days. Robinson became a national hero and received a Victoria Cross and reward of several thousand pounds. In a macabre publicity stunt, this financial 'prize' was raised by national newspapers and promised to the first pilot to shoot down a Zeppelin. A few days later the same newspapers carried headlines campaigning against the 'Zeppelin baby killers' being given a proper military funeral. Once British pilots voiced disgust at this attitude, the crew of SL.11 received an official military escort at their burial service. In 1964 their bodies were exhumed and reburied along with other airship crews in a special plot at Cannock Chase German Military Cemetery.

For some time after its destruction British authorities claimed SL.11 had been destroyed by bombs. This was partly to prevent the Germans realising effective incendiary ammunition had been developed, but also for political reasons. There was still concern about the legality of incendiary bullets under the terms of the Hague Convention. Once the British had devised the tactics to shoot down airships they followed in quick succession – with two coming to grief on the same night. On 23 September 1916 Second Lieutenant Frederick Sowery, of 39 Squadron RFC, shot down Zeppelin L.32 near Billericay, Essex. Commander Oberleutnant zur See Werner Peterson is now buried with his crew of twenty-two at Cannock. Also over Essex, L.33 was struck by anti-aircraft fire and crash landed near Great Wigborough. Kapitanleutnant Alois Bocker and his crew of twenty-two then surrendered to a startled local police constable. On 1 October 1916 Zeppelin L.31 was shot down near Potters Bar, north of London. Kapitanleutnant Heinrich Mathy and his crew of nineteen are also buried at Cannock. The loss of three airships in a month affected the morale of the other crews, especially as a burning Zeppelin could be seen from over a hundred miles away. Watching one's comrades die in this way prompted grim discussions about what to do in this situation; burn or jump. L.31 commander Heinrich Mathy was asked by a newspaper what he would do. He said he didn't know; but he would at the time. On 1 October Mathy jumped and his body was found unmarked a few yards from the wreckage of his Zeppelin.

In September 1916 Max Dietrich was assigned to a new Zeppelin, L.34. As was usual the crew who helped him bomb the Black Country in January went with him. His next raid was on the 27 November 1916 - his 47th birthday. It is said the mess at Nordholz was decorated for his birthday celebration as the officers sat down for lunch at about noon. Peter Strasser's adjutant then came in and said "*Gentlemen we have attack orders, the industrial areas of Middle England, we have to be in the air by 1.00pm. (Noon GMT) we have excellent prospects*". At that point Kurt Frankenburg, who had replaced Dietrich as commander of L.21, evidently said "*leave the birthday decorations, we can celebrate tomorrow.*" However, his Executive Officer, Hans-Werner Salzbrunn, turned to a friend and said, "*I know we won't be coming back from this flight*". He was correct; Dietrich and Frankenburg never returned for the birthday party. We can be sure those comrades who did, needed a stiff drink after this raid. L.34 left Nordholz with a crew of twenty at 1.00 pm on 27 November 1916 and her target was Newcastle. She arrived over England at 10.45 pm, making landfall at Black Hall Rocks, north of Hartlepool. L.34 was picked up by a searchlight near the Hutton Henry Lighthouse and fired on by anti-aircraft guns. Dietrich dropped thirteen high explosive bombs but failed to destroy the searchlight battery, hitting farm buildings instead and injuring two cows. Dietrich then turned for home, heading over West Hartlepool, where he was caught again by searchlights while dropping sixteen high explosive bombs. Two fell in Ward Jackson Park and a memorial stone plaque now marks the spot. L.34 then bombed working class homes in Harley Street, Lowthian Road and Poplar Grove, damaging a number and killing four people and injuring eleven. Dietrich then bombed allotments and hit the grandstand of Hartlepool United Football Club, causing major damage.

By then L.34 had been spotted in the searchlight beams by a British night fighter. Its pilot was Second Lieutenant Ian Vernon Pyatt; of 36 Home Defence Squadron, RFC, flying a B.E.2c aircraft. He had taken off from Seaton Carew and engaged L.34 over Hartlepool. In his combat report Pyatt said he caught up with the airship at about 11.42 pm over the mouth of the River Tees, and fired seventy-one rounds from his Lewis gun. He noticed a small area on her envelope become incandescent where he had seen his tracer bullets entering: "*this patch rapidly spread and the next thing the whole Zepp was in flames*". He watched L.34 fall into the sea still burning, half a mile off shore. The next day only a patch of oil marked the spot where Dietrich and nineteen other crew members had died. A few parts of L.34 later washed up on shore and in early 1917 the bodies of two crewmen also drifted in on the tide. However, they had been in the sea too long to be identified and were buried at Seaton Carew before being transferred later to Cannock. They are not buried in the main Zeppelin plot, but amongst the other unknown German soldiers.

A Bilston soldier named Private Cyril Morell, of the East Yorkshire Regiment, provided an eyewitness account of another Zeppelin that night. He was stationed at Cowden Camp, near Hornsea, East Yorkshire, and described events in a letter to his sister who lived at 1 Cemetery Road, Bilston. In his letter of 1 December he said he had never seen such a sight as he did on 27 November. *"We thought we were in the battlefield; a Zepp came over the next field where there were airmen and searchlights. The Zepp stood still for about five minutes with the searchlight on him, they were dropping bombs all the time, and the guns all going off. 'It was a noise'. It went off and there was a second one which was hit in the tail by an AA gun, and flew out to sea lit up by the searchlights. It must have been the one that went down."* Cyril was incorrect; he had not been watching Dietrich's L.34, but L.14, commanded by Hauptmann Kuno Manger. This Zeppelin did drop forty four bombs on Mappleton, near Hornsea, in answer to gunfire from Cowden Camp. Poor Cyril got to the battlefield soon enough - 4 February 1917 - where he was hit by shellfire and died of wounds near Hebuterne on 12 March 1917. He is buried at Sucrerie Military Cemetery, Colincamps, France. [44]

It is perhaps fitting that Zeppelin L.21 met the same fate as her old commander Max Dietrich that very night. Since the raid on the Black Country, L.21 had been involved in twelve more bombing raids and seventeen reconnaissance operations, including the Battle of Jutland. Her new commander was Kapitanleutnant Kurt Frankenberg and on this flight his Executive Officer was Leutnant zur See Hans-Werner von Salzbrunn. On 27 November 1916 Zeppelin L.21 took off from Nordholz at about the same time as L.34. At 10.20 pm she crossed the coast near Atwick, East Yorkshire, and flew to Leeds before bombing Wakefield and Barnsley. L.21 then headed south to the Stoke-on-Trent area where she dropped bombs on Kidsgrove, Goldenhill, Tunstall, Chesterton, Fenton and Trentham. After leaving the Potteries Frankenburg headed back to the coast but L.21 made slow progress over the East Midlands, probably due to engine trouble. At 2.50 am, as she passed south of Nottingham, she was caught in an airfield searchlight at Buckminster. Captain George Hornby Birley, 38 Squadron RFC, made contact with L.21 and followed her for about fifteen minutes. He fired at her but lost the airship in the dark when he changed the ammunition drum on his Lewis gun. Several other pilots saw L.21 and gave chase, but she escaped. An hour later she was intercepted again near East Derham, but the attacking aeroplane had to crashland when its engine failed. However, L.21's luck ran out when she reached the coast near Lowestoft in the early dawn. The system of air defence was working well. Given the code name 'Mary' the Zeppelin had been tracked throughout her nine-hour flight over England. When she reached the Suffolk coast at 6.05 am three RNAS aeroplanes were in the air waiting for her. The pilots were Flight Lieutenant Egbert Cadbury, of the Birmingham chocolate family, Flight Sub Lieutenant Gerard Fane and Flight Sub Lieutenant

---

[44] Morrell, C., *Letters from the Trenches*, Ed. Kathleen Carter, Brewin Books, 2000.

Edward Laston Pulling. All three attacked L.21, but Pulling received the credit for her destruction - he fired the final shots and was scorched by flames as the airship caught light. He was also close enough to witness a particularly grizzly scene, when the Zeppelin's machine gunner - stationed on top of the airship's envelope – left his platform, ran and dived straight off its nose to escape the flames. Pulling reported that after a few seconds the Zeppelin became a *"fiery furnace"*. L.21 fell into the sea about eight miles east of Lowestoft at 6.42 am on 28 November 1916. There were no survivors from its crew of seventeen and search vessels recovered only a broken propeller blade found floating in a great pool of petrol and oil. The rest of L.21 sank to the bottom of the North Sea. As far as we know it is still there.

It is fitting to end with the destruction of L.21. This Zeppelin ranged over the Midlands without opposition on 31 January 1916. However, ten months later on the night of 27/28 November she was the hunted not the hunter. The British had learned the lessons of the January raid, but the Germans had not. Much to their credit those responsible for Home Defence had built an effective air defence system. In a war where commanders are usually criticised for lacking the moral courage to accept and learn from their mistakes, the development of the British air defence system deserves special credit. In some ways defeating the Zeppelins was as much to do with the efforts of failed generals, politicians and bureaucrats, as it was pilots' bravery and the genius of scientists. Success occurred thanks to trial and error and implementing strategies that were seen to work. After 1916 the German army continued strategic bombing but focused on London using large fixed wing aeroplanes like the Gotha G.IV, based on airfields in Belgium. The German navy persisted with Zeppelins for long range attacks but developed the height climber airships to operate at 20,000 feet; well above an aeroplane's ceiling. Attacks continued in 1917 and 1918 but operations at great altitude made navigation and accurate bombing much more difficult. Britain also took the offensive using flying boats, equipped with radios, and primitive aircraft carriers to attack Zeppelins where they were most vulnerable; on the German side of the North Sea.

The Black Country was bombed again by a Zeppelin on 19 October 1917. This time L.41, commanded by *Hauptman* Kuno Manger, dropped bombs near the Grazebrook Foundry and blast furnace at Netherton.   Railway wagons were damaged near Hall Lane Farm where a bomb killed a cow and a number of pigeons in their pen. L.41 then flew a few miles south-east and dropped more bombs on Hayward Forge, Coombeswood. This was described locally as being *'lit up like a Christmas tree'*. One bomb fell near Firtree Farm, Mucklow Hill, but failed to explode and another that did landed on Leasowes Golf course, Halesowen. The remains of the crater can still be seen but sadly the story that the golf club used it to make an additional bunker is just a myth. It seems L.41 then turned towards the Austin Motor Works at Longbridge where she dropped five more bombs, three of which failed to explode. One man was injured and buildings damaged to a cost of about £500.[45]

[45] Powis, M., *The Last Zeppelin Raid on the Black Country*, The Blackcountryman, No.3, Vol.49, 2016.

Fregettenkapitan Peter Strasser never lost his conviction that precision bombing would win the war for Germany and was personally involved the final act in the Zeppelin campaign against Britain. On the night of 5 August 1918 he was present aboard the L.70 as it carried out the last air raid on England in the Great War. Although L.70 was the most technically advanced Zeppelin built in the war, it was shot down by a DH4 two-seater aeroplane that outperformed it in every way. The British plane was flown by Major Egbert Cadbury, of the Birmingham chocolate dynasty, with Captain Robert Leckie as his observer: both experienced airmen. Cadbury had participated in the destruction of L.21, almost two years earlier and Leckie had been a crewman on the Curtis flying boat that shot down L.22 on 14 May 1917. At 9.05 pm on 5 August 1918 Cadbury and Leckie took off in their DH4 from Yarmouth and observed L.70 and two other airships about forty miles away. It took over an hour for their plane to reach the same altitude as the Zeppelins but once it did they went into action. Cadbury attacked L.70 head on and swooped below to give his observer the chance to fire at her with his Lewis gun. Leckie emptied a whole magazine of Pomeroy explosive ammunition into the airship's hull, starting a fire at the stern which spread along the whole length of the Zeppelin in less than a minute. L.70 fell as a blazing mass, hitting the sea about eight miles off the Norfolk coast north of Wells-next-the-Sea. Peter Strasser died along with the other twenty-one airmen aboard. Zeppelin parts were recovered and examined by the British, as were the bodies of a number of its crew. Following protests from local people the dead Germans were not buried in the nearby cemetery but given military funerals at sea. However, the ultimate significance of this event was that the wreckage of the L.70 included Germany's dreams of defeating Britain by a strategic air offensive. This was the last Zeppelin raid of the Great War.

What remains?

Nowadays, the Black Country is a very different place to the one bombed by the Germans in the Great War and Tipton, Bradley, Wednesbury and Walsall are all struggling with the blight of de-industrialisation. However, some evidence of the Zeppelin raids still exists. The Bradley canal bank and pumping station, where William Fellows died and Maud was fatally injured, appears almost unaltered. In 1994, after a campaign by local historians and Maud's son, a memorial was placed on the wall of the old pump house. It was erected by British Waterways who own the site and unveiled by Dennis Turner MP and the Rev Richard Walker, vicar of Saint Martin's, Bradley.

Left: The Memorial plaque erected in 1994   *Right:* The Old Bush Inn, Bradley Lane, where Maud worked as a barmaid.

William Fellows was long known in the Bradley area as *'Fred'*, but there is no doubt about his real name; the inquest and his death certificate clearly identify him as William. The Old Bush pub in Bradley Lane, where Maud received first aid on a table, is also much as it was. It is also fitting that the facade of Wolverhampton General Hospital, where Maud died, is to be preserved. While the remains of L.19 and L.21 lie deep below the North Sea, the Imperial War Museum, Lambeth, and RAF Museum, Hendon, both have excellent exhibitions on the Zeppelin raids. In Germany, Nordholz - home of the L.21 - is still a naval base and contains an impressive museum; *'Aeronauticum Nordholz'*, recording the history of German naval aviation. Exhibits relating to the Zeppelin raids include letters in the bottle thrown into the North Sea by L.19's crew. Finally, the German War Cemetery at Cannock Chase includes a memorial garden containing the bodies of seventy-three men who were shot down over England in four airships. Many took part in the Black Country raid of 31 January 1916.

Sources used:

Documents and Articles.

Mick Davis and Bill Morgan, *Gazetter of Flying Sites*, Cross and Cockade International, Vol 44/3, 2013

Mick Davis, *The RFC in the UK, December 1916*, Cross and Cockade International, Vol/47/4, 2016

Intelligence Section GHQ Home Forces - Secret document, probably written by Lieutenant Colonel H G de Watterville: Air raids 31st January – 1st February 1916. Air Raids, 1916. 2nd – 3rd September 1916. Air Raids, 1916 23rd September to 2nd October 1916. H.B.M. Government. GHQ. H.F (1) November and December 1916.

David Mechan, *The Silent Raid - The Untold Story*, Cross and Cockade International, Vol 45/4 2014

The Rev. W.L.T Merson, *Zeppelin Raid on Walsall*, article in: 'Borough of Walsall, Programme of the Peace Celebrations', Borough of Walsall, 1919.

Chris Percy and Noel Ryan, *Lincolnshire Aviation in World War 1*, Airfield Research Group. 2012.

Mick Powis, *Zeppelins over the Black Country*, article in 'The Blackcountryman', numbers 3 and 4, Vol. 29, 1996.

Mick Powis, *The Last Zeppelin Raid on the Black Country*, article in 'The Blackcountryman', Number 3, Vol 49, 2016.

Walsall Local History Centre, Walsall Chronicle No 8: *Walsall at War*, Walsall Library and Museum Service.

Various, *Wolverhampton and the Great War*, Wolverhampton Archives and Local Studies, 2014.

Newspapers.

The Black Country Bugle. August, September, October 1983. July, November 1994.

The Dudley Herald. Editions from 1916.

The Express and Star. Editions from February and March 1916. Also see articles by Mick Powis in the editions of 25 January 1996 and 6 January 2000.

The Tipton Herald. Editions from 1916.

The Walsall Herald. Editions from 1916.

The Walsall Pioneer. Editions from 1916.

The Wednesbury Herald. Editions from 1916.

Books.

Ian M Bott, *The Midlands Zeppelin Outrage*, Black Country Society Publications, 2016.

Alec Brew, *The History of Black Country Aviation*, Alan Sutton, 1993.

Horst Treusch von Buttlar-Brandenfels, *Zeppelins over England*, George G Harrap, 1931.

Ian Castle, *London 1914 – 1917 - The Zeppelin Menace*, Osprey, 2008.

Christopher Cole and F G Cheeseman, *The Air Defence of Great Britain - 1914 – 1918*, Putnam, 1984.

Gwynne Dyer, *War*, The Bodley Head, 1986.

Bill Gunston, *Night Fighters - A Development and Combat History*, Patrick Stephens, 1976.

Henry Albert Jones, *The War in the Air*, Claredon Press, 1931.

Ernest A Lehmann and Howard Mingos, *The Zeppelins - The Development of the Airship, with the Story of the Zeppelin Raids in The World War*, J. H. Sears 1927. Reprint by P.S. Chapman 2014.

Cecil Lewis, *Sagittarius Rising*, Penguin, 1983.

Cyril Morrell (Edited by Kathleen Carter), *Letters from the Trenches*, Brewin Books, 2000.

Derek Nicholls and Chris Smith, *The Great Tipton Zeppelin Raid*, Tipton Civic Society, 2016.

Ian Mackersey, *No Empty Chairs*, Pheonix, 2012.

Joseph Morris, *German Air Raids on Britain 1914 -1918*, Sampson Lowe, 1925.

Michael Pearson, *The Black Country in the Great War*, Pen and Sword, 2014.

Mick Powis, *Zeppelins over the Midlands*, Pen and Sword, 2016.

Mick Powis, *The Defeat of the Zeppelins*, Pen and Sword, 2018.

Raymond Rimell, *Zeppelin Vol 1*, Albatros Publications, 2006.

Raymond Rimell, *Zeppelin Vol 2*, Albatros Publications, 2008.

Raymond Rimell, *The Last Flight of the L.48*, Windsock, 2006.

Raymond Rimel, *Zeppelins at War! 1914 – 1915*, Albatross Publications, 2014.

Raymond Rimell, *The Airship VC*, Aston Publications, 1989.

Raymond Rimell, *The Last Flight of the L.31*, Windsock data file special ,2016.

Raymond Rimell, *The Last Flight of the L.32*, Windsock data file special, 2016.

Douglas H Robinson, *The Zeppelin in Combat*, Schiffer Publishing, 1994.

Jerry White, *Zeppelin Nights - London in the First World War*, Vintage Books, 2015.

James Wyllie and Michael McKinley, *The Code breakers: the Secret Intelligence Unit that changed the course of the first World War*, Ebury Press, 2015.

Chapter 6

Grandad's War – Gallipoli, Egypt, the Somme and Ypres

Mark R. Cooper

This is the story of my grandfather, Corporal Bertie Henry Crick, 9362, of the 7th (Service) Battalion South Staffordshire Regiment, who fought and died in the Great War. It is based on family memories, passed down over the generations, and research from various regimental histories. Bertie was born in Wolverhampton on Sunday 13 April 1890 to John Henry Crick and Bertha Elizabeth Crick (née Harrison). His father was a baker who moved to Staffordshire from Northampton and his mother was from Leominster, Herefordshire. By the time of the 1901 census the family were living at 111 Green Lane, Walsall. When he started work Bertie became a caster in a local foundry. On 26 December 1913 he married my grandmother, Edith Meek, at St. Michael's Parish Church, Caldmore, Walsall. Edith was born in Wednesbury in 1893 and was working as a laundress when they first met. After their marriage they lived at 32 Orlando Street, Walsall.

Bertie enlisted in Kitchener's New Army at Walsall soon after the outbreak of war, joining the 7th Battalion of the South Staffs Regiment (7 South Staffords). This unit had been raised in Lichfield in August 1914 and was part of the 33rd Brigade, 11th Northern Division. After several weeks of induction at Belton Park, Grantham, Bertie and his comrades were sent for their final training at Frensham, Surrey, in April 1915. The 7 South Staffords set sail from Liverpool at the end of June 1915; destination Gallipoli, via the Greek island of Mudros. They briefly landed at Cape Helles, between 23 and 28 July before being re-embarked to take part in an amphibious assault against the Turks at Suvla Bay, on 7 August. After the failure of the August offensive Allied forces were eventually withdrawn from the Gallipoli peninsula in December and January 1916. Bertie's battalion were evacuated on the night of 19/20 December 1915 first to the island of Imbros, and then to Egypt by the end of January. Here they were concentrated at Sidi Bishr, and took over defensive positions along the Suez Canal, on 19 February 1916. Four months later Bertie's battalion was ordered to France to support the British offensive on the Somme, and its departure from Egypt was completed by 3 July. The 7 South Staffords took part in the capture of the German strongpoint known as Der Wundt-Werk, 14 September; the Battle of Flers-Courcellette, 15-22 September, and the Battle of the Thiepval Ridge, 26-28 September. In early 1917, after a period of operations in the Ancre valley, Bertie's unit was moved north to Flanders, ready to participate in the Battle of Messines, in June 1917.

In the meantime, Bertie had been promoted to the rank of Corporal on Saturday 24 February 1917. This meant he was now in charge of a 'section' of around sixteen men, there being four sections of infantry in a platoon. By early July 1917 Bertie's battalion had arrived at 'Camp O' near Poperinghe, in order to prepare for what is now called the Third Battle of Ypres, or Passchendaele. Evidently this site was nicknamed *"Ack 30 Central"* because it was such a popular target for German artillery who could clearly see it from the ridge to the east of Ypres. On Sunday 15 July 1917 Bertie's battalion moved from this hotspot into the trenches about a mile north of Ypres, relieving the 4/5th Battalion Black Watch. They were now positioned about three-quarters of a mile east of the Yser Canal in front of La Brique, with C and D Companies in the front line and A and B in support. The 7 South Staffords were meant to hold the line and improve the position ready for 51st Division, who were going to take a leading role in the great attack due to begin on 31 July. Unfortunately this location was one of the most dangerous on the Western Front because it was completely overlooked by the enemy and constantly raked by artillery fire. The battalion also suffered such dreadful losses from snipers it had to send out regular patrols into no man's land to flush them out and kill them. It was whilst working in the trenches at this lethal location that Bertie was fatally wounded by either shellfire or a sniper's bullet. We will never know for sure. The battalion war diary for 17 July 1917 records: *"9362, Cpl. Crick, B, died of wounds"* that day. Fortunately for the family the circumstances of Bertie's death meant he received a proper burial and he lies in La Brique Military Cemetery, No.2, in the north of the city of Ypres. On 18 August, my grieving grandmother placed a personal announcement in the Walsall Observer: *"O Lord, grant him eternal rest."* Bertie is commemorated locally on the Roll of Honour in Walsall Town Hall and on the war memorial in St. Matthew's Church, on the hill, Walsall. He is also remembered on the new Wolverhampton Roll of Honour together with 4,272 men and women from Wolverhampton, who died during the Great War. Obviously I never knew Bertie myself, but I have been looking for a photograph of him for many years without success. After all, it is more than a century since the conflict and all of his contemporaries have long since passed away. Yet, he is not entirely forgotten. My grandmother, Edith Sarah Crick, remarried in 1919 to another soldier; Sergeant Joseph Booth Gretton, and they settled in Clay Street, Penkridge. He was a veteran who survived being gassed and was discharged as unfit for service. They had two further children together - a boy and a girl.

The Passchendaele ridge was eventually taken by British and Canadian forces on 10 November and the Third Battle of Ypres brought to a close on 20 November 1917. More than 250,000 Commonwealth soldiers were killed or wounded in the campaign, with a similar number lost on the German side.

Chapter 7

Thomas Clarke – A Boy Soldier of the Great War

Chris Twiggs

Thomas Clarke lies buried in New Munich Trench Cemetery on the Somme in northern France. He was killed, aged eighteen, on 14 November 1916 during one of the last actions of the Battle of the Somme - one of an estimated 250,000 underage soldiers who served in the British army during the Great War.

Thomas Clarke's grave with his photograph.

He was born in 1898, the third son of Alfred and Mary Clarke. In 1901 the family lived at 4 Boscobel Place, off Stafford Street, before moving to 53 Stafford Road, Wolverhampton. By the time of the 1911 Census Mary had given birth to eight children and it would be fair to say that life for the Clarke family was tough. A clue to this was that thirteen-year-old Thomas was not living at home, but listed as a sailor and resident on board Training Ship *Clio*. This former Royal Navy gunship was moored in the Menai Straits near Bangor, off the North Wales coast. TS *Clio* had been used as a training ship since 1877 and was certified to receive boys under the terms of the 1908 Children's Act. It was part of range of institutions such as Reformatories, Farm Schools and Industrial Schools which existed to deal with children 'at risk'. As an industrial training ship TS *Clio* was not allowed to take boys with a criminal record but took eleven – sixteen-year-olds of all denominations – most of whom were sent by education committees from the Midlands, North Wales and

North West. Children such as Thomas, whose home circumstances meant they were not being adequately looked after, were deemed in danger of falling into criminality. The initiative of sending vulnerable boys to establishments such as TS *Clio* was made by parents or, as was usually the case, by local education committees. With Thomas it was almost certainly at the behest of the latter. In the early 1900s his parents were brought before the local courts in Wolverhampton on at least two occasions. The first of these was for allowing a child to beg and the second for failing to ensure one of their children regularly attended school. These offences were exactly the sorts of infraction that could see a child removed from *"a harmful home influence"* and sent to an institution of the type mentioned. Although the child involved in the case is not referred to by name in all likelihood it was Thomas.

The TS *Clio* took 260 boys and trained them for a life at sea, possibly leading to employment with the Royal Navy or the merchant navy. Life on the TS *Clio* was dedicated to inculcating values of regular hard work and above all a sense of personal responsibility. Boys received a basic education and instruction in all matters pertaining to a nautical career. Conditions on board were clean but basic and at weekends they would sometimes go on land to undertake other supervised activities. Particularly important in this respect was the ship's band which often performed in locations around North Wales and, on one occasion in the early 1900s, in Wolverhampton. Boys stayed on TS *Clio* for up to three years and were then expected to be ready to enter the adult world as responsible citizens. This was the case for many boys associated with the ship who went on to have fruitful careers at sea. Unfortunately Thomas Clarke was not one of their success stories.

The Training Ship Clio in the Menai Straits.

In 1914, when the Great War broke out, Thomas was at Feltham Borstal Institution in Middlesex, having been sentenced to two years imprisonment for theft. However, in April 1915 he was released under licence into the army. He was one of many inmates of young offenders' institutions, such as borstals, who was afforded such an opportunity. Britain had been at war since August 1914 and it was becoming clear that the war was not going to be a short one. Many had responded to Lord Kitchener's call for volunteers in the first weeks of the war but there was a constant demand for more men. There was a belief that service in the armed forces would do 'troubled' young men such as Thomas a power of good by allowing them to 'do their bit' for King and country. In 1915 Government policy was clearly laid out by Home Secretary, Sir John Simon, in the House of Commons: "*In the Borstal Institutions of Great Britain, where youths are received under sentences of one to three years, steps have been taken since the beginning of the War to release for enlistment selected prisoners who had profited by the training of the Institution, which includes drill and gymnastics, and who appeared likely to make good soldiers. The result of the experiment has been most satisfactory; a large number have been released and have enlisted, and in the great majority of cases good reports have been received of the conduct of the lads in the fighting services both at home and abroad. It is not possible to take similar steps in the local prisons, as in the large majority of cases the sentences are too short to allow of similar training; but the services of those who are received have been utilised in the manufacture of war stores. I may add that the number of young prisoners shows a very great reduction since the beginning of the War.*"

Thomas's first few weeks in the army were clearly sufficiently preferable to life at Feltham as in June 1915 he signed on for seven years with the 3rd Battalion of the Royal Berkshire Regiment (Service number: 17546). This was a home-based battalion responsible for training new recruits and usually based at Reading barracks. At the time Thomas joined, it was based at the Victoria Barracks, Portsmouth. Here he undertook several months of training before being sent to join the regiment's 1st Battalion in France towards the end of the year. His service appeared to go well until April 1916, at which point his battalion was ordered into the frontline and he deserted. This was an extremely unwise course of action as in many cases it led to death by firing squad. He was quickly apprehended and charged with desertion and theft. Clearly, with regard to the latter offence, the army had not ironed out Thomas' earlier criminal inclinations. Like many men who found themselves before a court martial, he was poorly educated and probably did not realise the seriousness of his situation. The likelihood of being shot for desertion increased if it occurred in the period leading up to a major offensive. His offence occurred in the weeks leading up to the Battle of the Somme. Thomas's court martial took place on 28 April and he was found guilty and sentenced to death. However, like the eighty-nine per cent of similarly condemned men in the British Army during the Great War, he was reprieved and his sentence commuted to ten years in prison. In reality this lasted only a matter of weeks and he was subsequently released to rejoin his unit. Shortly after his return he was quite badly wounded and sent back to a military hospital in Britain. He does not appear to have returned to Wolverhampton during the period of his recovery and it seems as if he was returned to France immediately he was deemed fit to serve.

The Battle of the Somme began on 1 July 1916 with disastrous consequences for the British Army. In the weeks and months that followed a steady advance was made, albeit with heavy casualties on all sides. By November the British had pushed the Germans back about five miles at the furthest point and the offensive was drawing to an end. A combination of increasingly poor weather, growing casualties and exhaustion meant that a halt to proceedings was only a matter of time. The 1st Battalion Royal Berkshires were to be involved in one of the last actions of the Somme campaign. Along with other units, they were tasked with driving the Germans from their positions on the Redan Ridge beyond the village of Beaumont Hamel. Their attack on the morning of 14 November 1916 did not go well. Conditions were poor and the featureless ground over which the attack was launched was pitted with shell holes and shrouded in dense mist. Some units spent hours even attempting to get to their starting positions and matters were chaotic. The attack started at 6.30 am and advancing units soon began to lose their bearings and the line of attack. Some troops entering German trenches misidentified their location which added to the sense of confusion. The advance by Thomas' battalion went very badly wrong and as they advanced across no man's land they appeared to be hit by a British artillery barrage. Whether this was a case of the barrage falling short or the men moving too quickly is disputed but the end result was that their advance resulted in 116 casualties from a force of 159. A small party of the 1st Royal Berkshires got into German positions at Munich Trench but were unable to hold off a counter-attack and what was left of the men had to fall back and create a new defensive position. Official records do not recount the exact fate of Thomas Clarke. He may have been in the small group that got as far as Munich Trench but in all likelihood he was one of the victims of 'friendly fire' on that fateful day. It was a sad end to his short and troubled life.

Sources used:
Van Emden, R., *Boy Soldiers of the Great War*, Headline Book Publishing, 2005

Chapter 8

From Flanders Fields to Wolverhampton

How wounded soldiers were evacuated to - and treated - in the town.

Roy Stallard

"A batch of twenty-one wounded soldiers arrived at the Wolverhampton General Hospital yesterday. Five were stretcher cases. The men had received their injuries in the recent fierce fighting at Ypres and Hill 60."

Birmingham Gazette, 8 May 1915

During the Great War Wolverhampton's contribution to the war effort went far beyond providing the brave servicemen and industrial resources needed to achieve victory. The town's hospitals also played a crucial role in providing vital medical care and support for many hundreds of sick and wounded soldiers. Wolverhampton's part in helping servicemen from all over Britain to recover from the physical and the mental damage caused by modern warfare has been overlooked. Therefore, a study of how wounded soldiers were brought to the town and how they were treated in local hospitals is long overdue. This research provides a rare insight into life on the Home Front, as well as illustrating the dedication and generosity of people from Wolverhampton and the surrounding area.

The Wolverhampton and Staffordshire General Hospital in 1910.
Photograph courtesy of Wolverhampton Archives & Local Studies.

Long before the outbreak of the Great War, the War Office had authorised the British Red Cross Society (BRCS) to maintain 'military' beds in hospitals across Staffordshire (the Northern Command). In 1905, the BRCS reported that the Wolverhampton and Staffordshire General Hospital, as it was then called, had thirty beds that were already occupied by sick or wounded military personnel.[46]   On 28 June 1914 Archduke Franz Ferdinand, heir to the throne of Austria-Hungary, was assassinated in Sarajevo. A few weeks later two officials from the War Office arrived in Wolverhampton to inform the hospital managers that the General was going to become a military hospital giving precedence to wounded service personnel. However, when the war broke out on 4 August concerns were expressed at a meeting of health professionals in Birmingham, about the overall efficiency of medical provision in the West Midlands. A letter from Lord Rothschild was read out in which he warned against repeating the mistakes of the South African War (1899-1902), where the efforts of the Red Cross were crippled by *"the evils of over-lapping, uncoordinated and disunited work."*[47]   He welcomed the well-intentioned sentiments of wealthy individuals, such as the teenage Lady (Cynthia) Blanche Curzon, who wanted to support the war effort by turning their stately homes into hospitals and sanatoria. Lady Curzon offered her family home, Kedleston Hall, Derbyshire, as a Voluntary Aid Detachment (VAD) hospital, and the mansion operated as such between December 1914 and February 1915. However, only twenty-two officers ever made use of its six beds during that brief period.[48] Rothschild cautioned that such laudable private initiatives would actually produce serious confusion; a dilution of skilled personnel and shortages of medical supplies. He argued it was vital that the operation and expansion of hospital provision in Britain should be solely managed by the BRCS.[49] In reviewing the situation at the Wolverhampton General Hospital in August 1914, the media acknowledged that War Office demands had already affected the staffing situation. Although none of the ordinary wards were closed, the admission of inpatients was restricted to *"actual cases of emergency,"* and by changing the days for outpatient appointments and minor surgical procedures, work at the General was temporarily reduced. However, this was to be the lull before the storm, as the depletion of the honorary and nursing staff was already *"heavy, owing to the War Office calls."*[50]

In September 1914 the Wolverhampton General was initially selected as an *"overflow hospital for the reception of convalescent cases among British troops."*[51] However, the General was soon identified as one of sixty Auxiliary hospitals linked to the 5th Northern General Hospital; a Territorial Unit formed in 1909, and based in Leicester.[52]   On the Leicester site, Lieutenant-Colonel Louis K. Harrison was in overall command, along with Major R. Wallace Henry. In only six weeks, these officers oversaw the transformation of a semi-derelict Victorian 'lunatic asylum' into a functioning military hospital, occupying a thirty-seven acre site now occupied by the University of Leicester.[53] The Principal Matron of this 'base' hospital was Miss C.E. Vincent, from Leicester Royal Infirmary, but Miss H. Hannath was appointed as the

[46] *Staffordshire Advertiser*, 6 March 1905
[47] *Birmingham Daily Post*, 15 August 1914
[48] Henry, R.W., *Fifth Northern General Hospital Leicester 1914-1919*, Unpub. MS, 1919, p.42
[49] *Birmingham Daily Post*, 15 August 1914
[50] Ibid, 15 August 1914
[51] *Staffordshire Advertiser*, 19 September 1914
[52] Henry, *Fifth Northern General Hospital, op. cit*, p.1
[53] *Melton Mowbray Mercury and Oakham & Uppingham News*, 22 October 1914

'resident Matron'. The formidable Henrietta Hannath (1863-1939) was seconded to Leicester from her position as Matron in charge of Wolverhampton General. Born in Worksop, Nottinghamshire, her first job was as a teacher in her widowed mother's private school – *Carlton Road Ladies Boarding School*. However, by 1898 she was Superintendent Nurse in the workhouse hospital at Eastville, Bristol. In December that year she placed an appeal in the local newspaper to encourage the donations of treats *"to brighten the Christmas season for the inmates."* In particular, she asked for pot plants and toys for the children, as well as oranges, cakes and sweets *"for the Boxing-night entertainment."*[54] Before her appointment as Matron at Wolverhampton, in 1906, Hannath worked in London and as a Night Superintendent at a Birmingham hospital. Her outstanding reputation led to her redeployment to the 5th Northern General Hospital in Leicester, on 10 August 1914.[55] Henrietta Hannath did not return to Wolverhampton until November 1919.[56]

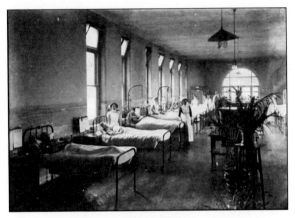

Edward Ward. Photograph taken in July 1914.
Courtesy of Wolverhampton Archives & Local Studies.

As the Wolverhampton General made initial preparations to receive wounded servicemen, space was set aside in the recently opened King Edward VII Memorial Wing; with thirty-five beds allocated in the Edward and Alexandra Wards. Most astonishingly once doctors Armitage, Boyd, Dent, Stidston and Strange had been despatched to the frontline their residential medical posts were made available to women! In December 1914 the local Press reported how the hospital governors had found it necessary to embark on the radical step of engaging *"lady doctors,"* as so many key members of staff were now absent on military duties and Miss Hannath, along with twelve other nurses, had also departed to work in other military hospitals.[57] Mr W.H. Harper, the house governor and secretary, explained that this serious situation had occurred because *"the whole of the residential medical staff volunteered at the outbreak of hostilities and extreme difficulty had been experienced*

[54] *The Western Daily Press*, 12 December 1898
[55] Henry, *Fifth Northern General Hospital*, op. cit., p.9
[56] *Staffordshire Advertiser*, 28 January 1939
[57] Ibid, 19 December 1914

in getting substitutes." In spite of a widespread advertising campaign, the hospital governors were now compelled to *"fall back on medical ladies;"* one of whom had already started work, with two more due to begin in January 1915.[58] Wolverhampton General's 'revolutionary' decision was reported nationally and generally welcomed, with positive Press comments such as: *"We must all try and extend the use of competent women in work they can do as well as men!"* [59] With Miss Hannath now despatched to the base hospital in Leicester a replacement Matron was urgently needed in Wolverhampton. The position was filled by the thirty-six-year-old senior Hospital Sister, Miss Eleanor Elizabeth Meadows, of Gnosall, Staffordshire.[60]

On Tuesday 27 October 1914 the first group of wounded soldiers arrived by train in Wolverhampton and were transferred to the General Hospital by *"motor-cars."* Only four days earlier, on Friday 23 October, most of these thirty men had still been *"in the fighting line at Armentieres."*[61] After a fortnight at Wolverhampton, they were released on sick furlough, and replaced by a new batch of men from the *"fierce fights around Ypres."* This second group of twenty troops arrived in Wolverhampton, via Leicester, and were also driven to the hospital in motor cars, *"lent for the occasion."* Three of the wounded were stretcher cases but most could walk as their injuries were mainly to the head and arms. According to the local Press: *"one man had been blown out of a trench by the explosion of a shell. He was uninjured, but rendered stone deaf."* [62] On 27 November, another consignment of wounded soldiers was admitted to the Edward Ward: men of the Cameron Highlanders Regiment. In the following weeks the number of wounded soldiers grew rapidly and it became necessary to use beds in the McLaren Ward. By December 1914, the hospital governors reported that much extra work was now being generated due to the presence of eighty wounded soldiers.[63] Records from the 5th Northern General Hospital indicate that the maximum number of *'equipped beds'* at the Wolverhampton General, throughout the war, was eighty-two.[64] In order to defray the costs involved, the Government paid the hospital £85 to pay for the treatment of every soldier who was admitted.

These injured soldiers reached Wolverhampton as a result of a transportation process that developed and improved during the course of the war. The initial evacuation of wounded men from the forward edge of the battle area was carried out by teams of stretcher-bearers or the injured soldier's own pals. At the Regimental Aid Post (RAP), usually found in a dugout or old cellar, basic first aid would be applied by the battalion Medical Officer, or one of his small team of Royal Army Medical Corps (RAMC) orderlies. Here, shell dressings and tourniquets were applied, along with the dispensing of basic analgesia, before the casualty was passed back to the Advanced Dressing Station (ADS). Still within range of the

---

[58] *Birmingham Daily Post*, 15 December 1914
[59] *West Sussex Gazette*, 17 December 1914
[60] *Staffordshire Advertiser*, 27 October 1917
[61] *Birmingham Daily Mail*, 28 October 1914
[62] *Birmingham Gazette*, 13 November 1914
[63] *Birmingham Daily Mail*, 15 December 1914
[64] Henry, *Fifth Northern General Hospital,* op. cit., p.43

German guns, the ADS was run by RAMC 'Field Ambulances', which were units of men, not vehicles. There were no facilities for surgery here, but dressings were checked and refastened before the walking-wounded were sent further back, along marked routes, and the stretcher-cases placed in motorised or horse-drawn ambulances. During the great British offensives on the Western Front the battlefield work of the RAMC has been described as both: *"heroic and horrifying, as they struggled to cope with a continuous tide of men with a vast and unpredictable range of wounds."*[65] The next stop for the injured soldier was the Casualty Clearing Station (CCS), which could be as much as ten miles behind the frontline and theoretically out of the range of enemy artillery. Wounds were classified at the CCS and basic, life-saving surgery carried out in tented hospitals which could accommodate as many as 2,000 patients. This was the point in the evacuation process where men were placed on ambulance trains, which carried as many as 400 men to other hospitals in France. The scale of these operations is shown by preparations made before the Battle of the Somme. On that occasion, General Sir Henry Rawlinson requested that eighteen ambulance trains should be made available to receive the 10,000 British casualties that were expected every day. Rawlinson wanted to avoid the casualty bottlenecks he had witnessed at Loos in September 1915. Yet, in spite of his request only five trains were available on the infamous first day of the battle - 1 July 1916. The wounded were eventually loaded onto trains at railheads, such as the one at Vecquemont, between Corbie and Amiens, and transported to the base hospitals in Rouen.

During the war, although ninety per cent of wounded British troops were carried by ambulance trains, barge transport was also utilised throughout the Somme campaign (July-November 1916). An overnight service along the River Somme took wounded soldiers to an inland port in Amiens, staffed by the RAMC. However, despite this being a *"particularly restful method"* of transporting wounded soldiers, each barge could only carry forty men.[66] The final stage of the continental leg of the evacuation process was by road or another ambulance train to one of the French Channel ports such as Le Havre, Dieppe or Boulogne. At every stage of the journey home, supportive medical staff redressed wounds, administered the necessary analgesia and provided copious cups of tea. As Martin Middlebrook has commented: *"the farther back a wounded soldier could get, the more considered and skilled the treatment he could expect."*[67]

Having arrived back in *'Blighty'* the initial transportation of casualties to places such as Wolverhampton was laborious and slow, with the rail network through London a particular bottleneck. In 1916 a more direct route, via Reading, was organised to cope with the huge number of casualties generated by the Battle of the Somme. The junction at Reading, almost halfway between the Channel ports and Wolverhampton, was a suitable place to administer fresh analgesics and redress wounds. From that point, the journey to Wolverhampton continued via the Great

---

[65] Brown, M., *Tommy Goes To War*, Dent, 1978
[66] Middlebrook, M., *The First Day On The Somme*, Penguin, 1971, p.84
[67] Middlebrook, Ibid, p.83

Western Railway route through Oxford, Worcester and Stourbridge; arriving into the Low Level station, for onward transfer to the hospital. En route, ambulance carriages were disconnected from the train at various points for hospitals in Oxford, Worcester and Wordsley, before arriving at Wolverhampton in the early evening. Carriage from Low Level station to the hospital presented problems because of a lack of ambulances; horse-drawn or motorised. In 1911 the General had taken possession of its one and only motorised ambulance thanks to a donation of £500 by the Wolverhampton Police. The local St. John's Ambulance had one vehicle and two more were provided by local industrial firms. However, drays from the local railway companies' goods depots and other local contractors provided welcome support. Fortunately, Low Level station had a very large booking-hall atrium, where stretcher cases and walking-wounded could wait for the slow process of hospital transfer to be completed. Once arrived at the hospital, soldiers were admitted and triaged through the admission block to their respective wards; most still wearing their torn and bloody uniforms. Due to the scale of the influx of wounded men by March 1917 it was decided to increase the Wolverhampton General's capacity by erecting temporary buildings in the hospital grounds. It was hoped this would permit the treatment of an additional fifty wounded soldiers.[68] The two new temporary wards were duly opened, by Colonel Harrison, on 8 June that year, at a cost of almost £2,000.[69] After the war, these buildings were used as nursing accommodation and a classroom.

Much of the surgery carried out on the wounded men admitted to the Wolverhampton General was of a secondary nature, including debridement; the removal of infected tissue surrounding a lesion and the resuturing of wounds. This treatment was no doubt carried out on a party of twenty-one soldiers who were transferred to the General, from Leicester suffering from *"shrapnel wounds,"* in January 1915.[70] The lack of antibiotics was a serious drawback in the treatment of wounded soldiers in the Great War - gas gangrene was a particular problem which occurred when bullet and shrapnel wounds became infected by contaminated soil, not by poison gas. It was, perhaps, no coincidence that Alexander Fleming, the man who later discovered penicillin, had been a British Army doctor, based at Boulogne, during the war. In the absence of antibiotics default treatments included poultices, leeches and the liberal use of antiseptic fluids, to prevent the spread of sepsis. Although the lack of antibiotics limited the work of surgeons and slowed down the pace at which many patients recovered, the use of ether as an anaesthetic was of great value. During the war the medical staff became very active in experimenting with new treatments especially to combat infection. However, as 'improving' soldiers prepared for home leave or demobilisation, chronic problems of chest disease and osteomyelitis often became apparent as did psychiatric conditions - often labelled as 'shell-shock' at the time. The full impact of modern warfare on those involved was only just becoming understood and treatments regarded as commonplace today were still in their infancy.

---

[68] *Birmingham Daily Post*, 29 March 1917
[69] *Birmingham Gazette*, 9 June 1917
[70] *Birmingham Daily Gazette*, 15 January 1915

The slow process of wound healing meant soldiers often spent many weeks in hospital. To them a bed bath, clean clothes and bed linen, along with regular hot meals were a tremendous aid to recovery. Nursing care was provided by voluntary bodies such as the Salvation Army and St. John's Ambulance. Patients were provided with free cigarettes, courtesy of Alfred Dunhill, and free beer from William Butler's local brewery. In fact all of the local pubs offered an open-door and free beer policy to wounded men in town and the *Express and Star* newspaper started a shilling fund which raised £3,400 to support the men. Seats for wounded soldiers were made available at *The Empire* and *The Grand* theatres and the grounds of the nearby St. George's Church became a popular spot to relax and socialise in good weather. The first group of wounded men to arrive at the General Hospital, along with several Belgian refugees, were invited to attend the football match between Wolverhampton Wanderers and Preston North End, on Saturday 31 October 1914. However, there is no evidence to indicate whether watching Wolves win 2-0 actually assisted in their recuperation![71]

Military patients received routine visits by welfare and pay officers; receiving their mandatory wages of one shilling a day. They also received the fruits of the many fundraising and donation schemes that were organised by local people. The Red Cross and Salvation Army were very active here, as were local businesses and market stallholders. As well as cigarettes and beer, soldiers received gifts of chocolate, fruit and writing materials. On 1 July 1915, for instance, a well-attended open-air meeting was held at Cheslyn Hay, to promote the work of the Red Cross Society and help raise funds. Since the start of the war, the chairman announced, that particular parish had raised £81,18s and 11½d for the Red Cross. Colonel C.H. Wright, of Stafford, thanked the audience for their generosity and then told them about the experiences of his own daughter, who was nursing at a Red Cross hospital in France. She wrote how it was a great help for wounded troops to be *"attended to in the hospitals by English ladies from their own counties...it heartened them to feel that they were in touch with someone from near home."* At the end of the meeting, a further collection was taken on behalf of *"the wounded soldiers in Wolverhampton General Hospital."* [72]

The increased workload created by the war affected every department in the hospital. The staff in the pharmacy, laundry, kitchen, stores and the hospital porters all worked unpaid overtime. The unrelenting routine of the hospital continued throughout the war, with patients roused from their slumbers at 5.30 am every day even if their injury was just a scratch on the nose. They had to be washed and shaved before breakfast was served at 6 am, and would receive any post at 6.30 am. The 'mid-morning' drink, at 9 am, would be followed by redressing of wounds and the distribution of medicines before the doctor's rounds. Lunch was at 12.30, tea at 4 pm, a final check of TPR (temperature, pulse and respiration) and then lights-out at 8 pm.

---

[71] *Birmingham Daily Post*, 2 November 1914
[72] *Staffordshire Advertiser*, 3 July 1915

Soon after the start of the war the Wolverhampton Eye Infirmary also became one of the sixty auxiliary hospitals, linked to the 5th Northern General Hospital. It prepared twenty-one ophthalmic beds, to deal with soldiers with eye injuries, and also received a payment of £85 per patient.[73] Eye Infirmary pharmacy records show a large increase in the amount of cocaine purchased during the war. This was added to eyedrops, known as guttae, along with antiseptic argyrols, zinc and adrenaline. The Institute of St. Dunstan's, which opened in London in 1915, gave much-needed support to soldiers who lost one or both eyes as a result of battlefield trauma. The grounds of Wolverhampton Eye Infirmary also provided a pleasant location for the wounded to socialise and they were allowed to visit the local hostelries, with sister's permission. Local church groups in Chapel Ash, especially St. Mark's, Trinity Methodist and the Presbyterian Church were very generous and supportive of the men. As eye-injured troops entered the period of post-operative convalescence many were sent to Milford on Cannock Chase, or to the newly reopened Manor House, Tettenhall. Generous local people also offered board and accommodation to recuperating soldiers and joined them in services at the hospital chapel, where attendances increased during the war. Senior members of the clergy often visited the hospital, along with prominent members of local Jewish groups.

Several members of staff at the Wolverhampton General received awards for their work during the war. In April 1917 Henrietta Hannath received the Royal Red Cross Award, First Class, for her work as Matron of the 5th Northern General Hospital, Leicester.[74] In August 1919, she received a Bar to add to this award: *"in recognition of valuable nursing services in connection with the war."*[75] In 1917 Matron Eleanor Meadows was also included in the London Gazette's second instalment of commendations presented by the Secretary of State of War, for her role in making *"special arrangements for the nursing of the sick and wounded"* at the Wolverhampton and Staffordshire General Hospital.[76] Meanwhile, many of the other medical and hospital staff who volunteered for military service abroad also received awards. Sister Sissy Spence (1886-1976) of the Queen Alexandra's Imperial Military Nursing Service (QAIMNS), was awarded the Military Medal for her actions in France, on the night of 6/7 July 1917. She was on duty at Bailleul Ambulance Siding, Casualty Clearing Station No.11; a tented medical centre, treating about 250 injured patients. During the night the CCS was bombed by the Germans, killing twenty-seven and injuring sixty-eight staff and patients. Throughout this terrifying episode Nurse Spence remained cool under fire and carried on with her duties; tending to the wounded and keeping them calm.[77]

Drs F.R. Armitage and C.A. Stidston were both awarded the Distinguished Service Order (DSO) for their work on the battlefield. In fact, Captain Frank Rhodes Armitage, MB, DSO, RFA, and RAMC became the only Wolverhampton doctor to be killed in action. He attended Wolverhampton Grammar and Oundle Schools before

[73] Henry, *The Fifth Northern General Hospital,* op. cit., p.43
[74] *Birmingham Daily Post,* 2 April 1917
[75] *Leicester Daily Post,* 2 August 1919
[76] *Staffordshire Advertiser,* 27 October 1917
[77] *London Gazette,* 17 September 1917

going on to Pembroke College, Cambridge. After completing his medical training at The London Hospital, he took up a position at Wolverhampton General in 1908, working alongside his father, Dr James Auriol Armitage.[78] Frank Armitage joined the RFA as a medical officer at the start of the war and was transferred to France early in 1915. Over the course of the next two years he acquired a reputation for leading a charmed life and being involved in *"many miraculous escapes from death."*[79] Described as *"absolutely fearless and never happier than when in the hottest part of the battlefield"*, he was unsurprisingly *"beloved by the men"* as *"he took all sorts of risks to search out and succour the wounded."*[80] Armitage received his DSO on 18 July 1917 and returned to France the following day. Less than a fortnight later he was killed when, on 30 July an *'8 inch'* shell crashed through the roof of the dugout he was sharing with another local officer, Captain C.E. Hickman.[81] In his letter of condolence to the captain's parents his colonel wrote: *"a braver and better man never walked on this earth and his place can never be filled."*[82] Thirty-four-year-old Captain Armitage was buried in Brandhoek New Military Cemetery, which lies beside the main road between Ypres and Poperinge.

Left: Dr Frank Armitage. *Right:* The Armitage memorial plaque at New Cross Hospital.

Charles Algernon Stidston, DSO, MD, BS, first arrived at the Wolverhampton General in 1907, having studied at St. Bartholomew's Hospital, London. In 1909, he was elected honorary assistant surgeon and he was also an officer in the Territorial, RAMC. When hostilities began Stidston was immediately called up with his field ambulance - the 2/3rd North Midland Brigade - and served throughout the war. He spent about eighteen months on the frontline, particularly *"during the difficult and anxious fighting which followed the battle of Cambrai,"*[83] and received the DSO for his efforts, in January 1918. On 18 May 1918 the British Medical Journal reported that he had been wounded. In fact, Stidston was gassed twice during the war, and this probably contributed to his premature death, aged only forty-nine, on 15 December

---

[78] *Staffordshire Advertiser*, 25 August 1917
[79] *Hastings and St. Leonards Observer*, 18 August 1917
[80] Ibid, 18 August 1917
[81] *Birmingham Gazette*, 10 August 1917
[82] *Hastings and St. Leonards Observer*, 18 August 1917.
[83] British Medical Journal, 3 January 1931, p.37, www.bmj.com

1930. He reached the rank of Lieutenant Colonel before returning to become full surgeon at Wolverhampton in 1920. Charles Stidston's brilliant career came to an untimely end in his own, recently renamed, hospital.[84] On 28 December 1928, the Wolverhampton and Staffordshire General had become the Royal Hospital, Wolverhampton. Matron Henrietta Hannath also returned to her post in Wolverhampton in November 1919 and remained until after the visit of the Prince of Wales on 13 June 1923. Having then reached the age of sixty she retired to Devon, where she died on 21 January 1939.[85]

During the Spring and early Summer of 1919, Wolverhampton General and the Eye Infirmary said farewell to their last military patients.[86] In five years as Auxiliaries to the 5th Northern General Hospital, Wolverhampton General treated a total of 1,450 patients, and a further 184 wounded soldiers passed through the Eye Infirmary.[87] It is a pity we still know so little about the work of Matron Eleanor E. Meadows and her dedicated staff. Likewise, few personal details exist about the wounded men they treated; their injuries, or what happened to them after they recovered and left Wolverhampton. However, some clues can be found by searching through newspapers from the time. For example, Private M. Britton, who hailed from Annesley Woodhouse, Nottinghamshire, was in the 2nd Battalion Leicestershire Regiment. He was invalided home after being wounded in the Battle of Neuve Chapelle (10-13 March 1915) and one month later he was recovering in the Wolverhampton Eye Infirmary.[88] As his name does not appear on any memorial rolls, Private Britton probably survived the Great War. So too did Sergeant G.L. Grieve from Enzie, near Buckie, Aberdeenshire. In December 1916, whilst fighting with the London Scottish, he was awarded the DCM. As he lay in Wolverhampton General recovering from the wounds sustained in this engagement, Sergeant Grieve learned that he had also been nominated for the Military Medal, making him *"the only one in the London Scottish to have both."* [89] Private Joseph Southworth, of the 4th Battalion Loyal North Lancashire Regiment appears to have recovered in Wolverhampton only to die later in the war. In June 1915 he wrote a letter home from the hospital describing the deaths of his two officers and how he had received *"a flesh wound in the thigh and crawled over two miles"* through mud before getting his wound dressed.[90] Sadly a soldier with the same name and in the same unit died on 1 April 1916 and is buried in Douchy-Les-Ayette British Cemetery, almost midway between Arras and Albert, France. It is more than likely to be the same man. A comment made by Private Southworth, in his letter home to Chorley, should stand as a fitting final tribute to the work carried out by the all of the medical staff at the Wolverhampton General and the Eye Infirmary, between 1914 and 1919: *"Thank God I am safe, for a little while."*[91]

---

[84] *Birmingham Daily Gazette*, 16 December 1930
[85] *Staffordshire Advertiser*, 28 January 1939
[86] Henry, *The Fifth Northern General Hospital*, op. cit., p.43
[87] Henry, Ibid, p.43
[88] *Nottingham Daily Express*, 23 April 1915
[89] *Aberdeen Weekly Journal*, 19 January 1917
[90] *Preston Herald*, 30 June 1915
[91] *Preston Herald*, 30 June 1915

Chapter 9

Remembering Private John Vincent Thomas

John A. Thomas

On 28 August 2018 a brief ceremony was arranged to commemorate the centenary of the death, in the Great War, of our grandfather John Vincent Thomas. This took place at the municipal war memorial, St. Peter's Square, Wolverhampton, and was accompanied by a standard bearer, bugler, and officials from the Royal British Legion; and Rev. Richard Reeve, Rector of St. Michael's and All Angels, Tettenhall. Afterwards we had a brief lunch in the adjacent Lych Gate Tavern, where I organised a small exhibition of items concerned with our grandfather, and his wife Fanny. Sadly we know very little about John's life but felt this was an appropriate occasion to pay tribute to a man who obviously played a significant role in our own lives, although we never met him.

John's parents were Emmanuel and Lucy Thomas, who lived at 83 Owen Road, off Great Brickkiln Street, Wolverhampton. His father was an "engine fitter", but John became a shoemaker in Upper Zoar Street, perhaps being apprenticed to Ike Jones. He was the brother of Fanny who John married in October 1910. Their marital home seems to have been in North Road and they had two sons who survived beyond infancy: Alfred Edward Arnold (1912-1962) and Arthur Wellesley (1916-1921). Another son, Eric Vincent, lived for only a few weeks in 1913, and it appears there were other children who were either stillborn, or succumbed to neonatal deaths. John worked with Ike; reputedly making bespoke shoes for his son, Alfred, who had a small bony lump on each foot.

Unfortunately little is also known for sure about John's war service, as his army records, like so many relating to the Great War, were destroyed on the first night of the London Blitz, 7/8 September 1940. He originally joined the King's Own Yorkshire Light Infantry, but also served in the Royal Army Service Corps, where his new army number, R/277025 'Remount', reveals that he worked with horses. When John was transferred to the 10th Battalion of the Lancashire Fusiliers he acquired the number 62971. Information gleaned from medal records confirms that he arrived on the Western Front sometime after January 1916. The Lancashire Fusiliers' activities during 1916-17 seem to have involved constantly moving around many places in northern France, and being deployed in various roles. In early August 1918 the Fusiliers saw much action on the old Somme battlefield during the great Allied attack which initiated the final '100 Days Offensive.' By the 27th and 28th they were being held in reserve, first at High Wood and then west of Gueudecourt, a village to the south of Bapaume. It was whilst the battalion was waiting here that John died on 28 August. Family tradition originally maintained that he had been confined to a field hospital, following a non-life-threatening condition. This might have been related to an "accident" mentioned in a letter to Fanny, dated 17 August, or maybe it was

Spanish flu? For many years it was believed that whilst John was receiving treatment, the hospital received a direct hit from a shell fired by the retreating German artillery. An army padre apparently wrote to Fanny giving some details of his death, although no such letter survives amongst the family papers. However, a recent find suggests he died following an active engagement with the enemy. The truth will probably never be known. Private John Vincent Thomas has no known grave and is remembered 'with honour' on the memorial at Vis-en-Artois, south east of Arras. This memorial bears the names of 9,843 men who also died in the period from 8 August to the Armistice on 11 November 1918. He was twenty-eight years-old at the time of his death, and like all of those who served and died, his family received his Victory Medal and British War Medal.

Although the end of the war brought joy to many people Fanny is reported to have said that *she* felt she had little to celebrate. Not only was she left with two young sons to bring up, but tragedy struck again in 1921, when five-year-old Wellesley was killed by an out of control vehicle. However, that same year, Fanny began to rebuild her life when she married Harry Smith, an engine driver on the Great Western Railway, from Berkshire. They had a daughter, Winifred Mary, and for many years Fanny kept two fruit and vegetable shops, in North Street and Worcester Street. She died in 1967.

Among the items displayed in the Lych Gate Tavern on 28 August 2018 was a letter from Fanny to John, dated 17 August 1918, which he may never have received. There was a Vesta matches case, a cigarette case, and a lighter that were all taken to France, but returned to Wolverhampton after his death. There were also John's Victory and British War Medals, inscribed with his name around the edges, as well as the Memorial Plaque that was given to Fanny, his next of kin, after the war.

Left: Pte John Vincent Thomas. *Right:* His wife, Fanny.

Chapter 10

Missing In Action – Arthur Stokes' Great War

Chris Twiggs

On 12 March 1917 a concerned Mrs Bessie Stokes wrote to the authorities at Whittington Barracks, Lichfield, as she had not heard from her husband for several weeks. Arthur was reported missing following an action by his regiment – 2nd Battalion South Staffordshire Regiment - near Courcelette, France, on 17 February 1917. Mrs Stokes would have to wait several weeks before receiving official confirmation that he was a prisoner of war (PoW). One can only speculate what it must have been like for her, but it was a predicament faced by thousands of families during the war - for many their relatives would remain missing without any confirmation of their fate.

Arthur Stokes was born in 1886, one of four sons of Arthur and Mary Ann Stokes. The 1901 census showed him living in the Whitmore Reans area of Wolverhampton and working as a boot operative. Ten years later he was still employed in the same occupation. In September 1912 he married Bessie Gibbons and the following year she gave birth to their first child, a daughter named Eleanor but usually referred to as Nellie. The family lived at 23 Gibbs Street, Whitmore Reans, close to Arthur's parents. Arthur was working at the boot and shoe manufacturer, James Baker & Sons Ltd, Cleveland Road, Wolverhampton. This building still exists, on the eastern side of the town centre. The outbreak of war did not initially affect Arthur's situation. He was a man in his late twenties whose priority was looking after his wife and young child. However, on 7 December 1915 he enlisted in the 2 South Staffords.

It has been possible to piece together Arthur's military experience through a range of source material. His service papers - unlike many others - survive as they were not destroyed during the Second World War Blitz. The war diary of the 2 South Staffords provides a valuable record of Arthur's short experience of life on the Western Front. His time as a PoW might well have remained something of a mystery but he kept his own diary of his time in captivity and this now provides a valuable insight into life behind enemy lines. Now in the possession of his granddaughter, it records in some detail events in the period from February 1917 until February 1918. Unfortunately, pages that may have recorded the months following have been ripped out, although he did mention the camps in Germany which he passed through whilst a prisoner. The records of the International Committee of the Red Cross have also helped confirm the names of the German PoW camps at which Arthur was registered.

Arthur was sent to France on 11 November 1916 following the completion of his training. The war diary of the 2 South Staffords shows that on 26 November they received a new draft of 148 men and Arthur was one of these. He was sent to Louvencourt, northern France, and then to billets behind the frontline on the Somme sector where he and the others underwent several weeks training. Arthur arrived just as fighting, which had raged there since 1 July, drew to a close. He first went into the frontline trenches on 24 January 1917 near the village of Courcelette, and remained for a few days before going back into reserve positions. His next visit to the frontline was in the action of 17 February 1917. The 2 South Staffords were to be involved in a subsidiary attack to support the main objective which was to capture the German strongpoint - Hill 130. This secondary attack was meant to occupy a position known as *"The Nose"* and surrounding German-held trenches. The battalion marched up to the frontline during the night and although conditions were poor they managed to arrive at their allotted positions on time. Just before 5 am a German artillery bombardment of British positions intensified and continued until about 5.30 am. Arthur and his comrades had to make the best of the cover provided by the very shallow trenches they occupied. At 5.45 am, following a British artillery bombardment, the 2 South Staffords started their attack. Initially it appeared to be successful but, as the hours went by, the full picture became clear, and it was not very pretty. The German defences were far stronger than expected - particularly the number of machine guns being deployed against the British attack. The four companies involved all suffered heavy casualties and very few men actually got into the German positions. No man's land was littered with the dead and wounded. Arthur was in A Company. Their attack had initially made progress but, when they reached the German barbed wire they found it had not been cut. Where there were gaps in the wire the enemy had trained machine guns on those precise locations. Later in the day the Germans launched a counter-attack which drove the surviving remnants of the 2 South Staffords back to their original starting point.

Those few who got into any of the German trenches had no option but to retreat or be killed or captured. Once the situation along the front was calm the Germans emerged from their trenches and collected the wounded British troops who were left behind. Lieutenant Colonel George Dawes, Commanding Officer of 2 South Staffords, made clear a number of factors in his report. He mentioned: *"The great strength of the enemy positions was not expected"* and *"the nature of casualties was remarked on by the Medical Officer:- there was a large proportion of bullet wounds."* Another report claimed a deserter had informed the Germans of the impending attack - hence the strengthened defences and subsequent heavy losses. Arthur was captured along with other men from his unit. Surrendering was always a risky business. Although the rules of war were meant to ensure a soldier's safety there were many examples on both sides where those attempting to surrender were killed. In the heat of battle on the Western Front, with machine gun and artillery fire prevalent, it was not unknown for those who had successfully surrendered to still be killed. Arthur's diary records events from his capture onwards: *"Taken a prisoner on Sat Feb 17-1917 after an attack on the Germans at Courcellettes (sic), which I am afraid turned out a failure. We were marched to their headquarters behind the line where we were searched for knives and other things. Pay books were taken off us, some were returned and some lost, mine were amongst the taken. We were* marched a good many kilometres to a place where we had to wait for others, and then on again until 1 o' clock when we were put in a loft for the rest of the night (I lost my prayer book and darling's photos). We had a loaf of bread between three of us at 10 o' clock, the first since the previous afternoon and the first given us this side and it was needed.," he wrote. Arthur's march eventually brought him to the Cambrai Citadel which was used by the Germans to house British and French prisoners. He added: "The conditions were very fair under the circumstances, each man having a clean pallias and clean straw." Food was basic but adequate. Coffee and bread at 7.30 am, soup at 11.30 am and for supper at 5.30 pm sausage or soup on alternate days. After a few days at Cambrai Arthur and his fellow prisoners were put to work by the Germans. Unlike officers - who were not expected to work and enjoyed generally better conditions - those in the ranks were expected to carry out a range of tasks. Under the terms of the 1907 Hague Convention prisoners were not supposed to be employed in any work which helped the war effort. However, just about any form of work could ultimately be seen as helping the war effort. For example, working on a farm could be seen as assisting the war if it resulted in another man being made available for war service. While at Cambrai Arthur found himself employed in unloading barges on the local canal. Material being unloaded was being used by the Germans for road building. Other men were engaged in building the roads. Work started at 6.30 am and continued until 4 pm. It was hard, particularly when the weather was poor and "especially when done on a quarter of a loaf and sometimes not that." Arthur's time at Cambrai left him to comment in his diary that: "Cambrai is a very fine place. Would be alright for a visit and holiday in peace time."

During June 1917 Arthur was moved north east from Cambrai to the area around Maubeuge and was detailed on working parties assisting with agricultural work. It was a time that had its positive and uplifting moments. On his party's first march to a local farm the German corporal in charge managed to get them lost. During a rest period, while the situation was being sorted out, the local population emerged to provide the prisoners with what Arthur described as: "afternoon tea. Bread, butter and tea with lump sugar". Arthur went on to comment that the experience: "made new men of us." Such events, of which this was one of a number he recorded, did much to lift the spirits and made the men aware that the French fully appreciated their involvement in the war. In late June Arthur was diagnosed with an ankle problem and was sent to a military hospital for treatment. He noted in his diary that his treatment was very good. He was discharged after five weeks and returned to join his men at the work camp. They had now moved to another location – Louvroil, near Maubeuge. At about the same time as his discharge from hospital and return he received his first letter from home. The next few weeks, at the height of summer, saw him working on farms helping to bring in the harvest. This meant a routine of plenty of fresh air and food rations regularly supplemented by donations from the local people.

Arthur's diary after September 1917 is much briefer. Each month was given just a single page and most days a single line. His comments tend to focus on the food situation, parcels and letters received or sent and specific events such as an outbreak of diphtheria which led to isolation for a week or so. Arthur was fortunate not to witness any ill-treatment during his time as a prisoner. The only comment in his diary that alludes to this is a copy of a declaration he made, while at Cambrai, about possible retaliatory action if German PoWs in British hands were not moved away from dangerous zones, close to the frontline. Use of prisoners in dangerous areas was an ongoing issue during the war and both sides engaged in a war of words and threats when it became known that the other side was not treating their prisoners with due respect and care. Arthur's diary ends in February 1918 with the pages which may have covered the period through to November 1918 missing. Apart from his record of events his notebook contains some handwritten copies of prayers and notes on the workings of a petrol engine. He was known to be quite a religious man, which explains the prayers. Notes about the engine suggest self-improvement and, as with many prisoners, he was looking to find activities to relieve the monotony of incarceration.

Records of the International Committee of the Red Cross helped to confirm Arthur was registered as a prisoner at Limburg, Friedrichsfeld and Stuttgart 2 PoW camps in western Germany. He was registered at the latter two camps by early 1918 and his diary indicates he was sent out for work in the local gasworks and the railways. Freedom for Arthur came fairly quickly following the Armistice on 11 November 1918. Red Cross records reveal he returned to Britain on 1 December 1918 and was granted leave from 4 December until 2 January 1919. A letter from James Baker & Sons, dated 28 January 1919, offered Arthur re-employment at their Wolverhampton boot factory. He was demobilised in March that year and transferred to the Army Reserve. Arthur spent the rest of his life working in the boot and shoe manufacturing industry.

Left: Arthur Stokes – courtesy of Margaret Flanagan. *Right:* James Baker's Boot Factory.

Sources used:
- Van Emden, R., *Prisoners of the Kaiser*, Pub Pen & Sword, 2009
- Yarnall, J., *Barbed Wire Disease*, Pub Spellmount, 2011
- https://grandeguerre.icrc.org for Red Cross records of POWs

Chapter 11

The Midland Railway at War, 1914-21

Forgotten railway servicemen of the Wolverhampton District

Quintin Watt

"As we travel the same tracks and pass through the same stations – still dominated by war memorials – we can try to enter into the mindset of those who lived through the dark days of the First World War." [92]

In the Great War, 186,457 railwaymen served in Britain's armed forces – representing between thirty and forty per cent of the total workforce.[93] As many as 21,517 of these died (11.5%) – highlighting their huge contribution to Britain's war effort.[94] These men are commemorated on memorials like the one on Wolverhampton railway station; currently located on the footbridge linking platform 1 with platforms 2 and 3. This brass plaque was originally unveiled at the London and North Western Railway (LNWR) offices, Five Ways, Wolverhampton on 11 September 1921. It records sixty-eight employees of that company's goods department from the *"Wolverhampton District"* who *"made the supreme sacrifice"* in the Great War. Sadly no comparable memorial exists to honour the sacrifice made by local men of the Midland Railway (MR) – a company that also had a presence in south Staffordshire. It seems as if these railwaymen have been largely forgotten, like the line they worked on, which has long since been lifted and lost. This chapter is about the MR in the Great War and it begins with an examination of how that company was affected by state control, increased transportation demands and the loss of much of its workforce to military service. The second section is an examination of the experiences of the fifteen 'lost' MR employees who worked in the Wolverhampton area before going off to fight and die in the Great War.

Part One – The Midland Railway and the Great War.

It has been suggested that the Great War marked a significant watershed in the history of British railways and the once *"powerful, self-confident, male-dominated industry of Edwardian times never again returned to its pre-war form."*[95] When the war began the MR (1844-1922) was the fourth largest private employer in the United Kingdom, with nearly 67,000 members of staff.[96] Centred on Derby the MR first developed in the Birmingham-Leicester-Nottingham region before stretching northwards to Manchester, Leeds and Carlisle. To the south-west it extended to Bristol and Bath and built its own line into London in 1868, along with St. Pancras

---

[92] Hooper, C., *Railways of the Great War*, Bantam Press, 2014, p.225
[93] Higgins, J., *Great War Railwaymen*, Uniform Press, 2014, p.32
[94] Ibid, p.32 and p.314.
[95] Hooper, op. cit., p.225
[96] Jeremy, D.J. The Hundred Largest Employers in the UK, Business History, 33:1, p.96

station and the iconic Midland Grand Hotel, which symbolised the *"gateway to the Midland main-line."*[97] It has even been claimed Sir George Gilbert Scott's Gothic masterpiece was partly inspired by the Cloth Hall in Ypres. Locally, the MR network reached Wolverhampton in 1876 when the company absorbed the Wolverhampton and Walsall Railway.[98] If this was the 'Golden Age' of the British railway industry, the MR probably *"attained its zenith by the summer of 1910,"* whilst struggling to maintain an essentially Victorian business model, based on a *"sophisticated atmosphere of suave opulence."*[99] Charged with leading the company as it confronted the challenges and uncertainties of the twentieth century was George Murray Smith (1859-1919). Appointed a director in 1901 and elected chairman in 1911, Murray Smith's recent biographer praised him in particular for the skill with which he *"steered the Midland through the difficult times of the First World War."*[100] Yet despite his best efforts, the tribulations of wartime operation and post-war economic depression highlighted the company's financial and technical vulnerabilities – problems that were far from unique to the MR. Starved of investment for almost a decade, the country's railways were virtually run into the ground during the war. The Government eventually took a reluctant half-step towards the nationalisation of the British railway industry on 1 January 1923 when the MR was incorporated into the London Midland and Scottish Railway (LMS) as part of the Railway Grouping Act.

When the Great War began the Government introduced the Railway Executive Committee (REC) to operate the British railway system. Even before August 1914 it recognised that some form of state intervention was needed to manage the transport network during a national emergency. However, few in Government probably anticipated the momentous struggle that lay ahead and the impact total war was to have on the railways. As forty-six railway companies were not 'nationalised' in 1914 it has been argued referring to these measures as state control *"is misleading for, in the main, it was anything but."*[101] However, the 130 most strategically important companies were taken over by the REC and that included the MR. One of the REC's well-founded concerns related to the number of essential railway employees who might be swept up in the tide of patriotic fervour and enlist to fight in the war – it was well known that many railwaymen were army reservists or Territorials. Therefore, on 4 September 1914 the REC issued an instruction that railwaymen had to provide written proof of approval from their employer before they could attest.[102] It has been suggested railwaymen were especially keen to enlist because of the similarity between their civilian occupation and that of a soldier, which was *"...often holistic, self-contained, and constrained by rules and rosters, arguably somewhat controlling, not too unlike the armed forces."*[103] In 1914 the MR produced a booklet which revealed *"how eager the employees of that railway have been to serve the King."* It proudly announced that in the week following the Mobilisation Order, 4 August 1914,

[97] Barnes, E.G., *The Midland Main Line, 1875-1922*, Allen and Unwin, 1969, p.267
[98] Haddock, J., *Walsall's Engine Shed – Railwaymen's Memories, 1877-1968*, 2006, p.15
[99] Barnes, op. cit., p.267
[100] McConnell, A. *Oxford Dictionary of National Biography*, Vol. 51, 2004, p.144.
[101] Earnshaw, A., *Britain's Railways at War 1914-1918*, Atlantic, 1990, p.8
[102] Pratt, E.A., *British Railways and the Great War*, London, Selwyn & Blount, 1921, pp.348-9
[103] Higgins, op. cit., p.214

1,838 army and naval reservists had re-joined the colours, and a further 1,462 Territorials "*had assembled at the allotted centres.*"[104] By the time Chairman Murray Smith made his first wartime annual report to shareholders in February 1915, the number of employees who had left to join the armed forces was nearly 9,000 - twelve per cent of the company's staff - and this was already causing "*a great shortage of labour.*"[105]

Previously employees of the MR who enlisted were regarded sympathetically by the company - a tradition that stretched back to the Second Boer War (1899-1902). At that time the company seriously underestimated the number of men who might be involved. When Army Reservists were instructed to re-join the colours in October 1899 the MR expected this would affect about 130 of their men.[106] By February 1900 the company chairman reported that 700 Reservists had been called away and a further seventy men had volunteered to fight in South Africa.[107] By mid-1900 this figure had increased to 1,148, including 820 Reservists and 109 volunteers – nine times more than envisaged when the Boer War began.[108] In January 1900 the company was forced to issue a statement warning that: "*any man in their service volunteering for service in South Africa*" would be reinstated by the MR but might "*not be given exactly the same position*" on their return, but one of "*equal value.*"[109] However, the sympathetic company continued to pay a proportion of the occupational pensions of servicemen serving with the colours. The MR could ill-afford to lose key personnel, but "*from the company's viewpoint, clerks were more expendable than skilled fitters and maintenance staff.*"[110] Fifteen years later this attitude towards losing men to the armed forces was repeated by the MR during the Great War (see Table Two). Sixty-eight Midland railwaymen eventually died in the Boer War and their names are recorded on a memorial at Derby station.

By February 1915 MR chairman Murray Smith reported the company was already "*working under great stress and difficulty*" and struggling with the new regulations imposed since the Government had taken control of the railways. However, he was confident they were equal to the great task imposed upon them thanks to the "*loyal and patriotic work of the salaried and wages staffs.*"[111] Murray Smith then proceeded to give a statistical breakdown of both the number of MR employees who had joined the armed forces and how many had become casualties. By February 1915 these figures already exceeded the totals from the Boer War: 102 dead, 369 wounded, 100 prisoners of war and twenty-nine listed as missing.[112] The fact Murray Smith reported these statistics at each of the succeeding wartime Annual General Meetings (AGMs) provides historians with a particularly useful source to monitor the impact of the conflict on the MR and its personnel (see Tables One and

[104] *Birmingham Post*, 28 January 1915
[105] *Birmingham Daily* Mail, 18 February 1915.
[106] *Derby Mercury*, 11 October 1899.
[107] *Derbyshire Advertiser and Journal*, 23 February 1900.
[108] Barnes, op. cit., p.200
[109] *Derby Mercury*, 3 January 1900.
[110] Barnes, op. cit., p.200.
[111] *Birmingham Daily Mail*, 18 February 1915.
[112] *Mansfield Reporter*, 26 February 1915.

Three).   As these numbers were processed by the company's statisticians and related directly to the current and future operation of the MR, one can probably assume they were as accurate as possible at the time. Murray Smith's decision to report such details may have been inspired by personal experience of loss. On 2 November 1914 his eldest son, Lieutenant Arthur George Murray Smith, 2ⁿᵈ Life Guards, died in a German military hospital in Lille having been wounded on 20 October near the village of Passchendaele. His youngest son, nineteen-year-old Lieutenant Geoffrey Murray Smith, was killed at Loos on 29 September 1915.

The MR continued its vital war work whilst losing increasing numbers of staff at all levels. In June 1915 Lloyd George seconded the company's chief mechanical engineer, Henry Fowler, and the head of its carriage and wagon department, W.D. Bain, to assist him in the Ministry of Munitions.[113] Despite this, Murray Smith was forced to defend MR employees against charges of lukewarm commitment to the war effort. In June 1915, whilst speaking at the Midland Railway Rifle Club Awards Evening, he responded to recent accusations his men were slackers because they *"did not happen to be in khaki".* This criticism was particularly unjust, he said, as: *"railways were an important link in military operations,"* and, like the navy, carried out vital, but *"silent work."*[114] By the end of August 1915, 92,658 railwaymen had enlisted across the UK but more men were still needed to replace ever-increasing losses, particularly on the Western Front.[115] At that time it was believed at least two million single men of fighting age had not volunteered and the impetus towards conscription gathered pace. The Earl of Derby, appointed Director-General of Recruiting on 5 October 1915, introduced a scheme to encourage men to attest, return to their normal work and wait until called up to begin their military service at a later date. In November 1915 the MR issued its own circular to clerical staff supporting those who wanted to enlist, providing they first obtained written authority from the company and then returned to work: *"until such time as called up, wearing in the meantime the khaki armlet."*[116] This reference to the so-called Derby Scheme indicates the REC had gained an additional commitment from the government that railwaymen still had to prove permission had been granted by their parent company before they could be released for military service.

By the time of the MR AGM in February 1916, Murray Smith had changed his opinion about some of the staff and confessed: *"he could not help thinking that out of the men who had neither enlisted or attested there must be some who could quite well join the colours, who were medically fit, had no responsibilities to keep them, and who could be spared by the company. These were shirkers, and no one could not but feel contempt for them. (Hear, hear.)"*[117] Lord Derby's scheme did increase recruitment, but not to the extent required by 1916. The Military Service Bill, introducing conscription for single men, received the Royal Assent on 26 May that year. The concern for each railway company was if the pruning effect of conscription

[113] *Huddersfield Daily Examiner*, 24 June 1915.
[114] *Sheffield Daily Telegraph*, 24 June 1915.
[115] Pratt, op. cit., p.358
[116] *Derby Daily Telegraph*, 2 November 1915.
[117] *Yorkshire Post*, 18 February 1916.

would trim their workforce to the point where the transport system ceased to function effectively. As in the Boer War the MR promised to find positions for men after their return from service – an issue that was discussed at a meeting of the Special Disablements Sub-committee of the War Pensions Statutory Committee in September 1916. On that occasion the MR insisted that efforts would be made *"to reinstate eligible men in similar positions or grades to those which they left, the salary or wage then paid being according to the scale to which they would have been entitled had they remained at work."* It also promised to *"find suitable employment for those who, through injury or disablement, cannot perform their old duties"*, but who could do other work.[118] However, the MR admitted that since 1914 a number of partially disabled men had not re-entered the company's service, although places had been found for every man who was *"well enough to resume railway work…though not in all cases in the same grade as occupied before the war."*[119] At that time almost 2,000 Midland men had been wounded in action, or disabled by illness. By the end of 1916, 15,165 men of the salaried and wages staff had left the MR to join the armed forces; a figure representing twenty per cent of the 1914 workforce. Most of these recruits would have been volunteers and by the end of the war this figure had risen to 21,813 men, or 29.38% of MR staff at the commencement of hostilities.[120] During the war a total of 184,475 men left railway employment in Britain to join the colours; which represents a staggering forty-nine per cent of all personnel of military age on 4 August 1914.[121]

To replace staff who joined up the MR employed unskilled men and women. As early as February 1915 the REC discussed the feasibility of using female labour to help release men for military service with Secretary of State for War Lord Kitchener. The prevailing view at the time was it would be *"admittedly impracticable"* to expect women to work as *"engine drivers, firemen and shunters."*[122] However, on 24 March 1915, an REC sub-committee proposed a range of alternative ways women could be used as substitutes so men could be released for military action. The *"greatest increase at first was naturally found in the employment of women and girls for clerical duties"*, but others soon followed, such as: booking clerks, parcel clerks, ticket collectors, ticket examiners, dining car attendants, porters, carriage cleaners and telegraphists.[123] In 1914 the MR employed 1,400 women but by the beginning of 1917 this figure had risen to 6,300. While most of these women worked in munitions production many were increasingly employed in traditional railway roles such as clerical work, engine and carriage cleaning, and *"porters, loaders and checkers"* in the goods department.[124] In February 1917, Murray Smith predicted that: *"presently the public will see many more women on the railway platform"*[125] and one year later the number of women employed by the MR had indeed risen by a further 2,700, with

[118] *Birmingham Daily Post*, 22 September 1916.
[119] Ibid
[120] Pratt, op. cit., p.371
[121] Ibid, p.370
[122] Ibid, p.475
[123] Ibid, p.475
[124] *Derby Daily Telegraph*, 15 February 1917.
[125] *Northern Whig*, 16 February 1917.

nearly 9,000 *"employed in the various grades."*[126] This reflected the national trend as in January 1918 women represented 50% of all clerical staff employed across the British railway network.[127] According to Pratt, *"the experience of the Midland was that, within their limitations, the women taken on did their work exceedingly well."* ! [128]

In 1918 Murray Smith gave MR shareholders an overview of the company's contribution to the war effort since 1914. As well as lending many of its chief officers and clerks to the Government it had produced *"remarkable statistics"* in munitions production - five million shell cases and two million fuses - and *"manufactured all sorts of other articles for the War Department, from picketing pegs to ambulance trains."*[129] Ninety-seven new munitions plants were built during the war on sites adjacent to the MR network and in the Birmingham area alone, the company transported 3,000 army G.S. wagons, 5,000 tons of barbed wire, 12,000 tons of saddlery, 500,000 bicycles and 40,000 motor cycles.[130] However, the MR management was still forced to deal with frequent criticisms of its services. In November 1915 one correspondent in King's Norton, Birmingham, complained about a shortage of domestic coal due to priority being given to local munitions works and the *"undue preference to Messrs. Cadbury Bros., who seem to get their supply through with great exactness."* In a swipe at the MR's state-controlled status, the writer declared the company had *"no right to give preference to private firms"* and, with colder weather approaching, said there was *"likely to be trouble in the district"* if nothing changed. The MR denied any favouritism towards Cadbury's and claimed they were: *"doing their best under the circumstances."*[131] Another matter that caused inconvenience to the general public was reduced passenger train services. During the autumn of 1915 passenger mileage was cut by 250,000 per annum, a trend that continued during the following year thanks to strategies like increasing the cost of rail fares by fifty per cent. By 1917 passenger journeys on the Midland were down to half of their pre-war mileage.[132] In his 1917 annual report Murray Smith defended the company and explained that due to government priorities the volume of *"freight train traffic"* being carried by the MR was *"greatly increasing"* and *"helping our soldiers at the front to win a great and convincing victory."* For this to happen the public had to *"ungrudgingly put up with a reduced train service."*[133] When trains did run they were invariably overcrowded, despite novel schemes like removing the armrests in First Class compartments, which increased the space for passenger seating by between fifty and 100%![134] The MR also played a key role in transporting industrial workers to munitions and other war-related factories. Every day 12,000 workers were carried by train to and from the Austin Motor Company plant at Longbridge, south of

---

[126] *Derby Daily Telegraph*, 14 February 1918
[127] Pratt, op. cit., p.476
[128] Pratt, E.A., *British Railways and the Great War*, Vol II, p.1050
[129] *Derby Daily Telegraph*, 14 February 1918.
[130] Barnes, op. cit., p.252-3.
[131] *Birmingham Daily Mail*, 18 November 1915.
[132] Barnes, op. cit., p.247.
[133] *Derby Daily Telegraph*, 15 February 1917.
[134] Barnes, op. cit., p.247-8.

Birmingham, where they produced aircraft engines, shells and re-lined artillery pieces.[135]

In March 1919 in his final act as company chairman, Murray Smith reported the total number of MR staff who had left to join the armed services was 21,813. This figure represented 29.38% *"of the staff employed immediately prior to the war."* Up until *"the day of the Armistice"* the MR suffered 6,934 casualties: 2,096 killed in action or died of wounds, 264 missing, 483 prisoners of war and 4,091 wounded or invalided home.[136] These figures would be revised considerably during the course of the next two years (see Table Three). Having guided the MR through the hectic years of the Great War, George Murray Smith died suddenly at his sister's home, 50 Park Street, Westminster, on 18 April 1919.[137] He was only sixty-one-years-old and never lived to see the construction of the company war memorial at Derby. This was initiated by his successor as MR Chairman - Charles Booth.[138] One year later Booth reported arrangements for the construction of a *"permanent memorial...had now been completed"* - a thirty-one foot tall cenotaph, designed by Sir Edwin Lutyens, the architect who created the original version in Whitehall. This was erected on land adjoining the Midland Hotel, Midland Road, Derby.[139] By the time the memorial was unveiled by Charles Booth on 15 December 1921, the final statistics indicated that 22,941 MR employees had served in the armed forces and 2,833 had *"laid down their lives."*[140] This final tally was so great the company decided it would be *"impracticable to accommodate"* the families of all the deceased at the unveiling. Instead, they were sent a Memorial Volume which included an alphabetical Roll of Honour that detailed their relatives' names, along with illustrations of the Derby Cenotaph. In his eulogy at the unveiling ceremony, Chairman Booth lauded the significant role played by the men and women of the MR as: *"a total war effort of great power and value...which undoubtedly played its part in achieving the ultimate victory."*[141]

Part Two – Forgotten Midland Railwaymen of the Wolverhampton area.

The second part of this article will focus on fifteen local railwaymen who worked for the MR in south Staffordshire before going off to fight and die in the Great War. A railway between Wolverhampton and Walsall was authorised on 29 June 1865 and opened to traffic on 1 November 1871. This eight mile length of line was initially purchased by the LNWR before being sold to the MR in 1876. To the east of Walsall the MR absorbed the Wolverhampton, Walsall and Midland Junction Railway on 30 July 1874 and finally completed their line from Wolverhampton to Water Orton, via Sutton Coldfield, on 1 July 1879.[142] This route also included a 5¼ mile branch line from Aldridge to Brownhills and Norton Canes which opened to goods and

---

[135] Pratt, Vol II, op. cit., p.1044
[136] *Derbyshire Advertiser*, 28 March 1919.
[137] McConnell, A. *Oxford Dictionary of National Biography*, Vol. 51, 2004, p.144.
[138] *Derby Daily Telegraph*, 19 February 1920.
[139] Derbyshire Advertiser, 18 February 1921.
[140] Ibid, 10 December 1921.
[141] *Derbyshire Advertiser*, 16 December 1921.
[142] Haddock, op. cit., p.15

passengers between 1882-4. The MR ran their trains into Wolverhampton High Level with the consent of the LNWR, via Crane Street Junction on the Stour Valley mainline to Birmingham.[143] The fifteen MR soldiers in this study worked at various points on the railway between Wolverhampton and Aldridge. Travelling eastwards from Wolverhampton High Level the passenger stations were: Heath Town, Wednesfield, Willenhall, Short Heath, Bentley, and North Walsall, before the line turned south at Rycroft junction into the LNWR station at Walsall. On leaving Walsall northwards, trains returned to Rycroft junction before turning eastwards towards Aldridge, Streetly, Sutton Park, Sutton Coldfield, Penns and Water Orton. It was here that the line connected with the main MR route from Birmingham to Derby. Several of the men in this study also worked at the goods depots at Wolverhampton and Walsall. As in other places with an overcrowded railway infrastructure, this MR line had to compete with routes of rival companies and it struggled from the start. As early as 1912 there were local concerns the MR might leave Walsall, prompting one Press correspondent to claim: *"If the Midland leave us our goods traffic to and from Walsall will soon get into a chaotic condition."*[144] The MR District Goods Manager responded that the company *"had not the slightest intention of withdrawing from Walsall,"* but locals were concerned about having to depend on the LNWR, which did not enjoy a good reputation in the area: *"it would indeed have been a calamity if a town the size of Walsall had to rely on only one company."*[145] However, by that time the MR had already closed its stations at Bentley - in 1898 - due to competition from trams and Heath Town, in 1910.[146] The Wolverhampton-Walsall line struggled on for the next twenty years before North Walsall station was shut in 1925, the branch line to Norton Canes ceased passenger traffic in 1930, and the rest of the line finally closed to passengers on 5 January 1931. According to Moors: *"although the line never generated the economic level of passenger usage enjoyed by the current ex-LNWR Walsall-Wolverhampton route, it survived as a viable goods line until 1966."*[147] This railway was eventually severed completely when the M6 motorway was cut through its route on 28 September 1964. The original site of Bentley station is now buried beneath the surface of the M6 carriageway a few hundred metres north of Junction 10.[148] Since then the old Wolverhampton and Walsall line and its associated railway infrastructure has been dismantled and forgotten like the fifteen MR soldiers who once worked at various points along its route. Luckily, we can identify where each man was based thanks to the Midland Railway Roll of Honour, published to coincide with the unveiling of the company war memorial in Derby in 1921.

These forgotten men will be recalled as if travelling on an eastwards journey from Wolverhampton High Level to Aldridge and Brownhills, via Walsall, including the MR goods depots at Wolverhampton and Walsall.

---

[143] Christiansen, R., *A Regional History of the Railways of Great Britain, Vol.7, The West Midlands,* 1973, pp.107ff
[144] *Walsall Advertiser,* 23 November 1912.
[145] Ibid, 30 November 1912.
[146] Boynton, J., *Rails Around Walsall,* 1996
[147] Moors, T., *Lost Railways of Birmingham and the West Midlands,* 2005
[148] Yate, B., *The Midland Railway Route From Wolverhampton,* Oakwood Press, 2018

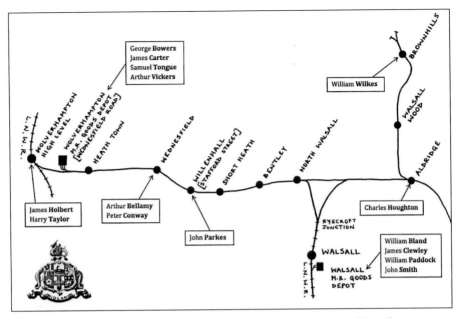

Map showing the MR route that forms the focus of this investigation and names of the railwaymen who worked at various locations along it.

Wolverhampton Queen Street station, as it was known between 1853 and 1885, was opened on 1 July 1852. It was officially renamed Wolverhampton (High Level) on 1 June 1885.[149] The only surviving part of that building is the original grand entrance in Victoria Square, on the corner of Piper's Row and Railway Drive, opened on 1 October 1851. The old station itself was completely demolished between 1964 and 1966, although a few sheds and warehouses survive nearby. It was here that (Henry) Harry Taylor worked for the MR as a labourer for the Way and Works department.[150] Way and Works came under the Engineer's Department and Taylor was probably a member of a team of at least six other men who were supervised by a ganger and sub-ganger. It was his job to help maintain the Permanent Way (track and ballast) near Wolverhampton station.[151] Harry Taylor had already served as a soldier before the outbreak of the Great War. The 1901 census locates him stationed at the 23rd Brigade Depot of the Royal Welsh Fusiliers (RWF), High Town Barracks, Wrexham. That year he was listed in the 5th Provisional Battalion RWF; a voluntary unit from the era before the creation of the Territorial Force. Taylor probably enlisted for seven years with the colours and five in the Reserve, but in 1911 he was back living at 12 Ward Street, Wolverhampton, with his wife Ann Maria and daughter Maud. His occupation was then listed as "*Railway Company Plate Layer's Labourer.*" On 19 September 1914, Private Taylor, No.6566, was called-up as a Section D Reservist. Although he enlisted into the 2nd Battalion RWF, he was almost

---

[149] Collins, P., *Rail Centres: Wolverhampton*, Ian Allan, 1990
[150] Midland Railway Co., *For King and Country, 1914-1919, Roll of Honour*, 1921, p.56
[151] Midlandrailwaystudycentre.org.uk

immediately transferred to the 1st Battalion (1/RWF), with whom he crossed from Southampton to Zeebrugge on 7 October. After a brief excursion to Ghent his regiment took their place on the Western Front, until the thirty-three-year-old Harry Taylor was killed during the first day of the Battle of Festubert, in May 1915. The previous week, the 1/RWF had been held in reserve at Essars during the Battle of Aubers Ridge. Then, on 15 May, its twenty-five officers and 806 NCOs and men were ordered up to the frontline.[152] Following a British artillery bombardment of the German trenches lasting exactly thirty-one minutes, Taylor and his comrades went 'over-the-top' at 3.15 am on 16 May 1915. The enemy frontline was breached and a 1,000 yard breakthrough made just south of an enemy strongpoint called the Quadrilateral. However, 1/RWF casualties were a crippling 221 dead, with hundreds more wounded – around sixty per cent of the total number involved in the operation. By the time they were withdrawn from the attack, Harry Taylor had become one of those listed as 'killed in action'.[153] Unfortunately, his body was never identified and he is commemorated on the Le Touret Memorial, between Bethune and Lille in northern France. He is also listed on the local war memorial at St Michael and All Angels Church, Tettenhall. Many of the 1/RWF officers who died that day are buried in Guards Cemetery, Windy Corner, Cuinchy, due south of the village of Festubert.

View of Wolverhampton High Level Station before the war. Note sign indicating the MR.
Photo courtesy of Wolverhampton Archives & Local Studies.

Another MR employee based at Wolverhampton station was Leicester-born, James Valentine Holbert - a constable with the railway police.[154] Like Harry Taylor, he also had previous military service, having enlisted into the 2nd Battalion of the Bedfordshire Regiment on 15 February 1897, aged twenty-one. This former milkman

[152] 1/RWF, *War Diary*, 15 May 1915
[153] Hancock, E., *Aubers Ridge*, Pen and Sword, 2005, p.147
[154] Midland Railway Co., *Roll of Honour*, op. cit., p.29

spent much of the next twelve years in India where he transferred to the No.9 Mountain Battery of the Royal Garrison Artillery and got married to Ella Rose in 1906. He was discharged from the army on 17 April 1909 and probably began his career with the MR soon afterwards. While working as a railway police officer Holbert probably encountered offences well-known to modern readers such as passengers travelling without valid tickets and others being drunk and disorderly. Cases of illegal entry onto railway property were also regularly reported in the local press, such as when *"two lads, aged 12 and 13 were summoned for trespassing on the Midland Railway at Rycroft."* Such was the frequency of this potentially fatal felony that a *'railway officer'* had to be stationed in that district for most of the time.[155]

James Holbert appears to have re-enlisted into the army in April 1915 but was not posted for duty until 29 July 1916 when he joined the 3rd Battalion Bedfordshire Regiment. He was eventually sent overseas on 31 January 1918 and, after a brief time at 'L' Infantry Base Depot, Calais, transferred to the 1st Battalion North Staffordshire Regiment (1/North Staffords) as No.41212. In March 1918 Holbert's new unit was based at Pontruet, north of St. Quentin. According to the battalion war diary: *"Information was received from Intelligence reports that an enemy offensive was to commence on the morning of 21st…prisoners captured on the 20th confirmed this giving details etc."* Holbert's introduction to the Western Front was to be a genuine baptism of fire as he and his comrades made hasty last-minute preparations for the impending German Spring offensive – the *Kaiserschlacht*. This began exactly as predicted at 4.30 am on 21 March with a huge enemy artillery barrage and within fifteen minutes communications with all nearby units were cut. As the 1/North Staffs waited for the German infantry to arrive they were disorientated by a noxious blend of poison gas and fog. Then at 11 am, they received news that the enemy had broken through nearby and the Battalion HQ dugout had been abandoned. As a scratch force of *"servants, signallers and pioneers"* attempted to hold the "RED LINE" defensive perimeter word arrived that the 1/North Staffords had been outflanked. As they rushed to the rear at 11.30 am they *"came under enfilade fire"* as well as from enemy machine guns now firing from the positions they had only just vacated.[156] At some point on this traumatic first day of the great German offensive - planned to win the war before fresh American troops ensured victory for the Allies - James Holbert was taken prisoner. German PoW documents indicate he was placed under the auspices of Stendal Camp in Saxony-Anhalt. However, this was just for administrative purposes and Holbert actually spent the next five months working for the German army very close to where he was captured on 21 March. We have no records of his time as PoW until he fell ill in August 1918 and was admitted to the German military hospital at Bohain (now called Bohain-en-Vermandois) north-east of St Quentin. It was here that the 42-year-old Acting Corporal died on 12 August, *"infolge Darmkatarrh"* – as a result of enteritis: inflammation of the small intestine probably brought on by eating contaminated food. According to the German *"Totenliste"* James Holbert was buried in plot 525 of what became Bohain Station Military Cemetery. After the war his body was exhumed and reinterred in Premont

---

[155] *Walsall Advertiser*, 15 November 1913.
[156] 1/North Staffs War Diary, 20-21 March 1918.

British Cemetery, about fifteen miles north-north-east of St Quentin.[157] At the time of his death Holbert's home address was 11 Gladstone Terrace, St Andrews Road, Small Heath, Birmingham, but according to pension records his widow and three small children had moved to Portsmouth by the early 1920s.

View of Platform 1 at Wolverhampton High Level Station taken c.1910.
Photo courtesy of Wolverhampton Archives & Local Studies.

The construction of Wolverhampton's MR Wednesfield Road Goods Depot began in November 1878 and it opened for goods and mineral traffic on 4 October 1880.[158] During the century that followed it processed many tons of produce and even changed its use on several occasions in its final years. Being close to the town centre, the depot was a focus for much of Wolverhampton's trade and commerce - whether arriving, or departing, by train. The site contained offices, sidings, warehouses, sheds and even cattle pens. It was a busy location as a steady stream of goods trains pulled in and out, and freight transferred to or from a succession of horse-drawn drays. In the mid-1980s one writer described: *"the squat and squarish Wednesfield Road goods depot"* as the *"most substantial monument to the Midland's presence in Wolverhampton."*[159] The depot was demolished in 1995 and replaced by the current Royal Mail Sorting Office. Four members of MR staff from the goods depot died in the Great War. The first was a porter called George Bowers who, like Harry Taylor, was a Reservist with the Royal Welsh Fusiliers (2nd Battalion).[160] Born in 1881 in Eccleshall, Staffordshire, he was living at Lower Green, Tettenhall, by 1891. According to the 1901 census Bowers was working as gardener at Chillington Hall, near Brewood, but he enlisted with the 5th Provisional Battalion, RWF the following year. Like Harry Taylor, whom he must have known, he probably signed up for 'seven and five' and was immediately recalled when the Great War began.

[157] www.cwgc.org
[158] *Wolverhampton Chronicle*, 6 October 1880
[159] Christiansen, Rex., *Forgotten Railways – The West Midlands, Vol. 10*, 1985, p.83ff.
[160] Midland Railway Co., *Roll of Honour*, op. cit., p.7

Bowers identified his brother, Thomas, as his next of kin. He lived at 15 Gaddesley Road, King's Heath, Birmingham. Like Harry Taylor, Private Bowers, No.7000, fought in the early campaigns on the Western Front and was awarded the '1914 Star.' He eventually died when the 2/RWF were involved in the capture of Flat Iron Copse and High Wood during the Battle of the Somme. Between 3 am and 8 am on 20 July 1916 Bowers and his comrades came under sustained German shellfire and suffered many casualties as they waited to move up to their jumping-off positions. The intensity of the bombardment diminished late morning and the battalion entered the frontline at 2 pm, from where they took part in an attack that successfully cleared the enemy from the woods.[161] In this 2/RWF assault, twenty-nine other ranks were killed, 180 were wounded and twenty-nine were listed as missing. However, Bowers was probably killed earlier that day while the men were waiting to move forward. He is buried, along with many others from his battalion, in Caterpillar Valley Cemetery, west of the village of Longueval. His name is also listed on the St Michael and All Angels war memorial, Tettenhall. One of the eleven 2/RWF officers seriously wounded in this same action was the writer, Captain Robert Graves.[162] In his memoirs he later wrote: *"we lost a third of our battalion before the show started. I was one of the casualties."* [163] So too was George Bowers, the MR porter.

James Carter's grave in Holy Trinity Churchyard, Heath Town.

The second former MR man from the Wednesfield Road Goods Depot to die was another porter, James Carter. He was born in the south Staffordshire village of Wombourne in 1882. In 1901 he worked in the japanning trade but was listed as a *'Railway Porter'* in the 1911 census, where his address was given as 21 Wood Street, Heath Town, Wolverhampton. On 5 October 1912 Carter joined the Wolverhampton branch of the Amalgamated Society of Railway Servants, where his grade was also listed as *'Porter'.*[164] On 5 May 1915 he enlisted into the 2/6th Battalion South Staffordshire Regiment (2/6 South Staffords) in Wolverhampton and was given the service number 241128.[165] This battalion crossed to France on 25

---

[161] 2/RWF, *War Diary*, 20 July 1916
[162] Ibid.
[163] Graves, R., *Goodbye to All That*, p.180
[164] Register of Trades Union Membership, A.S.R.S., MSS.127/AS/2/3/26, p.50
[165] Midland Railway Co., *Roll of Honour*, op. cit., p.10

February 1917 and after a year fighting on the Western Front Carter was seriously wounded, possibly during the German offensive on 21 March 1918. At that time 2/6 South Staffords were defending the front line near the village of Écoust-St-Mein, near Croiselles. He was evacuated home to Britain but died from the effects of: *"gas poisoning received in action"* on 12 May 1918 at Wallfields VAD hospital, Hertford.[166] James Carter was buried in Holy Trinity Churchyard, Heath Town, and is currently the only one of the fifteen MR men in this survey to have a known grave in Britain.

Only a few weeks later, another man from the Goods Depot was killed. He was Samuel Walter Tongue, a twenty-one-year-old shoeing smith who helped to maintain the fleet of horse-drawn drays that transhipped goods in and out of the Depot.[167] Born in 1897, Tongue lived with his parents Samuel Senior and Alice, at 32 Alma Street, just around the corner from his place of work. He must have been destined to become a railwayman as the 1911 census lists his occupation as *'Newspaper Boy'* at Wolverhampton station and that of his older brother as a *'Number-taker for the LNWR'*. Private Tongue, No.8812, enlisted into the 3rd Battalion of the Worcestershire Regiment (3/Worcesters) in Wolverhampton. In 1918, his regiment was also involved in the momentous defensive battles which began when the enemy launched their Spring Offensive on the Western Front. On 9 April Tongue's battalion were in the front line at Ploegsteert in Belgium when the second phase of the German campaign began – *Operation Georgette*, or the Battle of the Lys. For the rest of that month, *'with their backs to the wall',* they fought to hold the line in the Bailleul-Kemmel area, south of Ypres. Having suffered serious casualties, the 3/Worcesters were withdrawn from the frontline on 4 May, and sent south to recuperate on a 'quiet sector' of the Western Front, near Reims.[168] Unfortunately they were deployed to a location directly in the path of the impending third phase of the great German onslaught: *Operation Blücher-Yorcke*, or the Third Battle of the Aisne. At 3.40 am on 27 May, following an intense artillery bombardment lasting almost four hours, the German infantry attacked Allied positions along a twenty-four mile front – taking the Chemin-des-Dames Ridge by noon and advancing about twelve miles by nightfall. The enemy captured Soissons the following day and by 6 June had reached the River Marne for the second time in the war. However, the Germans were completely exhausted and - although the Allied defensive line had bent - it had not broken. Private Samuel Tongue was probably killed defending a crossing-point on the River Aisne on the very first day of this second great retreat to the Marne - 27 May 1918. His body was lost in the chaos of battle and he is commemorated on the Soissons Memorial, along with forty-four other men of the 3/Worcesters and seventeen of the 1st Battalion. The British military cemetery which contains the highest concentration of Tongue's comrades who also died on 27 May is at La Ville-Aux-Bois, north-west of Reims. It is highly likely he died whilst fighting close to that position.[169]

---

[166] *Wolverhampton Express and Star*, 15 May 1918
[167] Midland Railway Co., *Roll of Honour*, op. cit., p.58
[168] www.plugstreet-archaeology.com
[169] CWGC.org

The last man from the Wolverhampton Goods Depot to die in the Great War was twenty-five-year-old former MR clerk, Arthur Benjamin Vickers.[170] Born in 1893, Vickers married Florence in 1915 and they lived at 25 Francis Street, Wolverhampton. He enlisted in the town and became a Gunner, No.161757, in the 479th Siege Battery of the Royal Garrison Artillery. Nothing is yet known about his military career, but Vickers died of wounds on 27 June 1918 and is buried in Aire Communal Cemetery, south-east of St. Omer, in France. Arthur Vickers had become yet another MR casualty to die during the war's deadly final year.

Travelling eastwards along the line from Wolverhampton next reveals the stories of two men based at Wednesfield station – one of whom was the youngest MR casualty in this study and the only one to die in the Gallipoli campaign. Peter Conway, aged nineteen, was listed in the MR Roll of Honour as working as a porter in the 'Traffic – Coaching Section.'[171] This meant he assisted the station master with the day-to-day running of the station: dealing with passengers, handling small goods and lighting the gas lamps.[172] In 1911 he lived at 14 Bentley Road, Darlaston, with Peter (senior), his furnaceman father, and mother Emma. Private Conway, No.7/9905, enlisted into the 7th Service Battalion of the South Staffordshire Regiment (7/South Staffords) at Lichfield in August 1914. The following month the battalion moved to Grantham for training and in April 1915 was briefly posted to Frensham Camp in Surrey. On 1 July 1915 the 750 men of the 7/South Staffords set off for the Mediterranean from Liverpool aboard HMT *Empress of Britain*. The ship docked first at Alexandria before arriving at the island of Mudros on 18 July. On 21 July Peter Conway and his comrades were landed at *V Beach*, Cape Helles, on the Gallipoli peninsula and spent the next four days preparing a rest camp.[173] In this *"gruesome introduction to warfare"* the 7/South Staffords took over reserve trenches on the slopes of Achi Baba where the parapets were *"built up of the bodies of dead British and Turks, smelt abominably and attracted millions of loathsome flies."*[174] On the 25 July they went into the firing line to relieve the Drake and Plymouth Battalions of the Royal Naval Division. It was on that day that Conway became one of the battalion's *"first casualties"* when the men moved forward to a place known as the *'Horseshoe'*. How he died is not recorded. On 28 July the 7/South Staffords were redeployed to Imbros, before taking part in the amphibious landings at Suvla Bay on the night of 6/7 August. Private Peter Conway was buried in the Redoubt Cemetery, Helles, Gallipoli.

Also based at Wednesfield station was Arthur Thomas Bellamy, a *'Yardman'* in the MR Traffic Coaching Section.[175] Born in 1897 he lived with his parents, Arthur John and Ellen at 110 Wyrley Road, Witton, Birmingham. The 1911 census records the young Bellamy's occupation as *'Railway Van Boy.'* Between 18 February 1913 and 27 August 1916 he was a member of the Sutton Coldfield branch of the National

[170] Midland Railway Co., *Roll of Honour*, op. cit., p.59
[171] Ibid, p.13
[172] Midlandrailwaystudycentre.org.uk
[173] Ashcroft, A.H., *The History of the Seventh South Staffordshire Regiment*, London, 1919, p.9
[174] Ibid
[175] Midland Railway Co., *Roll of Honour*, op. cit., p.5

Union of Railwaymen, where his occupation was initially listed as *'Lampman'*, before being altered to *'Porter'*.[176] He enlisted in Birmingham with the 3rd Battalion of the Coldstream Guards, No.22169, and was killed in action on 13 April 1918 - another MR casualty to die during the great German Spring offensive. Bellamy's body was never recovered or identified and his name is recorded on the Ploegsteert Memorial in Belgium.

View of Stafford Street bridge from the site of Willenhall (Market Place/Stafford Street) station.

Continuing eastwards, the next station on the line was at Willenhall – which was originally subtitled Market Place, then Stafford Street by 1914. It was here that John Thomas Parkes worked as a labourer in the Way and Works department.[177] In terms of passengers this was the busiest on the Wolverhampton-Walsall line, with a peak annual usage of 149,000 in 1877. After that a steady decline took place which accelerated during the period of the Great War: in 1909, 80,000 passengers; in 1922, only 34,000.[178] John Parkes, was the son of William and Emma, and lived at 65 Stringes Lane, Willenhall. He joined up in Wolverhampton and his service number, 12948, indicates he did so in either September or October 1914. On 23 March 1915 Parkes' unit, the 2nd Battalion South Staffordshire Regiment (2/South Staffords), was posted to France and his brief period of service on the Western Front began. Two months later the twenty-four-year-old railwayman died during the Battle of Festubert, although there is some dispute about exactly when this occurred. Reports in the local Press referred to the 2/South Staffords being involved in *"particularly fierce fighting"* at the time, including bayonet charges and being under bombardment for two days and nights.[179] At first the battalion played a supporting role in the main British attack at Festubert, which began at 11.30 pm on 15 May. At 1 am the following morning the 60th Rifles requested reinforcements and 'D' Company 2/South Staffords was sent forward to the front line.[180] Throughout 16 May the three remaining companies suffered serious casualties from German artillery fire whilst

[176] Register of Trades Union Membership, N.U.R., MSS.127/NU/OR/2/44, p.57
[177] Midland Railway Co., *Roll of Honour*, op. cit., p.44
[178] Boynton, op. cit.
[179] *Walsall Advertiser*, 29 May 1915
[180] Jones, J.P., *History of the South Staffordshire Regiment (1705-1923)*, Wolverhampton, 1923, p.299

also waiting to go forward: *"...they held on grimly for eight hours on that bitter Sunday...shells falling everywhere and men being hit in all directions."*[181]   In the meantime they helped to carry fresh rations, water and bombs to their comrades in the frontline. At 8 pm they were finally ordered to relieve the 60th Rifles, a process that began at 1 am the following morning. At 10.30 am on 17 May the battalion finally launched the first of several unsuccessful attempts to capture Le Ferme Cour D'Avoine. After these, the 2/South Staffords were not withdrawn from the line until 1.30 am on 19 May. By the time they returned to Bethune their losses at Festubert had been awful. From a battalion that had gone into action on 15 May nearly 1,000 strong, *"only 130 could be mustered that night."*[182]   John Parkes was among those missing from that roll call and as his body was never recovered his name was inscribed on the Le Touret Memorial, north-east of Bethune. The Commonwealth War Graves Commission (CWGC) record the date of his death as 16 May but regimental medal and pension documents more tentatively state Parkes was *"presumed dead"* or had *"DoW"* – died of wounds - by 18 May 1915. This uncertainty is not surprising given the battalion's experiences during those four dreadful days.

The next group of MR servicemen worked at Walsall's Midland Railway Goods Depot. This was built between Walsall station and Pleck junction, on the town's former racecourse and received its first goods train on 1 July 1879.[183]   William Henry Bland was the first to die from a group of four soldiers who previously worked here; in his case as a porter.[184]   Born in 1886 Bland was an experienced soldier having joined the 1st Battalion South Staffordshire Regiment in October 1903. He served with the colours in the Transvaal (1903-04), Curragh Camp (1904-06), Bordon Camp (1906-08), Devonport (1908-11) and Gibraltar (1911-13). His military career was mainly routine garrison duty but Bland was listed in the 1911 census as *'Musician'* and according to his obituary *"played the saxophone in the regimental band."*[185]   A photograph of the 1/South Staffords regimental band, taken in 1907, shows William Bland with his instrument. After he left the army trades union records from 1914 reveal he was a member of the Walsall branch of the National Union of Railwaymen, where his occupation was listed as *'Goods Porter.'*[186]   At that time he lived at 53 Cairns Street, Walsall with his parents, George and Sophia. When he was called to rejoin the colours the 1/South Staffords were in South Africa which possibly explains why Private Bland, No.6919, was posted to the Regiment's 2nd Battalion (2/South Staffords). On 12 August his new unit sailed from Southampton for Le Havre aboard the troopship *Irrawaddy* and four days later arrived at Wassigny, near the Belgian border. During the next three months the battalion took part in the retreat from Mons and Battles of the Marne, Aisne and Aisne Heights – where it witnessed the genesis of trench warfare at Beaulne Spur, 7-15 October. On 17 October Bland's unit was sent north to Ypres where it took part in the Battle of Langemarck. In early November his family received what turned out to be his final field postcard home

---

181 Jones, History of the South Staffordshire Regiment, op. cit., p.300
182 Ibid, p.301
183 Haddock, *Walsall's Engine Sheds*, op. cit., p.15
184 Midland Railway Co., *Roll of Honour*, op. cit., p.6
185 *Walsall Observer and South Staffordshire Chronicle*, 12 December 1914
186 Register of Trades Union Membership, MSS.127/NU/OR/2/37, p.291

which *"stated that he was well."*[187]   Back in Walsall concerns amongst relatives were first raised when the army returned a packet of cigarettes addressed to him as *"untraceable."*   Confirmation of William Bland's death eventually arrived in early December in a letter written by *"a wounded comrade, who was engaged in the same railway department."*   He had been in *"an adjoining bed"* in the hospital where the saxophonist porter: *"succumbed to his wounds"* on 13 November 1914.[188]   William Bland was buried in Railway Chateau Cemetery, just west of Ypres and probably close to the site of the CCS that treated him and his wounded workmate.   That unnamed comrade explained that both men had been *"in the thick of the fighting in Belgium,"* a reference to the First Battle of Ypres.   On 1 November, the Germans attacked a line of trenches held by the 2/South Staffords in wooded country in front of Molenhoek, and for the next week the Battalion was left *"holding the most advanced line of the whole British Army, constantly being shelled."*[189]   Using the records of the CWGC it is possible to speculate when and where Private Bland was wounded.   The 2/South Staffords suffered particularly heavy losses while mounting a counter-attack against the Germans at Klein Zillebeke on 7 November 1914.   Consequently the names of many men from the unit are listed for that date on the Menin Gate Memorial.   There are also high concentrations of 2/South Staffords battle casualties buried in cemeteries south and east of Ypres: at Zantvoorde, Hooge, Zillebeke, Hill 60 and Bedford House.[190]   Bland was probably fatally wounded in this area and then transported to the field hospital, where he died later.   According to the Separation Allowance File in the Walsall Local History Centre, Bland's mother Sophia received a pension of eight shillings and six pence per week, beginning on 27 July 1915.[191]

The second MR porter at Walsall Goods Depot to die was John Norman Smith who lived at 30 Rutter Street, Walsall, with his wife Mary Ann.   He enlisted as a Private in the 2nd/5th Battalion of the South Staffordshire Regiment (2/5 South Staffords), No.36996, and was killed during the Battle of Cambrai.[192]   The Allied attack at Cambrai began on 20 November 1917 and was spearheaded by 437 Mk IV tanks.   These crushed the enemy barbed wire and created a breach in the Hindenburg Line which led to Allied advances of up to five miles.   Such was the unexpected scale of success that church bells were rung in Britain for the first time since the start of the war.   However, the celebrations were premature as the Germans responded with a massive counter-attack of their own on 30 November. The following day Smith's unit was defending positions on the Fontaine Notre-Dame Sector during which *"the enemy put down a very heavy barrage"* and attacked both their right and left flanks.[193]   The Battalion HQ was shelled all day and the telephone lines were cut several times.   The 2/5 South Staffords suffered seven Other Ranks killed and although they managed to hold the Germans back that day, within a week the enemy had regained most of the territory lost in November.   When the battle

[187] *Walsall Observer and South Staffordshire Chronicle*, 12 December 1914
[188] Ibid
[189] Jones, *History of the South Staffordshire Regiment*, op. cit., p.286
[190] CWGC.org
[191] Navy & Army Separation Allowances 78/11 – Separation Allowance File, 759.
[192] Midland Railway Co., *Roll of Honour*, op. cit., p.53
[193] 2/5SStaffs, *War Diary*, 30 Nov-1 Dec. 1917

ended, casualties on both sides were roughly comparable and these included Private John Smith. He died on 1 December and was buried in Orival Wood Cemetery, Flesquières, south-west of Cambrai. According to battalion records his outstanding pay was forwarded to his sister Gertrude and brother Sydney, although his wife also received a weekly pension of eight shillings.[194]

The sinking of HMT *Aragon* off the Egyptian coast, 30 December 1917.

The third porter from Walsall Goods Depot to lose his life was William John Allan Paddock.[195] He was born in 1894 and according to the 1911 census was then living at 35 Upper Walhouse Street, Walsall, and employed in a woollen warehouse. On the 19 September 1915 Paddock joined the Walsall branch of the National Union of Railwaymen and his occupation was recorded as *'Porter'*.[196] He enlisted in Wolverhampton and became the first soldier in this survey whose military role had a direct railway connection: he was a Sapper in the 96th Light Railway Operating Company [ROD] Royal Engineers, No.322809. Paddock was also the only MR man to die at sea, when the convoy carrying him to fight in Palestine was attacked by German U-boat, UC-34 on 30 December 1917. Along with the rest of HMT *Aragon's* other 2,700 passengers, Paddock probably experienced a *"most enjoyable Christmas aboard,"* as the troop-ship sailed through the Mediterranean.[197] However, for reasons that are still unclear, *Aragon* was instructed to wait: *"within sight of Egypt"* for permission to approach Alexandria harbour.[198] Eyewitness accounts of what happened next appeared in the British Press when surviving members of *Aragon's* crew arrived home in early February 1918. They claimed a torpedo struck the transport with *"a terrific crash"* at 9 am on the 30 December and the ship foundered in only fifteen minutes.[199] As the destroyer HMS *Attack*, attempted to pick up survivors it was itself *"cut in two"* by a second torpedo fired by UC-34 and those left struggling in the sea had to be rescued by several trawlers that rushed to the scene. In spite of this confusion, every one of the 160 VAD nurses on board *Aragon* were rescued

---

[194] Walsall Local History Centre, Navy & Army Separation Allowances 78/11 – Separation Allowance File, 4482.
[195] Midland Railway Co., *Roll of Honour*, op. cit., p.44
[196] Register of Trades Union Membership, MSS.127/NU/OR/2/44, p.245
[197] *Belfast Newsletter*, 11 February 1918
[198] *Londonderry Sentinel*, 2 February 1918
[199] Ibid

safely; *"without even wetting their feet."* [200] Unfortunately, this was not the case for the troops on board. Lieutenant H.O. Hinchcliffe, RE admitted: *"the losses amongst our boys was appalling. It nearly broke my heart when we called the roll next morning."*[201] In the event 610 passengers and crew aboard *Aragon* drowned, including at least seventy-seven railwaymen of the 96th Light Railway Operating Company. One was William Paddock.[202] According to Higgins, this was one of the worst single days for railwaymen casualties during the whole war.[203] Sapper Paddock's body was never recovered and he is commemorated on the Hadra Memorial in Alexandria. His mother, Clara Ann, received a pension of eight shillings per week.[204]

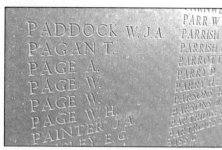

Left: Sapper William Paddock. *Right:* His inscription on the MR Cenotaph in Derby.

The final Walsall casualty was James Edward Clewley, a drayman at the goods depot.[205] He was born in 1894 and by 1911 was living at 43 Miner Street, Walsall. At that time, Clewley's occupation was noted as a *"Labourer in the Midland Railway Sheds."* He enlisted into the 256th Siege battery of the Royal Garrison Artillery in September 1916, leaving his wife, Elizabeth, and a child living at 23 Bath Street.[206] Lance Bombardier Clewley, No.117799, died from pneumonia in an army hospital in France, on 1 July 1918. His Major sent a letter to his grieving widow, in which he wrote: *"Your husband was one of the original members of __ Battery, and certainly one of its most popular ones, and one who, in particular of late months, had earned the esteem of all the officers and men of the unit, both in all his work and for his prowess on the football field...one who was a good and faithful soldier in all the best sense of the words."*[207] Clewley was buried in Ligny St. Flochel British Cemetery, Averdoingt, north-west of Arras. His wife received a pension of ten shillings per week.[208]

---

[200] *Belfast Newsletter*, 11 February 1918
[201] *Londonderry Sentinel*, 2 February 1918
[202] cwgc.org
[203] Higgins, *Great War Railwaymen*, op. cit., p.113
[204] Walsall Local History Centre, Navy & Army Separation Allowances 78/11 – Separation Allowance File, 4973.
[205] Midland Railway Co., *Roll of Honour*, op. cit., p.12
[206] *Walsall Observer and South Staffordshire Chronicle*, 20 July 1918.
[207] Ibid
[208] Walsall Local History Centre, Navy & Army Separation Allowances 78/11 – Separation Allowance File, 3648.

Travelling eastwards to the Aldridge – Brownhills branch line finds another MR soldier famed for his footballing prowess. William Joseph Wilkes was a labourer in the MR Way and Works department based at Brownhills (Watling Street) station.[209] When the war broke out his precise job title was *"platelayer."*[210] Wilkes was the son of Sarah Bowen (formerly Wilkes), of Lime Tree Cottages, Pelsall Road, Brownhills. Before he enlisted, he was a well-known local footballer having played for Brownhills Albion and Chase Terrace Athletic. He was also a referee in the Lichfield and District League and officiated at matches in the Brownhills Charity Cup competition.[211] Trades union records show that Wilkes became a member of the Brownhills branch of the Amalgamated Society of Railway Servants on 15 September 1910. His occupation was then given as *'Plate-layer'*, as it was in another leger entry for 23 June 1912.[212] Wilkes enlisted as a Pioneer in the North Midland Field Company, Royal Engineers, No.1481, where he no doubt had many opportunities to deploy both his tracklaying and football skills. Nothing is yet known about his military career. Wilkes died on 15 October 1915, aged thirty-one, and is buried in Lillers Communal Cemetery, west-north-west of Bethune.

Finally the Midland Railway Roll of Honour records that Charles Reginald Houghton was a porter in the *'Coaching Section – Traffic'*, at Aldridge station.[213] Houghton came from a railway family based on another part of the Midland network south of Birmingham. His father, George, was a signalman on the line at Defford, near Pershore and at the time of the 1911 census the family lived at 3 Railway Terrace, Stoke Works, near Bromsgrove. Like William Paddock, Houghton became a Sapper with the 96th Light Railway Operating Company, No.WR/290231, when he enlisted on 29 June 1917. Nothing is currently known about his army career but the Silver War Badge Roll indicates he was discharged from military service due to *'sickness'* on 30 October 1918 and issued with his badge two days before the Armistice. Charles Houghton eventually died in Bromsgrove Cottage Hospital on 11 March 1920, due to *"(1) injury to pelvis and spine (2) Psoas Abscess."*[214] This suggests he never recovered from the condition that led to his medical discharge seventeen months earlier. According to the CWGC website, Houghton's name appears on Panel 5 of the Brookwood Memorial, in Surrey. This memorial to the missing commemorates service personnel who: *"died in the care of their families"* after the war but whose burial site was never confirmed with the Imperial War Graves Commission as it was then known.[215] Sapper Houghton was actually buried in St Godwald's Cemetery, Finstall, near Bromsgrove, on 16 March 1920.[216] This is a particularly appropriate spot for a Midland man's grave as it lies at the foot of the Lickey Incline and is regularly shaken by trains thundering by on the steepest stretch of mainline railway in the country. Sadly, the precise location of Houghton's grave in

[209] Midland Railway Co., *Roll of Honour*, op. cit., p.63
[210] *Birmingham Mail*, 17 November 1915
[211] *Staffordshire Advertiser*, 13 November 1915
[212] Register of Trades Union Membership, A.S.R.S., MSS.127/AS/2/3/19, p.280
[213] Midland Railway Co., *Roll of Honour*, op. cit., p.30
[214] Death Certificate of C.R. Houghton.
[215] CWGC.org
[216] St Godwald's Burial Register, The Hive, Worcester.

the cemetery has been lost. At the time of writing this case had been referred to the *'In From The Cold'* organisation. They campaign to ensure 'lost' service personnel who died from war-related issues, like Charles Houghton, finally have an official CWGC headstone erected above their graves.

Men who gave their lives in the Great War—*continued.*							
NAME.	SERVICE IN H.M. FORCES.		RAILWAY EMPLOYMENT.				
	RANK.	REGIMENT, &c.	POSITION.	DEPARTMENT.	STATION.		
HOPWOOD, F. E.	Lieut.	R.O.D., R.E.	Privileged Apprentice..	Chief Mechanical Engineering	Derby.		
HORN, T. B.	Private	K.O.Y.L.I.	Porter	Traffic—Coaching Section	Sandal & Walton.		
HORNER, F. C.	Private	Royal Fusiliers	Clerk	Traffic—Coaching Section	Plaistow.		
HORNER, W.	L.-Cpl.	West Yorks.	Caller-Off	Goods	Leeds.		
HORSFIELD, T.	Private	York and Lancaster	Labourer	Way & Works	Wath.		
HORTON, L.	Private	Worcester..	Porter	Traffic—Coaching Section	Bromsgrove.		
HOUGH, F.	Private	Yorks.	Carriage Washer	Carriage & Wagon	Nottingham.		
HOUGHTON, C. R.	Sapper	R.T.E., R.E.	Porter	Traffic—Coaching Section	Aldridge.		
HOUGHTON, F. J.	Private	Suffolk	Porter	Goods	London (St. Pancras).		
HOUGHTON, L.	A.B.	Royal Navy	Porter	Traffic—Coaching Section	Rowsley.		

Extract from page 30 of the Midland Railway *Roll of Honour* showing details relating to Charles Reginald Houghton.

Part Three – Conclusion

This study now concludes with an examination of the statistical evidence about the wider contribution made by men of the Midland Railway Company and how this compares with the experiences of the fifteen men in the local sample.

Table One: Midland Railway Recruitment during the Great War

	During 1914	During 1915	During 1916	During 1917	During 1918	1919-1921
No. recruited from MR	c.9,000	2,923	2,188	6,058	1,644	1,128
Running Total	c. 9,000	11,923	14,111	20,169	21,813	**22,941**
Percentage	*39.2*	*12.7*	*9.53*	*26.4*	*7.1*	*4.9*

Table One is based on the statistics presented by MR Chairman George Murray Smith at each of the wartime AGMs and those recorded in the company Roll of Honour produced in 1921. The table demonstrates the initial surge of enthusiasm shown by MR employees to enlist or re-join the colours soon after the war began. As fifty-two per cent of the final total of 22,941 joined up in 1914 and 1915 alone it is probably safe to assume the majority of these MR servicemen were volunteers. This table also indicates the impact of continued government recruitment of railwaymen during the 'conscription era' after 1916, when the army's manpower shortages caused serious problems for the MR. The final tally of 22,941 men recruited between 1914 and 1921 represents 30.9 per cent of all MR staff at the start of the War. Of the fifteen local MR men in this study, at least eight are known to have rejoined the colours or enlisted during the first year of the war - 1914-15 (53%) - which is remarkably similar to the overall company figure for the same period.

Table Two: Midland Railway Offices and Departments providing most recruits.

	Goods	Traffic - coaching	Carriage & Wagon	Way & Works	Traffic – Motive Power	Chief Mechanical Engineers	Hotels
Number recruited from total of 22,941.	5,835	4,121	3,230	2,855	2,376	1,527	1,095
Percentage of total recruited	*25.43*	*17.96*	*14.07*	*12.44*	*10.35*	*6.65*	*4.77*

Table Two shows the seven leading MR departments that provided men for the armed forces during the war. It clearly indicates that essential railway personnel such as drivers, firemen and signalmen were retained by the MR for vital war work, whereas office clerks and labourers were 'expendable'. Of the fifteen men in the local sample, seven worked in the goods department (47%) which was an even larger percentage than the 25.43 per cent for the MR as a whole. James Holbert was one of the 157 MR policemen to enlist and became one of the unfortunate twenty-seven who never made it home.[217]

Table Three: Midland Railway Casualties during the Great War

Casualty	During 1914	During 1915	During 1916	During 1917	During 1918	1919-1921	Final Totals
KIA/DOW	102	355	440	541	658	737	
Running Total	*102*	*457*	*897*	*1438*	*2096*		*2833*
Wounded	369	742	859	864	1257	2977	
Running Total	*369*	*1,111*	*1,970*	*2,834*	*4,091*		*7,068*
POWs	100	10	34	19	320	255	
Running Total	*100*	*110*	*144*	*163*	*483*		*738*
Missing	29	34	64	30	107	-	
Running Total	*29*	*63*	*127*	*157*	*264*	*-*	
Annual Total	**600**	**1,141**	**1,397**	**1,454**	**2,342**	**3,969**	
Running Total	*600*	*1,741*	*3,138*	*4,592*	*6,934*		**10,903**

Table Three reveals more than 47 per cent of all MR men who enlisted became a casualty in some form. In terms of fatalities the figures indicate the rising annual death toll throughout the conflict, leading to a wartime peak in 1918. The death rate in 1917 and 1918 was 42.2 per cent of the total experienced by men of the MR. In the local study, eight of the fifteen MR men died in those final two years (53.3%) indicating their fates also reflected the war's lethal crescendo. What is more startling, however, is the fact that 737 MR men (26%) from the final company death toll of 2,833 were recorded in the three years *after* the cessation of hostilities. This discrepancy casts doubt on the accuracy of chairman Murray Smith's annual reports,

---

[217] Midland Railway Co., *Roll of Honour*, op. cit., p.67

the last of which listed the 'final' totals for the period up to the Armistice in November 1918.[218] Conversely, it may indicate the MR kept particularly accurate data about former employees who died as a result of injuries sustained in the years immediately after the war. In this context it is pertinent to consider the case of Sapper Charles Houghton, whose death was not initially recorded by the IWGC but whose name did appear on the MR Roll of Honour published in 1921. This disparity begs the question: how many others on the MR final death toll of 2,833 are absent from official government records of British war dead? This statistical discrepancy is not unique to the MR but also evident in the national records of railwayman deaths. At the time of the official ceremony to commemorate Britain's railwaymen, held at St. Paul's Cathedral on 14 May 1919, the total number of casualties listed in the Order of Service was 19,195. However, Higgins' research, based on information gathered from each of the individual railway companies, such as the MR Roll of Honour, has produced a revised national total figure of 21,517. Post-war accounting apparently 'discovered' an additional 2,322 railwaymen who died as a result of the Great War - an increase of 10.8% on the figures recorded in 1919.[219] This statistical inconsistency indicates further research is urgently needed to calculate the true cost of the Great War.

This numeric anomaly is also evident in the fact that 2,977 (42%) out of the total of 7,068 MR wounded men were recorded *after* the end of the war. This might indicate MR records became more accurate as the company assessed the individual cases of hundreds of returnees attempting to take up their old positions - or judging them incapable of doing so. There are no official records about the many MR men from south Staffordshire who were wounded in the war - only occasional newspaper references to people such as the unnamed colleague of William Bland, who lay beside the saxophonist during his final hours at a field hospital near Ypres. The local Press contains a few random mentions of named individuals such as Private H. Horton, 5th Battalion South Staffords who had been a *"member of the Walsall clerical staff of the Railway Goods department,"* [220] or Private John Small of 25 Marsh Street who was *"invalided home from Gallipoli with dysentery, and now in a Manchester hospital...Formerly in the employ of the Midland Railway Company as a carman,"* [221] and Bombardier Leonard Allmark, 9 Miner St. Walsall, who enlisted in the RFA in August 1915, *"now severely wounded in the side and arm...before enlisting he was employed by the Midland Railway Company."* [222] Although it is impossible to state exactly how many local MR men were wounded in the Great War, some estimates can be made based on the experiences of Wolverhampton's LNWR employees as well as those of MR men as a whole, as indicated in Table Three. When the LNWR memorial plaque was unveiled at Wolverhampton in 1921 it was reported that the sixty-eight names inscribed on it came from a total of 606 company employees who had joined up from the local area – representing a death rate of 11.22%.[223] Applying

---

[218] *Derbyshire Advertiser*, 28 March 1919
[219] Higgins, op. cit., p.314
[220] *Walsall Advertiser*, 17 April 1915
[221] *Walsall Observer and South Staffordshire Chronicle*, 9 October 1915
[222] Ibid, 21 September 1918
[223] *Wolverhampton Express & Star*, 12 September 1921

the same percentage death-rate to the fifteen MR men suggests a figure of about 135 men originally enlisting from that company in the area. If about 31 per cent of all MR employees were wounded in the war, then about forty-two men from the estimated total of 135 local recruits were probably wounded too. As already mentioned the sheer scale of the discrepancy between Murray Smith's final reported figures concerning both deaths and wounded, with those in the MR Roll of Honour clearly requires further investigation.

Table Four: Midland Railway – Distribution of Casualties by Armed Service.

	Army	Royal Navy	RNR	RNVR	RNAS	Royal Marines	RND	RAF
Number died from total of 2,833.	2,740	37	7	3	2	8	25	11
Percentage of total war dead	96.7	1.3	0.03	0.10	0.07	0.28	0.88	0.30

Table Four is also based on the statistics recorded in the MR Roll of Honour and clearly shows the vast majority of MR employees died whilst serving with the army rather than other branches of the armed services. This picture is also accurately reflected in the local study where all fifteen railwaymen died whilst serving in the army.

The Midland Railway Cenotaph at Derby.

Colette Hooper has written that *"viewing the war through the lens of the railways allows us to glimpse unseen aspects of that terrible conflict."*[224] The original purpose of this chapter was to use the experiences of fifteen forgotten local

[224] Hooper, Op. Cit., pp.224-25

railwaymen to present one such view of the Great War. However, the overwhelming and unexpected conclusion now reached is that the railwaymen of the Wolverhampton – Walsall area, as well as their colleagues across the whole of the United Kingdom, made a truly outstanding contribution to the achievement of victory in the Great War - perhaps an exceptional one? As the *Derbyshire Advertiser* commented in December 1921: "*Some day, perhaps, a memorial will be erected to the memory of all the railwaymen who fell in the war, but even then the full story of the great service which the railways rendered to the country will be little more than half told. Probably no class of men did more than railway workers at a time when every class did its utmost.*"[225]

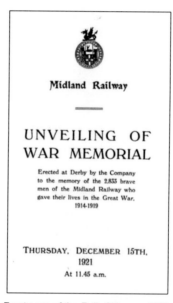

Midland Railway

UNVEILING OF WAR MEMORIAL

Erected at Derby by the Company to the memory of the 2,833 brave men of the Midland Railway who gave their lives in the Great War. 1914-1919

THURSDAY, DECEMBER 15TH, 1921
At 11.45 a.m.

Front page of the *Roll of Honour*, 1921.

The author would like to extend his thanks to the following people for their help in writing this chapter: Jim Barrow, Julian Crute and Mike Plant (RWF Archives, Wrexham); Dave Harris (Midland Railway Study Centre); Jeremy Higgins; Chris and Judy Rouse ('Wyvern' Railway Ancestry Advice); Sue Satterthwaite; the Staffordshire Regiment Museum Research Team, and staff at Wolverhampton Archives and Local Studies, Walsall Local History Centre and Worcestershire Archive and Archaeology Service.

---

[225] *Derbyshire Advertiser*, 10 December 1921.

Chapter 12

Wolverhampton's Tank Week – February 1918

Richard Pursehouse and Ben Cunliffe

Shakespeare Press]　　THE WOLVERHAMPTON TANK　　[Hincklev Street, Birm.

Postcard sold in Wolverhampton but photograph actually taken in Birmingham.

The Great War began as one of rapid movement in Belgium and France as the German army's Schlieffen Plan was initiated to win the war for the Kaiser in only six weeks. However, the plan failed and by October 1914 the opposing armies started digging 'temporary' defensive positions across Flanders and France. Soon, mobile warfare stagnated into military gridlock as parallel lines of trenches were constructed for more than four hundred miles from the Swiss border to the English Channel coast. During 1915 the static Western Front solidified as both sides reinforced their positions with successive lines of interconnected support trenches, protected by barbed wire entanglements – defence in depth. Any attempt to advance required a head-on assault across no man's land to capture an enemy front line in the face of determined resistance with small arms, machine gun and artillery fire. Although frontal attacks occasionally succeeded in taking the enemy's front line positions, defending troops soon rushed to plug the gaps and trench deadlock returned. This trench stalemate continued until 21 March 1918, when the great German Spring Offensive marked a return to mobile warfare.

In the meantime attempts to break the impasse on the Western Front achieved mixed results. The casualty figures of Britain's first major offensive on the Somme in July 1916 are well documented with more than 58,000 dead and wounded on the first day alone. However, the British Commander-in-Chief, Sir Douglas Haig had a plan. Having watched early trials of a new weapon, he saw huge potential in the untried "tanks" - so named as a ruse to confuse enemy spies. He hoped to use

137

them for the first time at the start of the Somme offensive, believing they would simply flatten the deep belts of German barbed wire and plough on regardless of German machine gun fire. Delays and production problems meant that only about forty tanks were available when he eventually sent them into action for the first time on 15 September 1916. Despite numerous mechanical problems these tanks achieved some success at Flers-Courcelette and justified Haig's confidence in their 'war-winning' potential. As the Somme fighting drew towards its costly close Haig appreciated that many more tanks were needed if a breakthrough on the Western Front was to be achieved. However, it would take many months to build sufficient numbers to make a decisive impact in the war. On 20 November 1917 more than 430 tanks were gathered together for a dramatic and dynamic attempt to smash through the German Hindenburg Line defences at Cambrai in northern France. The initial success of this tank-led attack and its advance of over five miles on a six mile front resulted in church bells being rung in celebration across Britain for the first time in the war. Yet a successful German counter-attack pushed the Allies back to their starting positions by 7 December. Even more tanks would be needed if they were to play a truly decisive role in winning the war.

In early November 1917 two "female" tanks were included in the Lord Mayor's Show in London and the reaction to them was duly noted by the National War Savings Committee. A "female" tank was armed with two machine guns in her side turrets – sponsons - whereas a "male" tank was armed with two 6-pounder canons. The public clamour for information about these "land ironclads" - a phrase coined by author H. G. Wells - quickly resulted in two "male" tanks being sent to London's Trafalgar Square to help boost sales in War Bonds and Savings Certificates. The success of these two tanks in persuading people to invest in the *"war winners"*, as Prime Minister Lloyd George described them, metamorphosed into 'Tank Weeks' or 'Tank Banks'. Across the country, towns and cities soon vied with each other to raise ever higher amounts in subscriptions for War Bonds and War Savings Certificates. Eventually there were more than one hundred and sixty of these events held across Great Britain.

The Tank Bank, After Business Hours

Tank 130 in Trafalgar Square – *Photo courtesy of the Chase Project.*

In late 1917 Richard Kindersley, head of the National War Savings Committee, capitalised on the reaction to the Tank Banks touring the country. He recognised an opportunity to reinvigorate the lacklustre response to the recent issue of War Bonds in a nation still hurting from the recent Passchendaele casualty figures. Battles such as this one - which had finally ground to a bloody and muddy halt on 10 November 1917 - could be avoided if fleets of "landships" were built to win the war by smashing through the German barbed wire and defences. Kindersley wanted the British public to invest their savings in a series of Tank Weeks and lend their money to the British Government to buy more tanks - each costing £5,000. Tank Weeks took place across the Midlands after Christmas 1917 and by early 1918 it was the turn of the citizens of Wolverhampton to 'do their bit.'

"Old Bill" in Nottingham and en route to Wolverhampton

The touring tanks were sometimes named after sweethearts or wives of crew members. More humorous examples included *"Creme de Menthe"* and *"Fray Bentos"* - a brand name well-known to the British Tommy. *"Hunkiller"* requires no explanation and *"Lusitania"* was named after the Cunard passenger liner torpedoed by a German U-boat on 7 May 1915. Of the other touring tanks *"Egbert"*, which sustained damage in the recent Battle of Cambrai, may have been named in honour of the King of Wessex who was victorious over the Mercians at the battle of Ellendun, in 819 A.D. *"Nelson"* was the victorious admiral at the Battle of Trafalgar, *"Iron Ration"* named after army slang for ammunition or the detested dried food that was supplied to soldiers and *"Drake"* was inspired by the Elizabethan seadog who triumphed over the Spanish Armada. The tank called *"Julian"* was probably named after General Julian Byng - the Third Army commander responsible for the successful tank-led attack at Cambrai, in November 1917. His troops were nicknamed *"The Byng Boys"* after a popular West-End show.

Tank number 119 - *"Old Bill"* - arrived at Wolverhampton on Sunday 3 February 1918. The name *"Old Bill"* came from Bruce Bairnsfather's cartoon character - famous from numerous postcards and immortalised in the musical production *"The Better Ole."* At Birmingham, in the first week of 1918, *"Old Bill"* had raised £6,585,439. This was enough to "pay for a day" of the war according to the British government estimate of a daily cost of £6,500,000. Afterwards *"Old Bill"* visited Nottingham (£2,635,000), Leicester (£2,061,228) The Potteries – now Stoke-on-Trent (£1,123,000) and Derby (£1,284,574) and the challenge was now on for Wolverhampton to do as well, if not better. *"Old Bill"* was met at Wolverhampton railway station goods yard by police, local volunteers, and members of the Women's Volunteer Reserve. The tank made a *"preliminary triumphal tour round the centre of the town"* before proceeding towards its pre-prepared position in Market Square, accompanied by music from the Police Band. Progress was slow as the enthusiastic crowd strained for a glimpse of the weapon they had read so much about - but few had seen. The procession eventually halted at the Town Hall and a hush fell upon the crowd when *"Old Bill"* was officially received by Mayor, Councillor John Francis Wyatt, Town Clerk Sir Horatio Brevitt, council members and representatives of neighbouring local authorities. The convoy continued to the open wholesale market, where a guard was positioned around its enclosure. All was ready for the start of Wolverhampton's Tank Week the next day.

On Monday morning Mayor Wyatt made the first speech from the top of *"Old Bill"* expressing the belief that Wolverhampton would raise more than £1 million and investing £25,000 from his own company, West End Brewery, later part of Ansell's brewing empire. The next speaker was Brigadier-General Thomas Edgecume Hickman DSO, MP for Wolverhampton Bilston, who appealed for all to: *"steel their hearts and tighten their belts"* and whose exhortation: *"Men, Munitions and Money!"* was chanted by the crowd. Mr. Alfred Bird, MP for Wolverhampton West, was unable to attend but £30,000 was invested on his behalf. The ladies from the town Post Office were kept busy stamping 'Tank Bank' on the Certificates and Bonds being issued and within fifteen minutes the first £100,000 had been reached. The decision to use "male" tanks for Tank Banks was sensibly pragmatic as the rear-facing hatches in the side sponsons were larger than those on "female tanks". Investments from Pearl Assurance and Eagle Star Assurance (£10,000 each) and Wolverhampton and District Permanent Building Society (£5,000) were augmented by payments from individuals such as Alderman Dickson (£2,000). By 6pm the total raised on the first day was £350,000. Other local firms came to the Tank Bank on Tuesday - Bayliss, Jones and Bayliss (which eventually became part of GKN) and Old Wolverhampton Breweries Ltd were the highest investors - each depositing £25,000. The Police Band and Volunteers' Band alternated in entertaining the crowd, but expectant heads turned and ears strained to hear music when a contingent of New Zealand Rifle Brigade troops arrived with their band as vanguard. Having completed a route march from Cannock Chase Reserve Centre, the band took up residence and played a variety of music from the wooden platform next to the tank, while the New Zealand riflemen stood guard with 'swords drawn' (bayonets fixed). Wednesday was market day and despite poor weather two large payments were made: one of £50,000 from Sunbeam Motor Car Company Ltd, who built motorcycles, ambulances, trucks and aeroplane engines and 647 aircraft for the war effort and another from Bradley Bar and Sheet Iron Company Ltd (£30,000). The Wolverhampton Board of Guardians, who were responsible for operating the Poor Law Union and managing the workhouse, invested £1,000 although the Wolverhampton branch of the Independent Labour Party passed a resolution against this payment questioning its legality.

By the morning of Saturday 9 February the £1 million target was smashed and the mayor received a congratulatory telegram from Mr Andrew Bonar Law, Chancellor of the Exchequer, offering *"BEST WISHES ON BEHALF OF THE GOVERNMENT."* The crowd cheered after the telegram was read out, and the band of the Leicestershire Regiment (again from Cannock Chase Reserve Centre) paraded through the streets before ending up on the tank platform. Mayor Fryatt shook hands with *"Old Bill's"* commander Lieutenant Brocklehurst and further cheering merged into the singing of the National Anthem. An hour later saw the return of the riflemen and band of the New Zealand Rifle Brigade, accompanied by their commanding officer, British-born Lieutenant Colonel J.G. Roache DSO. Then *Freda*, the harlequin Great Dane mascot of the NZRB, 'inspected' the riflemen as they took up position around the tank, much to the amusement of the crowd. The New Zealand band did, *"sterling work"* throughout the week, entertaining the crowd despite the weather - *"rough and boisterous with occasional showers."* The mayor, councillors and other dignitaries gave final speeches congratulating everyone for their efforts and at the close of business that evening, it was announced that Wolverhampton had raised the grand total of £1,410,872 (around £125 million today).

Floral tribute attached to *"Old Bill"* in Wolverhampton.

Overnight, tank Number 119 *"Old Bill"* departed for Coventry, adorned on the front with *"a red floral decoration in a horseshoe of artificial flowers presented to the Tank by a little Wolverhampton girl"*. In comparison, Walsall raised £832,000 during a four day visit of tank *"Julian"* in March, Dudley and Brierley Hill almost £1,200,000, Coventry £1,370,000, and Nottingham £2,635,000. The "battle scarred" *"Egbert"* tank was offered as a prize for the town with the highest per capita amount raised for War Bond sales. West Hartlepool won *"Egbert"* with an average of more than £37 per person - much to the annoyance of Glasgow which raised a total of more than £14,500,000. It could be argued that Prime Minister Lloyd George's claim that the tank was a "war winner" on the battlefield is somewhat exaggerated. However, the tank was certainly a major contributor to Britain's financial ability to keep on fighting until the end of the war. More importantly support for Tank Banks showed soldiers abroad that people on the Home Front were buying War Bonds and War Saving Certificates to help them get home more quickly. There is a misconception that civilians did not fully understand what was happening in the mud and blood of Flanders and France - and to a certain extent this is correct. However, civilians realised that War Bonds would buy tanks and tanks would overcome German defences and barbed wire. The war would be won. Their husbands, brothers, sisters, fathers, sons and daughters could come home. The logic was obvious to the citizens of Wolverhampton and elsewhere who unanimously united in their support. British newspapers were sent to troops in France, Belgium and Italy and their contents were devoured avidly within days of being printed. Versions of national daily and weekly newspapers were available in neutral countries, such as Holland, and some even reached Germany, where people could read about the tremendous amounts being raised at these British Tank Weeks. Daily reports on the initial four, then six (eventually seven) touring Tank Banks greatly encouraged war-weary troops, as can be seen by the letters printed in local newspapers in the weeks following Wolverhampton's Tank Week. This mutually reciprocal encouragement resulted in more than £135 million being collected in War Loans between November 1917 and June 1918. More importantly the ability to raise credit abroad (on Wall Street for example) was unequivocal. The concept spread to the Dominion allies: Canada, South Africa, Australia and New Zealand, all of whom held their own Tank Weeks. The tank *"Britannia"* even toured America, successfully encouraging investors to participate in the sale of $2 billion worth of Liberty Bonds - an issue oversubscribed by fifty per cent. Perhaps the tank was a war-winning weapon in more ways than one.

"Old Bill" arrives in Coventry

Chapter 13

The 1918-19 Influenza Pandemic in the Black Country

David Taylor

Introduction

The worldwide influenza pandemic that occurred in the years 1918 and 1919 has attracted increasing attention in the last ten years for two main reasons. Firstly, recognition that similar pandemics of influenza or other diseases are still possible - the outbreaks of 'Swine Flu', 2009-2010, and Ebola in West Africa, 2014-2015, being recent examples. Secondly, historians are examining a wider range of issues associated with the impact of the First World War and its immediate aftermath. The scale of the 1918-19 global pandemic has been subject to a wide range of estimates due mainly to the lack of accurate contemporary information. In Britain this is less of an issue, although there is still a substantial spread in the estimates. Immediately after the outbreak the Registrar General, Sir Bernard Mallet, was requested to provide a statistical report on what happened, which he published in 1920.[226] He came to the conclusion that approximately 184,000 civilians died in the influenza pandemic in England and Wales.[227] More recent estimates have settled at about 200,000 deaths - a reasonably similar number given the difficulties in calculating such a figure.[228] Mallet stated in his opening paragraph that this was the worst death rate of any disease since detailed records were first kept in 1836. In England and Wales a clear chronological progression of three separate waves was visible with peaks in July 1918, November 1918 and March 1919. Other countries showed a similar pattern with some variations in intensity. In broad terms the causes and processes of any pandemic are well understood. Three factors need to coincide. Firstly, a new virus with the right characteristics of contagiousness, incubation and deadliness has to appear. Secondly, public health actions need to be inadequate or inappropriate to deal with the primary characteristics of the virus. Thirdly, a sufficiently large number of people have to travel substantial distances in a relatively short time period. These factors came together in the years 1918 and 1919 and form the focus of this investigation into the impact of the influenza pandemic in the Black Country.

Firstly, the source of the new virus in Europe has been widely commented upon, with France and the USA being the most often implicated. It appears that the

---

[226] Sir Bernard Mallet, *Supplement to the Eighty First Report of the Registrar General of Births, Deaths and Marriages in England and Wales: Report on the Mortality from Influenza in England and Wales during the Epidemic of 1918-19, Cmd 700*, (HM Stationery Office, 1920).
[227] Supplement to the Eighty First Report, p.7.
[228] N P A S Johnson, *The Overshadowed Killer: Influenza in Britain in 1918-19*, ch9 in Howard Phillips and David Killingray (eds) *The Spanish Influenza Pandemic Of 1918-19: New Perspectives* (Routledge, 2003) p.136.

first official recordings of a new influenza type disease were made in military camps in the USA. This was quickly followed by army medical staff of all nationalities, Central Powers and Allies, noting a strange new influenza type illness in France. Its spread to Britain has been identified through two broad routes. Firstly, directly from the USA when American servicemen landed in Liverpool and other northern and western ports on their way to training camps in Britain. Secondly from Europe, when British servicemen returned due to leave, injuries or the effects of the disease itself, landed in the southern ports on their way to hospitals and destinations all over the country. These two different routes meant that there was a two pronged influx of the disease into Britain, causing substantial anomalies in its rate and direction of travel.

Academic Interest

There has been an unusual combination of academic interests examining the 1918-19 influenza pandemic. Medical scientists, public health specialists, historians, geographers and statisticians have all examined various aspects of the pandemic. Questions raised have been wide-ranging. For example, what exactly was the disease? Where did it originate? What were its characteristics which allowed it to spread so widely and be so deadly? What environmental characteristics were involved? What steps were taken to combat the pandemic and why were they unsuccessful? How can we be better prepared for a future pandemic? What were the short and long-term outcomes of the pandemic?[229] The editors of *'The Spanish Influenza Pandemic Of 1918-19: New Perspectives'* noted in their introduction that the *'brevity of the pandemic ... posed great problems to doctors at the time ... [and to] historians ever since.'*[230] Further, it has been said that the *'universality of the pandemic has rendered "trivial" local variations'* in mortality rates, but that is not to say that there are no local variations deserving investigation.[231] Geographical variations in mortality rates in England and Wales were identified at the time and commented on, but in general they were not systematically investigated.[232] In 1920 Sir Bernard Mallet's report noted that districts in close proximity could suffer very different mortality rates.[233] Local investigations concentrated on two general topics. The first was to gain more information on what occurred - for example the studies on Leicester, Manchester, South Shields, Blackburn, Wigan and Widnes carried out by George Newman in his *'Reports On Public Health And Medical Subjects No. 4 Report On The Pandemic Of Influenza, 1918-19'*. The second was to investigate specific hypotheses of possible methods of reducing the impact of the disease. Few

---

[229] For a review of the academic interest in the subject see Howard Phillips and David Killingray 'Forwards and Introduction', in Howard Phillips and David Killingray (eds) *The Spanish Influenza Pandemic Of 1918-19 : New Perspectives* (Routledge, 2003).
[230] Howard Phillips and David Killingray, New Perspectives.
[231] Johnson, *Overshadowed Killer*, op. cit., p.132.
[232] Supplement to the Eighty First Report, p.12. The Registrar General is more specific in his comment on the variation of mortality rate at the local level. Commenting on the high mortality rates in Bacup and Rawtenstall in comparison to other local towns. George Newman, *Reports On Public Health and Medical Subjects. No. 4. Report On The Pandemic Of Influenza, 1918-19* (HM Stationery Office, 1920), pxiii. His comment that there was 'considerable local variations in periodicity, incidence, and case mortality' is directed more at differences between the three waves rather than specifically between localities overall.
[233] Supplement to the Eighty First Report, p.26.

tangible positive results have been produced since to explain the geographical variations in mortality rates. Large and small-scale studies have found few consistent reasons for this variation. For example, a study of two parishes in the Norwegian capital Kristiania, modern day Oslo, showed that once controlled for age, sex and marital status, *'apartment size as an indicator of wealth of a household, in addition to social status of place of residence, were the only socioeconomic variables that had an independent and significant effect on mortality.'* However, larger scale studies, such as those undertaken by the Registrar General Mallet in 1920, showed little correlation between wealth and health.[234]

In Britain little work has been done until recently on the geographic characteristics of the pandemic.[235] This point was emphasised by Gerardo Chowell et al in their 2008 study.[236] They noted that: *'local factors, including geographical and demographic characteristics, could play a role in disease transmissibility [and thus mortality rates]'.* However, their analysis concludes with little insight into what these 'geographical and demographic characteristics' might be. Chowell's study confirmed that the disease moved hierarchically through the population centres, striking the large population centres first. He concluded that these findings, along with the short timescales within which the majority of districts were first affected, were due to: *'strong population mixing and the small geographical extent of this region [England and Wales]'.* He finished by noting that an: *'important residual variability in ... death rates remained unexplained in our study'.* Chowell and his team speculated that it was *'unlikely that local differences in population age structure or public health interventions could have played a role.'*[237] Niall Johnson has identified the importance of communication routes, especially railways, in the spread of the disease in Britain, which might provide an explanation for this *'residual variability'.*[238] This chapter seeks to partially fill this gap by providing an in-depth review of the influenza pandemic in the Black Country county boroughs of Dudley, Smethwick, Walsall, West Bromwich and Wolverhampton, specifically exploring the anomalous mortality rate experienced in Dudley. Based on data from all county boroughs, the Black Country had the third worst mortality rate in the regions of England and Wales, after South Yorkshire and Tyneside.[239] Table 1 provides the summary and Appendix 1 the details of this calculation.

---

[234] S. E. Mamelund, 'A socially neutral disease? Individual social class, household wealth and mortality from Spanish influenza in two socially contrasting parishes in Kristiania 1918–19', *Social Science and Medicine* vol.62 (2006) 923–940. doi:10.1016/j.socscimed.2005.06.051.

[235] Johnson, *Overshadowed Killer*, op. cit., p.146.

[236] Gerardo Chowell, Luís M.A Bettencourt, Niall Johnson, Wladimir J Alonso, Cécile Viboud, 'The 1918–1919 influenza pandemic in England and Wales: spatial patterns in transmissibility and mortality impact', *Proceedings Of The Royal Society Biological Sciences* (2008). doi: 10.1098/rspb.2007.1477.

[237] Chowell et al.

[238] Johnson, *Overshadowed Killer*, op.cit, p.148.

[239] The data source for all statistics, unless specified otherwise are the Registrar General's Supplement to the Eighty First Report, Table XX, pages 51 to 80 and Table IX, p.24.

The Black Country Experience

Map 1: The Black Country and Birmingham

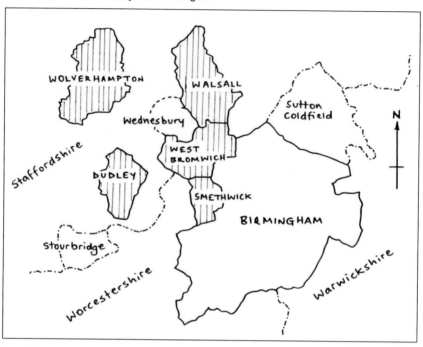

Map 1 shows the Black Country county boroughs and other places mentioned in this chapter. The distance between Smethwick and Wolverhampton is 13.5 miles with the average distance between the other five county boroughs being 8 miles.

Table 1: Mortality Rate by Region[240]

Cluster	Annualised Mortality Rate (per thousand of population)
South Yorkshire	6.44
Tyneside	6.08
Black Country	5.96
All county boroughs	5.10

Birmingham, the largest county borough contiguous with the Black Country, had a mortality rate of 4.10, substantially lower than its neighbour. The weekly profile of the disease, based on an annualised mortality rate, shows the importance of the second wave of October to December 1918 in the overall pandemic, especially in the Black Country. See Chart 1.

---

[240] See Appendix 1 for details on the calculation.

Chart 1: Weekly Annualised Mortality Rates for the Black Country and all County Boroughs.

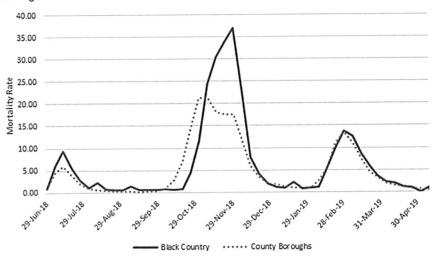

However, this general mortality rate in the Black Country was not replicated uniformly and Table 2 shows that there was a marked difference between Dudley and the other four county boroughs.

Table 2: Mortality Rates by Black Country County Borough

County Borough	Annualised Mortality Rate (per thousand of population)	Ranking In All County Boroughs
West Bromwich	7.70	2
Wolverhampton	6.80	4
Walsall	5.80	19
Smethwick	5.10	38
Dudley	3.60	77
Black Country	5.96	-

The chronological profile of the disease for Dudley reflects the anomalous mortality rate shown in Chart 2. It was the lowest in each of the three waves and its wave started later than any of the others, markedly so for the important second wave, although its drop-off at the end of the second wave was slightly longer.

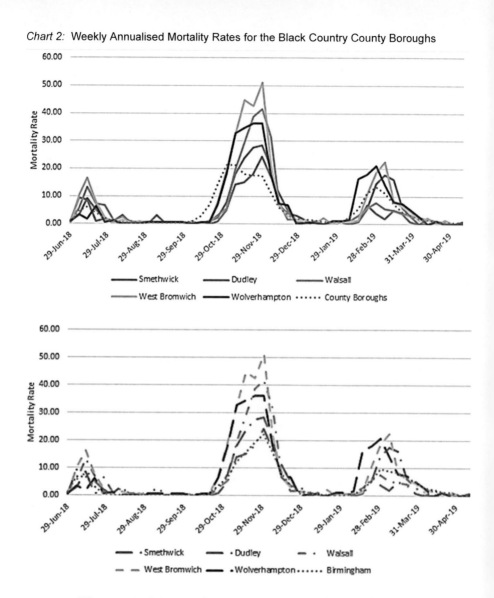

Chart 2: Weekly Annualised Mortality Rates for the Black Country County Boroughs

What caused these differences? – Eliminating Issues

The first concern of the Registrar General when analysing the mortality rates was the accuracy of the information provided by the local Medical Officers of Health (MOsH) on the deaths caused by influenza. He was aware that *'during influenza epidemics the mortality attributed to the disease does not represent the whole caused by it.* [241] The Registrar General concluded that at a country level the returns

[241] Supplement to the Eighty First Report, p.3.

from MOsH would have to be increased by approximately 43,000 or 30.0 per cent to reflect the full mortality rate from the pandemic. This adjustment was mainly due to the inevitable allocation of cause of death to different diseases, given the interaction between influenza and other diseases such as pneumonia. He made no comment on the accuracy of individual districts and his analysis was based on the returns adding up to 140,989 civilian deaths. The first question therefore needs to be whether Dudley's anomalous performance was due to under-reporting of influenza-related deaths. This can be examined by looking at the overall mortality rate for the Black Country county boroughs, as shown in Chart 3.

Chart 3: Overall Mortality Rates for the Black Country County Boroughs[242]

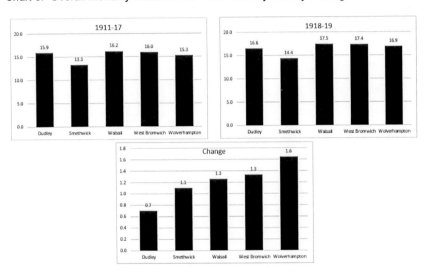

As can be seen, Dudley's average overall mortality rate of 15.9 in the years 1911-1917 was average for the five county boroughs, whereas for the years 1918-1919 it was slightly below average. This can be highlighted by the change in the mortality rate shown in the bottom graph of Chart 3. Dudley's increase in overall mortality rate was the lowest by a significant amount. It was less than two thirds of the next lowest, Smethwick, and less than half of the highest, Wolverhampton. This indicates that Dudley's anomalous influenza related mortality rate was not due to substantial under-reporting by local MOsH. The Registrar General considered a number of possible causes for differences in the mortality rates between districts - including primarily wealth and health - and came to the conclusion that these did not explain the variations.[243] This finding has been confirmed by Chowell et al who discerned no difference in county borough mortality rates due to *'measures of population density or residential crowding.'*[244] However, it should be noted that the

---

[242] Data sources : Local Government Board Medical Officer of Health Annual Reports 1911 to 1919, (HM Stationery Office).
[243] Supplement to the Eighty First Report, pp.27-30.
[244] Chowell et al.

149

Wolverhampton MOH, Dr Henry Malet, drew attention to the difference between East and West Wolverhampton in his Report in 1919. In East Wolverhampton - a *'poor and crowded district'* – the influenza mortality rate was 2.44, whereas in West Wolverhampton – a *'better one'* – it was 1.52. He noted this *'contrast remains almost more marked than ever.'*[245] Further Dr Harry Shore, MOH for Walsall, expressed similar but unsupported views that the pandemic was worst felt in working class areas affected by overcrowding, a *'vitiated atmosphere...physical fatigue from war conditions'* and *'lack of accustomed food.'*[246] Analysis of the Black Country county boroughs seems to support the general conclusion, rather than Dr Malet's, as shown in Table 3.

Table 3: Measures of Population Density and Crowding in the Black Country County Boroughs.[247]

	Dudley	Smethwick	Walsall	West Bromwich	Wolver hampton
1921 Census:					
Population Density	12.9	31.1	10.3	10.2	23.1
Families per Dwelling	1.03	1.06	1.07	1.04	1.06
Rooms per Family	4.11	3.08	4.50	4.18	4.65
1911 Census:					
Average Family Size	4.2	4.0	4.1	4.3	3.9
Percentage Crowded Dwellings	13.5	10.9	11.4	12.9	11.0
Area (acres)	3,546	1,929	7,483	5,859	3,525

Dudley's population density was substantially lower than Smethwick or Wolverhampton while it was slightly higher than that in Walsall and West Bromwich. The 'families per dwelling' rating in Dudley was the lowest of all the county boroughs but not by a significant amount. The average number of rooms per family in Dudley was lower than for three of the county boroughs, but significantly higher than that for Smethwick. Similarly, based on the 1911 census, the average family size was similar across the five county boroughs. The lack of consistency in these measures can be shown by the percentage of dwellings that could be considered crowded, with more than one person per room in the dwelling. This was significantly higher in Dudley, at 13.5, which intuitively would be expected to have encouraged the spread of the disease, and therefore increased Dudley's mortality rate rather than decrease it. Finally, Dudley's area of 3,546 acres meant that the other county boroughs were as

[245] Wolverhampton Medical Officer of Health 1919 Report, p.14, https://wellcomelibrary.org/item/b30289397.
[246] Walsall Medical Officer of Health 1918 Report, p.20, https://wellcomelibrary.org/item/b30230196.
[247] Data source, Supplement to the Eighty First Report and the 1911 and 1921 censuses as presented on http://www.visionofbritain.org.uk (accessed in January 2018).

easy to travel around and to provide medical cover for. It is difficult to discern a combination of factors which might explain Dudley's lower mortality rate. Even removing workhouses and other civilian institutions from the figures makes no appreciable difference to the findings, primarily because their numbers were too low.

If socio-geographic characteristics do not explain the variations, it is possible that different measures were taken in Dudley to combat the disease. Tomkins and others, including the British medical authorities at the time, came to the conclusion that the influenza pandemic represented a failure in public health management.[248] Whether their conclusions were fair is beyond the scope of this chapter.[249] However, it does raise the hypothesis that perhaps Dudley's performance represented a different, or more thorough, approach to combating the disease. The official guidelines from the Local Government Board (LGB) were not formally issued until 22 October 1918. These were given to the various MOsH who then passed them on to their council committees.[250] The LGB response to the outbreak was piece-meal as well as late. For example, the initial regulation was that public performances in places of entertainment, such as cinemas and theatres, were to be for no more than three consecutive hours, followed by a thirty-minute gap to air the building. Only two days later this 'instruction' was altered to four hours.[251] Other features of LGB advice concentrated on avoiding crowds, especially for children. Therefore, schools were closed if the local MOH and council committee believed it was necessary and children could also be barred from places of entertainment, especially cinemas. The other major feature of the advice was self-help, as shown in the advice that: *'at the first sign of catarrhal attack and every illness associated with a rise of temperature, go to bed, keep warm, eat a balanced diet and isolate oneself as much as possible.'* Plenty of fresh air was highly recommended for everyone. Medical staff were told to take precautions such as wearing a face mask when attending a patient.[252] There was a warning *'that the fever attacks the victim for at least four days and it can take a week or more to recover after an attack'*, therefore not to overexert oneself after a bout of illness. Finally, it was advised that the use of a nasal, mouth or hand wash might be of assistance in avoiding contracting the disease, and premises might be

---

[248] Sandra M. Tomkins, 'The Failure of Expertise: Public Health Policy in Britain during the 1918—19 Influenza Epidemic', *Social History of Medicine*, Vol.5, Iss.3,(1992) 435–454. For contemporary analysis see *The British Medical Journal*, 1 November 1919, p.570. See also *The British Medical Journal*, 25 October 1919, p.541, for a gloomy assessment of preparedness to deal with another outbreak in the near future.

[249] It should be noted that knowledge, at the time, of the microbiology of influenza was extremely limited. Some medical scientists thought they were dealing with a bacteria, Pfeiffer's bacillus was often cited, but it was noted that pneumococci, streptococci and pneumobacilli were often mentioned as being associated with the disease. Others disagreed and said that the microorganism responsible for influenza had not yet been discovered. Viruses, which were little understood, were beyond the technology of the time to investigate. See articles in The British Medical Journal, 8 June 1918, p.653; 30 November 1918, p.610; 14 December 1918, p.665; and 2 November 1918, p.494.

[250] Joan Knight, *The social impact of the influenza pandemic of 1918-19: with special reference to the East Midlands*. PhD thesis, University of Nottingham (2014) p.211.

[251] Niall Johnson, *Britain and the 1918-19 Influenza Pandemic: A Dark Epilogue* (Routledge 2006) p.128.

[252] Some of this advice was issued in a piece meal fashion as the pandemic developed and the medical profession searched for anything that might help the situation. Face masks were not mentioned until the 9 November 1918 by The British Medical Journal p.522.

disinfected.[253] At the time this advice was generally viewed by the medical authorities as sensible in the circumstances.[254]

In reviewing the actions of the medical and local authorities in the important second wave, these guidelines appear to have been uniformly implemented across the five county boroughs. In Wolverhampton, some schools were closed on the 21 and 22 October as a precautionary measure and because measles as well as influenza was apparent in the local community.[255] All schools in Walsall were closed towards to the end of October until the 11 November.[256] By 5 November, Wolverhampton MOH, Dr Malet, advised that all schools in the borough should be closed until the 18 November. Wolverhampton's Sunday Schools, operated independently by local churches, generally followed the same advice given by the MOH. Children were excluded from many places of amusement and limitations on performances were also enacted.[257] Cinemas were specifically targeted, which some turned to their advantage. For instance, the Queen's Picture House in Wolverhampton described itself as: 'The healthiest place in town.' In order to justify its claim the new 'hours of opening 2 to 5 and 6:30 to 10:30' were advertised to demonstrate how they were complying with official advice.[258] It would appear that Bilston UDC considered going even further than the official advice when they decided to ask cinema proprietors 'to discontinue children's performances [altogether] during the epidemic.'[259] However, if this was implemented, it appeared to make no difference to health of the town's citizens. Of the 161 towns in England and Wales with populations of more than 20,000, Bilston had the seventh highest mortality rate. There are no other examples of Black Country councils considering proposals to go beyond the general guidelines and take steps to close all places where the general public might assemble. A debate held in a council meeting at nearby Cannock succinctly summarised opinions held in the Black Country. When Cannock's MOH, Dr Clendinnen, suggested that 'all places of amusement should be asked to temporarily close,' Councillor Mr J. R. Winterton responded that 'if cinemas were closed places of worship would have to be closed as well.' Another councillor added that 'public houses' would be shut down too. Dr Clendinnen and others were 'instructed to make further inquiries and report to a future meeting of the council.'[260] In the meantime public meetings across the Black Country continued as normal and,

---

[253] There was severe criticism of the President of the Local Government Board, W. Hayes Fisher, for not taking the warnings from the June and July outbreak to plan for the widely expected early winter outbreak. The Medical Research Committee, an advisory body to the Local Government Board, published in the first week of August 1918 a resume stating that a second wave of greater severity was likely, see Hansard, 5 November 1918, report from Sir EDWIN CORNWALL, representing the National Health Insurance Commissioners and the Medical Research Committee. See the British Medical Journal, 2 November 1918, p.494 for comments on the expectation of a second wave; and 15 February 1919, p.195 regarding the expectation of the third wave. See Joan Knight Thesis p.210 for a fuller review of the performance of the Local Government Board in the pandemic and medical warnings.
[254] The British Medical Journal, 19 October 1918, p.440; and 26 October 1918, p.473.
[255] Wolverhampton Express & Star, 23 October 1918.
[256] Ibid, 30 October 1918.
[257] Ibid, 25 November 1918.
[258] Ibid, 25 November 1918.
[259] Ibid, 29 November 1918.
[260] Ibid, 6 November 1918.

just before the second influenza wave arrived in Dudley, a widely advertised meeting was held in the Congregational church to raise funds for the war effort.[261] In practice, even more public meetings were actually held and the Armistice on 11 November was an occasion when very large numbers of people gathered in crowded public spaces. Thanksgiving services were held all across the region and nearly every church held an event of some sort to mark the event. These took place either on the day itself or those following and especially on Sunday 24 November.[262] In Dudley it was reported that 11 November *'became a general holiday, men "downed" tools, factories closed and children were released from schools. That evening there was a torchlight progression to the Castle Grounds, with a display of fireworks. There were huge crowds in the Market Place during most of the day'.*[263] This situation then continued after the Armistice because large electioneering meetings took place across the Black Country when the month long General Election campaign was announced on 14 November.[264]

Communication of advice about the spread of influenza was promulgated throughout the local community in a variety of ways but, again, with no apparent substantial differences across the Black Country. The *Wolverhampton Express and Star* summarised the advice from the LGB as: *'The only safe rule is to regard all catarrhal attacks and every illness associated with a rise of temperature during the prevalence of influenza, as infectious...They should go to bed and stay there for three or four days.'*[265] There was obviously some appreciation of this guidance among members of the general public judging by the various letters sent to the editor of the *Express and Star*. These commented on the *'deplorable lack of ventilation'* on crowded trains and trams and suggested that their windows and doors should be fixed open.[266] One letter to the editor addressed the subject of *'Coughing in Church'*. The writer had attended a recent thanksgiving service in Wolverhampton and was *'horrified at the seeming carelessness of a large number of the members of the congregation. Cough! Cough! Cough! And in the majority of the cases direct into the atmosphere without covering their mouths. The place for these people is by their own fire sides – not in a crowded public building.'*[267]

It appears that strategies to combat the disease, as reported in the local newspapers and elsewhere, were roughly similar in each of the Black Country county boroughs. This raises the question of whether there were any differences in the vigour with which different MOsH and local authorities approached the pandemic? A study of the disease in American cities has shown that the speed, vigour and persistence in local authority responses to the outbreak were vitally important in

---

[261] *Dudley Herald*, 28 September 1918.
[262] *Wolverhampton Express & Star*, 18 November 1918.
[263] *Dudley Herald*, 28 December 1918.
[264] *Dudley Herald*, 14 December 1918.
[265] *Wolverhampton Express & Star*, 23 October 1918.
[266] Ibid, 2 December 1918.
[267] Ibid, 18 November 1918.

curtailing the mortality rate.[268]   Nevertheless, the experience in Alaska should be noted regarding the effectiveness of public health actions. Alaska had a high level of natural isolation from the main population movements at the time and the authorities were able to impose a stringent set of public health policies promoting that isolation. Yet in spite of these factors, the pandemic eventually reached Alaska with particularly devastating results.[269]   It is difficult to make a definitive judgement about the efficiency of the Black Country's MOsH and local authorities because there is little information available. The evidence that survives is mainly comments made by the officials themselves, as recorded in local newspapers and in their own official reports. These comments may reflect differences in approach but they may reflect only a public message, rather than private efforts and overall abilities. In the Black Country it appears a lack of speed and persistence was consistent across the five county boroughs, although there is no suggestion this approach was any different to officials across the country as a whole. Walsall MOH, Dr Shore, reportedly stated the mortality rate in Walsall had remained *'pretty normal'* whilst in other towns it had *'jumped up somewhat alarmingly.'*[270] However, Walsall was one of the first of the five county boroughs to close all its schools at the end of October. This suggests Dr Shore was relatively prompt in his responses to the pandemic once its presence became apparent in the borough. In comparison, Wolverhampton and Dudley did not close their schools until around 6 November, despite the pandemic starting in Wolverhampton at least two weeks earlier than Walsall.[271] In contrast, it was not until 10 December, just as the key second wave was finishing, that Walsall set up *a 'special emergency committee'* to take *'all possible steps to counter act the epidemic'*. There is no evidence that other county boroughs went that far, relying instead on the existing committees of the council and their normal arrangements to organise responses to the pandemic. Wolverhampton Borough Council's minutes for the period contain only four references to influenza. Two noted that it was referred to in Health Committee reports and two were about the imposition and then relaxation of the Public Health Act (Influenza) Regulations 1918, dated 9 December 1918 and 10 February 1919 respectively.[272]   Dr Malet, MOH for Wolverhampton, took his annual holidays in August 1918, which might suggest there was a more relaxed approach to dealing with the pandemic in that town than Walsall.[273] This could also explain why Wolverhampton's mortality rate was greater than Walsall's by 1.0 per thousand of population. However, this is a very small base upon which to establish such an hypothesis. Further, if a correspondingly greater effort was made in Dudley to produce its much lower mortality rate, it is difficult to imagine this would not have attracted contemporary comment in the Press and elsewhere. Typical of the many summaries of actions taken nearby was that of Dr Wilkinson in Cannock. His report

---

[268] Jason Socrates Bardi, 'Rapid Response was Crucial to Containing the 1918 Flu Pandemic', *US National Institutes Of Health* (2007) https://www.nih.gov/news-events/news-releases/rapid-response-was-crucial-containing-1918-flu-pandemic.

[269] Knight, p.107, referencing Alfred W. Crosby, America's Forgotten Pandemic, Cambridge University Press, 2003, Cambridge, pp. 231-232.

[270] *Wolverhampton Express & Star*, 5 November 1918.

[271] Ibid, 30 October and 5 November 1918.

[272] Wolverhampton Archives Wol – C – Cou/16 Wolverhampton Borough Corporation Minute Book No.16.

[273] Wolverhampton Archives D-TET/3/1 Signed minutes of committees (1918 - 1919, 1939 - 1966).

for 1918 stated that: *'There appears to be no real prevention'* of influenza and that the best treatment is to *'remain in bed while the fever lasts.'*[274]

There is no evidence to suggest that Dudley had more resources than the other Black Country boroughs. The shortage of medical staff was apparent across the region and the country, where skilled personnel were mainly deployed on military matters such as tending to wounded soldiers or assessing potential recruits to the armed forces.[275] At the Coseley District Council meeting in early August 1918 the shortage of doctors in the area was debated. One suggestion was to *'petition the army for the return of one of the doctors'* called up by the army.[276] The difficulty of redirecting medical staff from military to civilian matters was illustrated in a report in the *Express and Star* on 20 December 1918. This stated that the process would be implemented *'once the general demobilisation is underway'*, to give *'preference'* to *'experienced doctors'* from *'districts under the greatest shortage'* but that they will be replaced in the army by *'new and not yet qualified doctors'*. However, this inevitably meant the pandemic would be over by the time they returned to their civilian roles. Dudley suffered from the same pressures on medical resources as other boroughs, including the loss of key staff due to the sickness. Dr Smith, a local doctor in Quarry Bank, on the south-east border of Dudley, contracted influenza and was forced to go *'to his father's house in Derbyshire for a short rest'*.[277] Similarly, Dr Shore, Walsall's MOH, reported that *'nurses were included'* in the recent death toll and that *'several of the nurses at the hospital'* were ill with influenza.[278]

As for other potential causes for the anomaly in the Dudley mortality rate, the evidence points in different directions. For example Walsall appeared to have better resources than Dudley - even though its mortality rate was higher.   The Walsall Victoria Nursing Institute committee reported that it had made arrangements to use the very limited local nursing staff - six district nurses and four school nurses - as efficiently as possible. They visited patients *'2 or 3 times daily,'* to help with *'feeding and general care'* and the committee reported that *'4,308 visits were paid by the nurses'*.[279] In contrast, in Dudley, there were long-running complaints about the poor management of one of the town's major medical institutions: the Guest Hospital. A local newspaper questioned whether *'the Management of the Guest Hospital [is] archaic?'* and whether *'archaism'* was responsible for cutting the *'number of beds from 100 to 50'*?[280] In addition, public health provision in Dudley operated under two constraints in 1918. Firstly, for most of that year the MOH was only a part-time position - not becoming full-time until October. This was considered so important that the MOH's report at the end of 1918 said that *'the employment of a whole-time Medical Officer of Health'* was the *'most important matter'* that the committee had to

---

[274] Dudley Medical Officer of Health 1918 Report, p.17, https://dlcs.io/pdf/wellcome/pdf-item/b2917093x/0.
[275] Johnson, *A Dark Epilogue*, p.130.
[276] *Dudley Herald*, 17 August 1918.
[277] *Dudley Herald*, 27 July 1918.
[278] *Wolverhampton Express & Star*, 5 November 1918.
[279] Ibid, 20 December 1918.
[280] *Dudley Herald*, 6 July 1918.

deal with in the year. Secondly, Dr J. Howard Wilkinson, the MOH at the beginning of 1918, retired in September.[281] During September the recruitment of a replacement was not completed and a point of procedure threatened to delay the process.[282] At the October meeting of the council it was confirmed that the appointment of Dr C. W. Hutt had been made. However, when the mayor was asked when the doctor would start work, the reply was: *'[I do] not know the exact date, but that he had been here the other day'*.[283] Within three months Dr Hutt had resigned and was not replaced until early 1919, with Dr Wilkinson standing in until a new appointment was made.[284] While it is not possible to draw a definitive conclusion from this evidence there is a strong suggestion that contrasts between the effectiveness of the different MOsH was not responsible for the differences in mortality rates. If anything, Dudley appeared to be less well organised than the other local boroughs, and changing its medical personnel in the middle of the pandemic ought to have produced a higher, not lower, mortality rate.

One other explanation can be discounted. Some researchers have suggested influenza entered Britain through soldiers returning from Western Europe and as Dudley was not a military borough, this explains the low mortality rate.[285] If this theory was credible it would be expected that Cannock Urban District, with its substantial military presence, would have a higher mortality rate. While Cannock's rate was 5.70 - which was higher than Dudley's at 3.60 - it was also lower than the rates for the non-military boroughs of Walsall, West Bromwich and Wolverhampton. Therefore, the returning soldiers theory is unproven in explaining the variations in local mortality rates.

Was The Railway Network The Reason For The Anomaly?

The thesis that the national railway/communication network was the main conduit for the spread of the pandemic has been developed by Niall Johnson.[286] Once in the regions local transport networks spread the disease still further.[287] Finally, personal networks of contacts completed the transmission process. This thesis has been widely shown to be effective in describing the spread of the disease at a national or regional level. However, its efficacy in explaining its transmission at the micro level has not yet been systematically investigated. The ideal information required to test the thesis at county borough level would be the numbers of passengers travelling on each part of the transport network and which stations they used. Unfortunately, this information is not available and the quantitative data that does exist is a poor substitute. The number of locations that a county borough was directly linked to in a local network was likely to be high - which was the case in the

---

[281] Ibid, 29 June 1918.
[282] Ibid, 14 September 1918.
[283] Ibid, 5 October 1918.
[284] Dudley Medical Officer of Health 1918 Report, opening remarks, https://dlcs.io/pdf/wellcome/pdf-item/b2917093x/0.
[285] Dudley Medical Officer of Health 1918 Report, https://dlcs.io/pdf/wellcome/pdf-item/b2917093x/0.
[286] Johnson, *Overshadowed Killer*, op. cit., p.149.
[287] Johnson, *Dark Epilogue*, op. cit., p.47.

Black Country. Only West Bromwich and Walsall, West Bromwich and Dudley, and Walsall and Smethwick had no direct rail links. Further, all the county boroughs were linked via Wolverhampton and Birmingham - the two major network hubs of the region. Another measure would be the number of trains which ran between each location, but this is unsatisfactory for a number of reasons. The number of passengers boarding or alighting at a particular station was only one reason for running a train along a particular route. Other reasons included a desire to connect other stations along the line, or simply to re-position trains for a busier service. Also the measure assumes that each train should be equally weighted in the number of passengers using each station. As Table 4 shows the number of trains that visited each of the county borough stations per day from Mondays to Saturdays does not help to explain Dudley's anomalous mortality rate.

Table 4: Number of Trains Visiting Each Station

County Borough	Number of Trains Per Day (Except Sunday)
West Bromwich	47
Wolverhampton	105
Walsall	48
Smethwick	48
Dudley	40

Source : National Railway Museum, York, Archives, Bradshaw Timetable 1918.

Instead, looking at the layout of the railway network in general might produce a more qualitative approach to explain Dudley's statistical deviation. Map 2 shows the railway network across the Black Country for the two main companies in the region - the London and North Western (LNWR) and Great Western (GWR). For clarity, the Midland Railway (MR) which had only a small presence in the area - primarily linking Wolverhampton to Walsall and thence to Birmingham via a circuitous route - has been excluded from the map. Map 2 highlights three characteristics of the network which might indicate an explanation for Dudley's relatively low mortality rate. Firstly, there were essentially four main railway routes across the region, anchored on Wolverhampton and Birmingham; two for each company. Other railway lines were primarily based on portions of these main routes: the LNWR's two routes from Birmingham to Wolverhampton were via Walsall and Smethwick and the GWR's were via West Bromwich and Dudley. Of the four routes, the GWR's Dudley route and the LNWR's Walsall route were longer than the other two with the Dudley route being by far the longest and most circuitous. This suggests that passengers travelling between Birmingham and Wolverhampton were unlikely to choose either of these, especially the GWR Dudley route.

Secondly, Walsall and Dudley might be described as 'outliers' on this network. To the north Walsall was connected to Burton upon Trent and Stoke via the MR and North Staffordshire Railway. To the south Dudley was connected to Worcester via

157

the GWR. The marked difference between the two locations was that Walsall's links were to places with higher mortality rates. Specifically, Burton had a mortality rate of 8.7 and Stoke 6.5, whereas Worcester's was 4.9. Generally, mortality rates were higher in the north than the south and Staffordshire was identified by the Registrar General as being on the borderline between the two regions of England. Thirdly, West Bromwich and Smethwick were centrally placed on the railway network which suggests they were relatively well used by passengers of both the LNWR and GWR.

Map 2: The Railway Network of the Black Country showing the main lines of the LNWR and GWR.

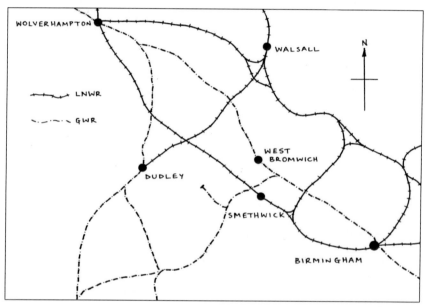

Source : W.P. Conolly, *British Railways Pre-Grouping Atlas and Gazetteer*, Ian Allan Ltd, 1976

These characteristics may offer an explanation for the low influenza mortality rate for Dudley - especially if they are placed alongside the possible direction of travel of the disease. The general hypothesis remains that the influenza entered Britain at different seaports, travelled to the main population centres, and from there spread out across the country. At face value this would suggest that the nearest main population centre affected would be Birmingham and from there the disease spread out into the Black Country. This should be indicated by Birmingham recording deaths from influenza earlier than the Black Country county boroughs. However, the evidence suggests influenza cases in Birmingham occurred slightly later than most of the Black Country county boroughs, as shown in Chart 4. Therefore, Birmingham did not appear to lead the region in the development of the disease, particularly in the key second wave – October to December 1918.

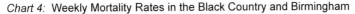

Chart 4: Weekly Mortality Rates in the Black Country and Birmingham

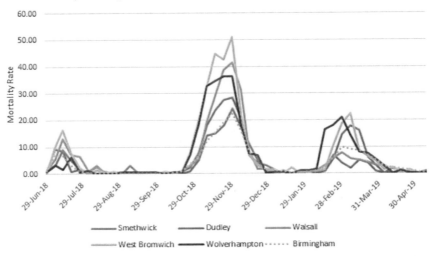

Chart Four indicates that Birmingham did develop the disease before Wolverhampton in the first wave, June-July 1918. However, there appears to be little significant difference compared with the other Black Country county boroughs; with some ahead and some behind Birmingham. In the second wave Birmingham started to register an increase at about the same time as the Black Country county boroughs, although the rate was much slower and, by early November, was slightly behind the other five local boroughs. This might indicate Birmingham actually 'received' the disease from the Black Country county boroughs, especially Wolverhampton, rather than transmitting it to them. In the third wave of the pandemic (January-March 1919), Wolverhampton cases clearly started a week or two earlier than Birmingham and also peaked slightly earlier. Thus Wolverhampton might be considered the central source for the influenza in the Black Country. Certainly it was noted at the time that Birmingham's mortality rate increased in the week ending 15 March 1919, i.e. towards the end of the third wave. It was one of only two English towns to record such an increase - the other being Oldham.[288] Again, this would suggest Birmingham was following rather than leading the development of the pandemic in the region. What this might point towards is that the direction of travel of the disease in the Black Country was from north to south rather than south to north. It arrived in the area from the northern ports before it arrived from London. However, one has to be very aware about the complicated effect of local factors and the arbitrary progress made by any disease of this type.

---

[288] *The British Medical Journal*, 22 March 1919, p.353.

Conclusion

This analysis finds that public health interventions and the other geographic characteristics studied, with the exception of the railway network, were unlikely to be the cause of Dudley's low mortality rate. However, Dudley's position on the railway network displayed two characteristics which might be considered important. Firstly, it was on the southern edge of the network and adjacent to districts that were less affected by influenza. Its Black Country neighbours were either centrally placed on the local network, or bordered districts to the north which were more seriously affected by the pandemic. Secondly, Dudley witnessed less through traffic and in consequence was marginally more isolated from neighbouring Black Country boroughs that were more seriously affected by the various influenza outbreaks. That the only effective widescale public health response to such an emergency was the isolation of individuals and communities at all levels was recognised at the time, and it is still a major tactic in dealing with infectious diseases. This was recognised by many authorities at the time, as indicated by comments made to the local council meeting by Dr A. S. Underhill, MOH for Tipton. After outlining the standard recommendations of the LGB he added: *'I fear that we cannot do more than I have mentioned'.*[289] Therefore, it is intuitive that those communities more isolated from their neighbours were likely to suffer less in the pandemic, all other factors being equal. This chapter has indicated that even a slight difference in public transport accessibility could affect the onset and severity of the pandemic. It may also explain the difference in mortality rates in Wolverhampton, noted by Dr Malet in 1919. West Wolverhampton, which bordered rural South Staffordshire, was less affected than urban/industrial East Wolverhampton which bordered more severely affected areas. It would be interesting to see if comparable findings are reached by studying similarly other anomalous districts in England and Wales.

---

[289] *Dudley Herald*, 7 December 1918.

Appendix 1: Calculation of Mortality Rate By Region

Mortality and mortality rate by County Borough was presented in the Registrar-General's Supplement in Table XX. Clusters of County Boroughs were identified on the basis that they were on average within 10 miles of each other.

	Deaths	Population	Mortality Rate per thousand
South Yorkshire:			
Rotherham	382	57,015	6.70
Sheffield	2,633	411,406	6.40
South Yorkshire Total	3,015	468,421	6.44
Tyneside:			
South Shields	669	92,917	7.20
Gateshead	420	102,439	4.10
Newcastle upon Tyne	1,299	236,182	5.50
Tynemouth	265	49,074	5.40
Sunderland	869	98,750	8.80
Tyneside Total	3,522	579,362	6.08
Black Country:			
Dudley	165	45,833	3.60
Smethwick	306	60,000	5.10
Walsall	445	76,724	5.80
West Bromwich	459	59,610	7.70
Wolverhampton	554	81,471	6.80
Black Country Total	1,929	323,638	5.96

It should be noted that there was a similar anomaly in Tyneside where the mortality rate in Gateshead was less than half that in Sunderland.

Acknowledgements : This chapter is based on an article published by *The Local Historian* in October 2018. Thanks are also due to Dr Alan Crosby of the British Association for Local History for the production of the two maps.

Chapter 14

Roland Edward Elcock and the story
of his Victoria Cross

Richard Pursehouse

Today, if you were aged fifteen years and four months, you might be concentrating on looming GCSE exams. In October 1914 the focus of Roland Edward Elcock was on one thing - joining up to fight for King and Country! He was born on 5 June 1899 at 52 Alma Street, Heath Town and educated at Causeway Lake Infant and Junior Schools. When war broke out he was a clerk at the Labour Assembly Rooms, Queen Street, Wolverhampton. After his elder brother, George Henry Elcock, enlisted the tall, well-built Elcock tried half a dozen times to join up as well. On each occasion he was caught out by the army doctor, until one day the recruiting officer threatened to *"put the policeman on his track"*. Later that day he heard a fresh doctor was in charge of examinations, tried again and managed to get himself into the 6th South Staffs Regiment. With the service number 3239, young Elcock was sent to train at Himley Park, near Dudley. After initial training Elcock's battalion was sent to Egypt to protect the Suez Canal and prepare for deployment in the Gallipoli campaign. The troopship never made it to the Dardanelles but carried them to Marseilles, France. Following a journey of several days travelling slowly northwards by train the battalion saw some hard fighting in the trenches of the Western Front. After one engagement Elcock was one of fewer than a dozen men in his company to answer the roll call. However, in August 1916 Private Elcock was discharged from service as the army could no longer ignore the fact he was only fifteen when he enlisted and was still under age.

Returning home to his widowed mother and two sisters in Alma Street, Elcock did clerical work for Wolverhampton Corporation Electricity Department before he was officially called up on his eighteenth birthday in June 1917. After going through basic training for a second time he was told he could not rejoin his original regiment due to manpower shortages and was sent instead to The Royal Scots (Lothian) Regiment, in Edinburgh. Thanks to a lineage going back to the 1630s, the Royal Scots were nicknamed 'Pontius Pilate's Bodyguard'. Elcock eventually joined the 11th Battalion with the service number 271401 and, after more training, was sent on garrison duties in Ireland, returning to France in February 1918. His frequent proximity to danger was evident when he reported having had a *"wristlet watch"* blown off his hand. Another indication of his determination to 'do his bit' was demonstrated in the summer of 1918 when he was awarded the Military Medal (MM). Brother George, a Lance Sergeant in the Royal Warwickshire Regiment, was also awarded the MM. Before enlisting George was an assistant master at Fox Street Schools, Aston, Birmingham and lived at 451 Lichfield Street, Aston.

In August and September 1918 Roland Elcock's battalion took part in many key battles of the '100 Days Offensive', especially on the Somme sector; at Bapaume, the Hindenburg Line and St. Quentin Canal. Then, as the war moved into its final weeks, they were transferred north to Belgium. It was here that Acting Corporal Elcock's courage led to him being awarded the Victoria Cross. At 5.35 am on 14 October 1918 the Battle of Courtrai began in an area of West Flanders to the east of Ypres. During the first day the British Second Army made rapid progress, occupying Werviq, Menin, Wevelgheim and Moorslede, before moving forward to Gulleghem and Steenbeek. Although German morale appeared to be crumbling and the end of the war seemed near, some units of the Kaiser's army continued to offer stiff resistance. In such circumstances the obvious strategy for a sensible Tommy was to keep one's head down and wait for the joyful news that he had survived the Great War - but not Roland Elcock. The following day, 15 October, he single-handedly rushed a German machine gun post with a Lewis gun and captured five prisoners of war. This heroic exploit, which occurred north of Courtrai at Capelle St. Catherine, or Sint-Katarina Kapel, as it is known today, earned Elcock his Victoria Cross. The day after that, as the British advance continued eastwards along the north bank of the River Lys towards Harelbeke, Elcock struck again. His commanding officer was so impressed by his bravery that he recommended him for the Victoria Cross - the highest award 'For Valour'. His Medal Citation later said exactly what he did to deserve the medal:

"For most conspicuous bravery and initiative south-east of Capelle St. Catherine on the 15th October, 1918, when in charge of a Lewis gun team. Entirely on his own initiative, Cpl. Elcock rushed his gun up to within ten yards of enemy guns, which were causing heavy casualties and holding up the advance. He put both guns out of action, captured five prisoners, and undoubtedly saved the whole attack from being held up. Later, near the River Lys, this non-commissioned officer again attacked an enemy machine gun and captured the crew. His behaviour throughout the day was absolutely fearless." The citation for Elcock's Victoria Cross was published in the London Gazette of 24 December 1918, Supplement 31082, p.15118.

Over the next few days Ostend, Lille and Brugge were all liberated by Allied troops and by the time of the Armistice, Elcock's battalion was en route to Brussels. It was while he was based in Cologne, as part of the Allied army of occupation in the demilitarised Rhineland, that he caught wind of his impending honour. He wrote home to his family telling them he was awaiting leave and had been put forward for another award: *"You ask me what I have been doing to get recommended again. Well, if I tell, you will fairly guess what I am going to get for it. So I will leave it till the decoration comes out. I am expecting the DCM, but, as rumours go in the battalion, I am in for the VC. So I hope I get it."*

Although this letter arrived home in Wolverhampton before an *Express and Star* reporter turned up to give his mother the 'good news', she *"expressed surprise"* at the announcement. Councillor Alfred George Jeffs, the Mayor of Wolverhampton, also promptly visited the Elcock residence to congratulate his proud mother on behalf of the town.[290] It was on 13 February 1919 that Roland Elcock was one of six Victoria Cross recipients presented to the King, with relatives of two other VCs, and alongside Bilston-born George Onions. The investiture at Buckingham Palace involved more than 320 other medal recipients including many Red Cross nurses. The next month he was presented with *"gifts from the townspeople"* of Wolverhampton, including £500 of War Savings Certificates and £30 in Bank of England banknotes.[291] On 26 June 1920 he was invited to Buckingham Palace again - for a Royal garden party with 300 other VC holders, including one old veteran from the Indian Mutiny in 1857! It began with the *"March of the Heroes"* from Wellington Barracks to the Palace led by the band of the Welsh Guards along a route lined by cheering crowds. The VC holders paraded in seven groups with no distinction made between officers and men.[292] King George V inspected them, and *"stood at the foot of the west terrace, as each V.C. was presented in turn"*. On 11 November 1920, the second anniversary of the end of the war, Elcock was one of the VC recipients chosen to march past the new Cenotaph in Whitehall. Afterwards he was included in the Guard of Honour who paraded at the tomb of the Unknown Warrior, at Westminster Abbey. His 'brush' with royalty did not end there as the Duke of York, the future King George VI, specifically requested to be introduced to him during his visit to Wolverhampton in 1922.

Life in Wolverhampton briefly returned to relative normality, despite Elcock being the town's only VC holder. However, in July 1921 the local Press announced the shocking news: "V.C. TO QUIT."[293] It said *"Corporal Elcock, Wolverhampton's only V.C. is to be turned out of the home in Alma Street in which he was born and reared, for yesterday an ejectment order was obtained by the owner Edward Neachell, a dairyman against the V.C.'s mother, Mrs. Fanny Elcock, on the ground that occupation of the house was required for the cultivation of the adjoining land. In support a certificate from the County Agricultural Committee was produced."*

Next month the plight of the Elcock family was in the news again, as the *Birmingham Daily Post* of 21 August 1921 ran an article: "CORPORATION COTTAGES THAT ARE TOO SMALL. *Wolverhampton's only V.C. is just now the centre of a little episode which is engaging plenty of attention, and though there is the possibility of him being homeless very shortly, the public do not know whether to treat the case as a tragedy or a comedy. Corporal Elcock, V.C. lives with his mother in Alma-street, the house in which he was born, but recently a new owner succeeded in an action for possession of the premises, under an agricultural clause, which did away with the necessity of offering alternative accommodation. In the few weeks at their disposal, Mrs. Elcock found the house shortage as acute as ever, and looked like being turned into the street with her V.C. son. A further short respite was secured, however, and meanwhile the case had been brought to the notice of the authorities, and the Housing Committee, stretching a point in such an exceptional*

---

[290] *Birmingham Daily Post*, 28 December 1918
[291] *Lancashire Evening Post*, 3 March 1919
[292] *The Scotsman*, 28 June 1920
[293] *Birmingham Gazette*, 21 July 1921.

case, offered the V.C.'s mother one of the new Corporation houses. Then came the anti-climax. This house proved so circumscribed that Mrs. Elcock's furniture, which is certainly not massive, would not go in, and now the police are trying to find someone who will exchange a suitable house for the new one offered by the Corporation. The time is nearly up, and so far no volunteer has come forward."[294]

Mike Jackson, of the Wolverhampton branch of the Western Front Association, researched what happened with the Elcock house and found that not only was the land not used for *'agricultural purposes'* at the time, but was never even used to grow vegetables in the 'Dig for Victory' campaign during the Second World War. It is believed Elcock was so disappointed at how the 'town of his birth' turned its back on him and his family, that he decided to move to India where he joined the Posts and Telegraph service, eventually becoming director-general on the North-West Frontier. On the outbreak of war in 1939 he joined the Indian Army with the rank of major, and was about to leave with his regiment for an active theatre of war when seized with a mysterious illness. This condition affected him for the next four years and ill health led to his premature death, aged only forty-five, at Dehradun, north of New Delhi, on 6 October 1944.

Elcock's Military Medal and Victoria Cross were passed down to his daughter, Mrs June Owen. Her widowed mother made her promise never to sell them, "even if she were destitute and starving". However, his widow was unable to work due to her own ill-health. Having returned from India, she was now living in Lower Oxford Road, Basford, Newcastle-under-Lyme. Without telling her mother, June decided to sell the medals. This was an agonising decision she told several newspapers: *"I offered the V.C. for sale without my mother's knowledge. It has been an awful business for me."* Having vowed to keep her father's medals in the family, she sold them to send her fifty-seven-year-old mother on a *"long health-restoring holiday."* In February 1958 Elcock's medal group including his VC and MM was sold for a then "record" sum of £650 at Christie's Auction House - beating the previous record of £480. As Elcock's daughter looked on tearfully, the brisk bidding soon saw Wolverhampton Royal British Legion outbid and the medals purchased on behalf of the Royal Scots Museum by Major General R. F. Johnstone, Colonel of the Regiment. Thankfully the medal group is now displayed at the regimental museum in Edinburgh Castle. Wolverhampton's Great War VC was also briefly commemorated in the naming of Roland Elcock House - accommodation to help former service personnel's transition to civilian life. This was opened in Barnfield Road, East Park, Wolverhampton, in 2014, but closed when funding ran out in August 2016.

On Monday 15 October 2018, the centenary of his act of valour, a dignified ceremony took place in Wolverhampton city centre to honour Roland Elcock. After the unveiling of the Victoria Cross memorial paving stone, wreaths were laid by Mayor of Wolverhampton, Councillor Phil Page, Elcock's grandson, Dominic Owen and Dominic's sister, Christine Kinsella. Dominic recalled that when he was fifteen

---

[294] *Birmingham Daily Post*, 21 August 1921

and considering his future, his father told him about his grandfather being awarded the Military Medal and the Victoria Cross. He then decided to join the same regiment in which his grandfather had served with such fame. He said that at times it was tough and he cried himself to sleep on some nights in the barracks, but eventually his Scottish comrades accepted and respected his determination. Wreaths were also laid on behalf of The Deputy Lord Lieutenant of the West Midlands, The Royal Scots Regimental Association, The Chase Project, the High Sheriff, a captain currently serving in The Royal Regiment of Scotland, the Staffordshire Regiment Association, the Wolverhampton branch of the Western Front Association and the Deputy Lord Lieutenant. Prayers and Blessing were led by the Reverend Richard Merrick, of Holy Trinity Church, Heath Town. The ceremony concluded with the Last Post and Reveille played by Don Somers and Stan Wilkinson, and the haunting skirl of "Flowers of the Forest" by piper Ian Reid Fleming.

The picture that never happened – showing a youthful Elcock with his VC whilst wearing the uniform of the South Staffords – an early example of photoshopping!

Left: Elcock at the time he received his VC. *Right:* The memorial unveiling ceremony in 2018.

Chapter 15

Roads of Remembrance in Wolverhampton

How trees were used to commemorate the fallen of the Great War.

Jim Barrow

"The idea of the living tree appeals more powerfully to those who have lost a loved one than a cold stone or marble monument." [295]

In the aftermath of the mass slaughter and trauma of the Great War the people of Britain cast around for the best ways to remember those who had served, died, or been injured and left to carry on with life as normal. Wolverhampton was no exception, but what constituted appropriate Remembrance became a contentious issue in the town. Some people wanted grand memorials of stone, brick, wood, and metal, as well as framed rolls of honour, to be kept on display in public buildings such as churches or government offices. Others, particularly ex-service people, had more important priorities such as work, food, and making *"Britain a fit country for heroes to live in."* [296] They preferred the idea of somewhere to go and meet others who had gone through the same or similar experiences to them; a place to talk, get help to find work, have a drink, throw darts, play snooker, cards, or dominoes. Opinion was divided between those who wanted a memorial that would be of practical use, such as an ex-service club, whereas others wanted Gardens of Remembrance, Memorial Parks or Recreation Grounds.

In Wolverhampton, although the trades unions and the Labour movement broadly supported creating 'useful' memorials, they did not believe this should exclude the possibility of other memorials. Even before the war was over a range of exterior and interior memorials appeared using photographs, wood, stone, brick, marble and metal. In factories, churches, business offices, sports clubs, schools, colleges, universities and council buildings, memorial statues, rolls of honour, plaques, boards and painted tributes were installed to commemorate those who served and fell. By the time of the Armistice on 11 November 1918, two of the town's most famous monuments had already been unveiled: the Able Seaman Douglas Morris Harris memorial in St Peter's Gardens, on 22 June 1918,[297] and the Little's Lane local plaque to the fallen from the *'Caribee Island'* district, between Stafford Street and the Birmingham Canal.

One year later, in November 1919, the town councillor for Dunstall Ward, Thomas Austin Henn (1871-1948), was elected as mayor of Wolverhampton. He

---

[295] *Western Morning News & Mercury*, 20 December 1922
[296] *Wolverhampton Express & Star.* Lloyd George's speech at Wolverhampton Grand Theatre, 23 November 1918
[297] *Birmingham Post*, 24 June 1918

lived at *Springhead*, on the Dudley Road in Sedgley, and his family owned the jewellery business that still operates in Princess Street. In his first mayoral address, Henn proposed to plant a thousand trees across Wolverhampton to: *"stimulate local patriotism and give residents a greater pride in their town."*[298] In particular, he wanted the honour of the plantings to be carried out by local schoolchildren as a mark of distinction for those *"who had excelled in conduct or progress."*[299] He appealed to the public to help raise the £1,200 needed to implement his idea, which was reported in the local Press as an *"interesting scheme"* to both literally improve the outlook *"of those who dwell in a drab and monotonous environment"* as well as *"lessen the contrast between the gloomy East and the verdant West"* of the town.[300] Mayor Henn may well have been inspired by events in other parts of the British Empire as the Australians planted memorial trees in Creswell Gardens, Adelaide, as early as 1914. By 1921 an avenue of trees seventy miles long had been *"planted at Ballarat in memory of the soldiers who fell in the field, a tablet being placed before each tree naming the hero to whom it was dedicated."*[301] On 8 January 1919, C.L. Pack of the American Forestry Association also made a call for: *"Memorial Trees for soldiers - thousands may be planted along boulevards and county highways"* - including the naming of a national highway to honour the memory of former President Theodore Roosevelt, who had just died.[302] Planting trees as memorials was not a new idea but a tradition that stretched back for thousands of years of human history - when they had been regarded as important symbols of life, renewal, death and continuity. The French had planted their 'Liberty Tree' in 1789 and the Americans said their own Boston Liberty Tree was: *"The tree that looks at God all day and lifts her leafy arms to pray."*

Perhaps Mayor Henn was inspired by events much closer to home - and actually in the West Midlands. In 1919 Coventry City Council purchased land for its famous War Memorial Park to commemorate local service personnel killed in the Great War. That park was formally opened on 9 July 1921 and memorial plaques could be purchased to dedicate particular trees to the fallen. However, due to financial difficulties, the final landscaping of the park was not completed until 1935. Nationally, the formation of the Roads of Remembrance Association (RRA) also provided an additional boost to Henn's ideas. Evidently founded in the Speaker's House at the House of Commons in 1919, the RRA sought to *"commemorate the sacrifices of our countrymen in the Great War"* by promoting the *"planting of memorial trees along suitable roads"* as well as in gardens, schools or public institutions.[303] One of the immediate objectives of the organisation was the planting of *'Tribute Trees'* and by March 1921 the RRA was appealing for another £1,500 to continue its work.[304] The RRA project was welcomed by Sphere Magazine, which commented that *"it has a spaciousness and dignity which are missing in most war*

---

[298] *Staffordshire Advertiser*, 14 February 1920
[299] *Wolverhampton Express & Star*, 10 November 1919
[300] *Staffordshire Advertiser*, 14 February 1920
[301] *Biggleswade Chronicle*, 7 October 1921
[302] Inventory of The American Forestry Association Records, 1875-1997, foresthistory.org
[303] *Western Morning News & Mercury*, 3 March 1921
[304] *Portsmouth Evening News*, 5 March 1921.

memorial schemes...the road of remembrance will guard the memory of the dead so that no man passing that way, beneath their own trees will forget them; they will have a living monument that shall endure when the others are broken and forgotten."[305] By the time of the Armistice commemorations in November 1921, the RRA had an Honorary Secretary, Mrs M.H. Morrison, and an office at 47 Victoria Street, London, S.W.1.[306] In October 1922 the RRA was described as *"strongly supported in the Midlands and the South of England"* with several roads having already been dedicated and planted with memorial trees.[307]

Locally, the campaigning of the RRA coincided with the planning and construction of the Wolverhampton to Birmingham New Road (A4123). On this road's route through the nearby urban district of Coseley, a cherry tree was planted to remember each of the 350 men from that district who made the ultimate sacrifice in the war. Every tree planted bore an oval plaque bearing the name of the dead serviceman. Among those Coseley men who served were six brothers; the sons of Mrs Isaac Morgan, of 48 Castle Street, Roseville. Of these, Isaac junior was a Gunner in the Royal Garrison Artillery, with a wife and two children. He died of wounds on 17 April 1916 and was buried at Coseley (Christ Church) New Churchyard. Another son, Abraham Malcolm Morgan, was a Lance Sergeant in the 1st/6th Battalion of the South Staffordshire Regiment, and died only a month before the Armistice, on 8 October 1918. This twenty-one-year old soldier was buried at Tourgeville Military Cemetery, near the base hospital in Normandy, suggesting he died from wounds or from some form of illness.

Finding money to create any war memorial was not easy in the dire economic aftermath of the Great War. Nationally, the huge cost of the conflict had been underpinned with massive loans and these war debts now had to be repaid. Post-war austerity affected people at the local level too, and it was hard to argue war memorials were a priority when thousands of demobbed servicemen were searching for work and the women, who had stood-in for them during the war were being hastily dismissed. In Wolverhampton, Mayor Henn's tree project was expected to cost £1,200 – nearly £61,500 in 2019 prices, so it was agreed from the start that the scheme would have to be funded by the planters themselves; in effect the pupils, parents and staff of Wolverhampton's schools.[308] In October 1920, this message was noted in the logbook of the Higher Grade School, Newhampton Road, by Headteacher, Jesse West: *"Remind scholars about collection towards Tree Planting Fund of Mayor and Carnival in aid of charities of town."*[309]

The first memorial trees in Wolverhampton were planted in All Saints Road on 22 March 1920, at a ceremony attended by Mayor Henn and his children, Thomas, Frank and Molly. In advance of the ceremony *"a miniature general election took*

---

[305] *The Sphere*, 26 March 1921
[306] *Yorkshire Post*, 2 November 1921
[307] *Shields Daily News*, 9 October 1922
[308] *Wolverhampton Express & Star*, 10 November 1919
[309] Wolverhampton Higher Grade/Secondary School Log Book, 1902-1921, Ref D-EDS-169, City Archives.

place at All Saints, St Joseph's and Dudley Road Schools, for the purpose of selecting by popular vote the boys and girls who were to plant the trees."[310] A large crowd assembled in All Saints Road as pupils from each of the three schools planted ten plane trees. Three children officiated at the planting of every tree, making the declaration that it was *"well and truly planted in memory of the brave men who died to make the world freer and brighter."*[311] By then the scheme's aims included remembering the ex-pupils from the schools in each area. Horace Belcher, an assistant at the town's Free Library, had lived at 247 All Saints Road before he enlisted into the 2nd/3rd Brigade of the North Midland Field Ambulance, RAMC. The son of Joseph and Mary Ann Belcher, Horace died on 27 September 1917, while fighting in the Third Battle of Ypres. His body was never identified and his name was inscribed on the Tyne Cot Memorial to the missing along with 35,000 other Commonwealth troops who died between July 1917 and November 1918. In Blakenhall pupils from the Dudley Road Schools planted trees in Vicarage Road, Mason Street, Thompson Avenue and Silver Birch Road. Private Ewart Barrett, who had lived nearby at 91 Napier Road, was the youngest member of the South Staffordshire Regiment to die in the war. On 27 May 1915 he was hit by a bullet that went through his side and into his heart. This sixteen-year-old soldier was buried at St Quentin Cabaret Military Cemetery, between Ypres and Armentières, Belgium. His grieving mother, Sarah, chose the words: *"He died a noble death"* to be inscribed on his headstone.[312]

On 31 March 1920 more tree plantings took place. In Bradmore, pupils from the Bingley Street, St Mark's and Brickkiln Street Schools planted a combination of London Plane and fir trees at Walford Avenue, near Bantock House. On the Stafford Road pupils from the Red Cross Street Schools planted saplings on the roadside coming out of the town centre. The Schools' logbook for 31 March records: *"Instead of ordinary lessons this morning the scholars assembled in the playground at 10am to hear an address by the Mayor on the occasion of the planting of memorial trees by the scholars of Red Cross Street School. After the address Classes 1(A) and 1(B) marched to Stafford Road with the children of the senior departments to do the planting."* On the afternoon of Wednesday 28 June, children from Old Hall Street, Walsall Street and Willenhall Road Schools planted a further thirty-six trees. Then, on 27 October, pupils from St Jude's School, Whitmore Reans, planted a mixture of nineteen elm and oak trees on either side of Avondale Road and another four in Riches Street. That same day Jesse West, headmaster of The Higher Grade School – at the junction of Dunkley Street and Newhampton Road – wrote in the school logbook, *"Our scholars had Dunkley Street allotted to them. There were eleven trees in all and three planters had been chosen from each form by the scholars themselves."*

---

[310] *Wolverhampton Chronicle*, 24 March 1920
[311] Ibid, 24 March 1920
[312] Evans, R.C., *Wolverhampton Warriors*, 2010, p.43

Coseley
Avenue of Remembrance

The Tree Planting In This
Area Is To Commemorate
The 350 Members Of The
Armed Forces Who Gave
Their Lives In The
Great War
1914 - 1918

Left: London Plane Trees in Old Hall Street, Wolverhampton. Right: Memorial beside the Birmingham New Road (A4123), near Ward Grove, WV4.

On the 10 November 1920, a year to the day after Mayor Henn had introduced his scheme, he officiated at a tree-planting ceremony by scholars in Old Hall Street. This event was also attended by the Mayoress, the Deputy Mayor and other town officers including the headmaster, Harry D. Jackson, who had enlisted in the Royal Field Artillery in 1915.[313] Having reached the rank of Sergeant, Harry Jackson resumed working at the school on 5 November 1917, after a medical discharge from the army due to being gassed.[314] The day after the ceremony, being Armistice Day itself, the pupils attended the 11 am service in a local park, before being dismissed for a half-day holiday. In his oration Mayor Henn hoped the scheme would continue after he became Deputy Mayor later that same month. It certainly did, and twelve trees were planted in Hordern Road, Whitmore Reans, by the pupils of Hordern Road Schools. These included one dedicated by a pupil to the memory of his older brother. Another local soldier remembered was twenty-year-old Acting Sergeant Frederick Wallace Watson, who lived with his parents, Wallace and Hannah, at 299 Hordern Road. He had trained as a bomber with the 1/6 South Staffords and took part in the assault on the Hohenzollern Redoubt at Loos, on 13 October 1915. During the German counter-attack, he kept the enemy at bay for five hours with Mills bombs/hand grenades and accurate rifle-fire until he was eventually killed. Not surprisingly, he was described by one of his men as *"the bravest and most daring fellow I ever knew."*[315] A few days later, the *Wolverhampton Express and Star* reported that Fred Watson's name was mentioned in a special memorial service to

[313] *Wolverhampton Express & Star*, 17 May 1915
[314] Wolverhampton's War – Lost Voices from The Great War – wolverhamptonswar.wordpress.com
[315] Evans, *Wolverhampton Warriors*, op. cit., p.61

the *"Brave men of Whitmore Reans"*, held at St Andrew's Church.[316] His name was eventually recorded on the Loos Memorial.

On the afternoon of Tuesday 3 November 1922, Mayor James Thompson watched children from St. John's and Graiseley Schools plant fourteen trees in St. John's Square and twenty in the streets surrounding Blakenhall Recreation Ground.[317] Thirty four more trees were planted by pupils from St Luke's School - in Blakenhall's Mason Street – as children from SS Mary and John and Monmore Green Schools set them in Vicarage Road, Blakenhall, and Bilston Road, Monmore Green. Councillor J. Walsh, Chairman of the Education Committee, presided at each of the plantings and was forced to respond to criticism that the school curriculum was being badly affected by the loss of valuable teaching time due to these ceremonies. However, the 1922 annual report of the Council Education Committee stated: *"The scheme inaugurated by Councillor Henn during his mayorality of 1919-1920 continues to progress. 230 trees have been planted by 20 schools and dedicated to their old boys who fell in action. Several schools are collecting and it is hoped shortly to complete the scheme by the planting of a further 80 trees. It is encouraging to find that the children in all parts of the town have redeemed their promises to protect the trees from ill-usage. The planting of the trees, in most cases under the name of the individual fallen men, has contributed much to the respect with which the trees are regarded."*[318] The minutes of the council Parks and Baths Committee of 9 November 1926 also reported: *"Your committee have supervised the planting of 56 trees by schoolchildren in Thompson Avenue and Silver Birch Avenue. This was the scheme inaugurated by Alderman Henn. Fifty trees have also been planted on Old Heath Road and Willenhall Road Housing Estate."*[319]

Elsewhere, on 4 June 1925, the Duke and Duchess of York visited T.W. Lench Ltd, Blackheath, where the former Yew Tree Colliery had been developed as a park with flower beds, walks and a garden of remembrance. The future King George VI and Queen Elizabeth witnessed the planting of trees to commemorate each one of the company's twenty-seven workers who died in the war. The Royal planting of a pine tree at Lench's was assisted by an employee called Bethnel Ness. At St Michael's Mission Church, Wolverhampton Street, Bilston, the memorial poplar trees planted to commemorate three men in the congregation, helped to pull the building down. The tree roots combined with those of others to undermine the 150-year-old building's foundations. However, parts of the original building were salvaged and incorporated into the new church that was subsequently built on the site, including a plaque listing the three local soldiers who died in the Great War.[320]

Today the significance of trees as memorials is demonstrated by the creation of the National Memorial Arboretum at Alrewas, Staffordshire. The 150 acre site, opened to the public in 2001, has more than 300 memorials and 30,000 trees that will

---

[316] *Wolverhampton Express & Star*, 23 October 1915
[317] *Staffordshire Advertiser*, 11 November 1922
[318] Wolverhampton Council, Education Committee Annual Report, 9 November 1922, p.19
[319] Wolverhampton Council, Parks and Baths Committee Annual Report, 9 November 1926, p.77
[320] Davies, R., 'St. Michael's Mission Church', *The Blackcountryman*, 1987, No.1.

eventually form a recreated Forest of Mercia. In 2015 the Woodland Trust, which owns more than 1,000 sites across the UK, also announced a £20 million project to commemorate those who died in the Great War. In Sheffield, a council decision to fell the fifty-three surviving war memorial trees in the city's Western Road provoked a huge public outcry. As a result, they trimmed the scheme and promised to plant hundreds of new trees in parks across the city. A Scarlet Oak Tree (Quercus Coccinea) was planted in memory of the ten man crew of the USAAF B-17 Flying Fortress 'Mi Amigo', that crashed in Endcliffe Park on 22 February 1944. This planting was carried out by Tony Foulds, who witnessed the crash, and the BBC's Dan Walker. In Canada, two million trees are being planted along Ontario's Macdonald-Cartier Highway - Highway 401 - linking Windsor with Quebec City. In 2007 a 170 kilometre section of the highway from the Canadian Forces base at Trenton, on Lake Ontario, to the Don Valley Parkway, Toronto, was designated the 'Highway of Heroes.' This reflected its use as the route for funeral convoys carrying fallen armed forces personnel from CFB Trenton to the coroner's office in Toronto, where inquests are held on every member of the Canadian armed forces who die in service.[321]

In Wolverhampton the legacy of the council's decision to promote tree planting after the Great War has been noted by Alec Brew. Commenting on how verdant the city had become, he said: *"time and again I found it impossible to take a photograph from the same spot as the early twentieth century photographers because there were too many trees in the way."*[322] However, although Britain's tree cover has more than doubled to thirteen per cent, since the low-point it reached in 1918, it still compares poorly with other European countries where the average cover is thirty-seven per cent. In February 2019 Wolverhampton Council also admitted that their tree replacement budget of £10,000 might be sacrificed in order to make general savings across all their services. In spite of this, fresh trees are still being planted in Wolverhampton, with some in the Wildside Centre, off Hordern Road, Whitmore Reans in 2018. This is close to the site of original memorial trees, as were recent plantings at Bantock Park – near to Walford Avenue. Perhaps this is a fitting tribute to Mayor Thomas A. Henn's grand project and a poignant reminder of the many trees that were planted by scholars from forty-eight different schools in Wolverhampton in the years immediately following the Great War.

---

[321] Highways of Heroes Tree Campaign, https://hohtribute.ca.about-hoh/
[322] Brew, A., *Wolverhampton Through Time*, 2019, Introduction.

Chapter 16

Able Seaman Harris – Poster boy in Bronze?

Quintin Watt

Bronze memorial bust of A/S D.M.H. Harris, St. Peter's Gardens, Wolverhampton.

St. Peter's Gardens in Wolverhampton city centre boasts a fine war memorial – a bronze bust dedicated to and depicting Able Seaman Douglas Morris Henry Harris, AB, Royal Naval Volunteer Reserve (RNVR), who died in action on 15 May 1917. Many sailors from Wolverhampton died in the Great War but why did local people subscribe to this particular monument? Could it be the Harris memorial came about as a result of a local sense of injustice that his undoubted bravery did not receive due recognition? Did the Admiralty show a parsimonious attitude when commemorating Royal Navy personnel for courageous actions in embarrassing military failures? There is little doubt that after his death the nineteen-year-old Wireless Operator became an heroic icon for the British media and a public aching for positive news and encouragement in the desperate final stages of the Great War.

Douglas Harris was born in Penn, Wolverhampton, on 7 April 1898. His parents, Leopold and Mabel Harris, were originally from London but lived at 49, Penn Road at the time of the 1901 census. Leopold was then working as a commercial traveller but by 1911 he was listed in that year's census as a sales manager for a local 'Motor Fittings' business and living at 42, Lea Road. Leopold's promotions meant the Harris family now employed two servants: a general domestic and a governess for their six children. Douglas had two older sisters, Irene and Doris, an older brother, Gerald, and younger twin sisters, Muriel and Olive. By the time of his death, in 1917, his father and mother lived at Eagle House, Penn Fields,

Wolverhampton, but soon afterwards returned south to a house called Winsmore Lodge in St. Albans Road, Watford.

Harris attended Wolverhampton Higher Grade School and worked for the Corporation Electricity Works before joining the RNVR on his eighteenth birthday; training to become a Wireless Operator.[323] He served on HMS *Admirable* (service number BZ9359) before being transferred to the drifter HM Trawler *Floandi*, a small ship forming part of the Otranto Barrage - the naval blockade guarding the entrance to the Adriatic Sea.[324] Drifters were small vessels stationed in a line across the 45 miles of the Straits of Otranto, from the 'heel' of Italy to the coast of Albania north of the Greek island of Corfu. Many of these small ships were trawlers from the north-east of Scotland, still manned by their crews of 'co-opted' fishermen. *Floandi* was a hired drifter (Admiralty number 748) built in 1914 and registered at Great Yarmouth (Reg, YH973). The anti-submarine nets strung between the drifters were meant to stop Austro-Hungarian and German U-boats, based in modern Croatia and Montenegro, from operating in the Mediterranean. The submarine menace had been growing since 1915 and one, the U35, sank forty-eight Allied ships during a nineteen day killing spree.[325] When Rear Admiral Mark Kerr was appointed Commander of the British Adriatic Squadron, in May 1916, he grasped the scale of the problem facing him: *"I realised that if we lost the war we should do it by being bled to death through the wounding or cutting of the vital arteries of our sea communications, of which one of the greatest ran through the Mediterranean."* [326] In effect the Otranto Barrage was the equivalent of the forward trenches on the Western Front, yet Rear Admiral Kerr failed to persuade the Admiralty, or his French and Italian allies, to deploy the destroyers and aircraft needed to make it a truly formidable barrier. The view in London was that the Adriatic 'backwater' was the naval equivalent of the other Mediterranean 'sideshows' that sucked valuable resources away from the 'most important' area of operations – those closest to Great Britain. Kerr admitted that this *'parochialism'* at the highest levels meant the barrage was so ineffective that enemy U-boats could simply pass through it with *"brazen effrontery."*[327] Therefore, the use of the term barrage is misleading - it was an obstacle in name only - and generally ignored by the Austrians and Germans because it was utterly ineffectual.[328] By April 1917 the Otranto Barrage was under the operational command of Commodore Algernon Heneage. His flotilla of seventy drifters worked in a rotation between the Italian port of Brindisi and "The Net" with major boat repairs carried out in Taranto. Most of the drifters were steam-powered North Sea trawlers with a top speed of 8-9 knots. On average, they were about 88 feet long by 19 feet wide and weighed about 30 tons. Although some drifters were lightly armed with Italian 57mm and 47mm guns and a few with British three-pounders, most boats in the barrage were completely defenceless and vulnerable to attack. As each drifter covered only about

[323] *Birmingham Daily Post*, 6 August 1917
[324] Portrait by George Phoenix, Wolverhampton Art Gallery.
[325] Kerr, M., *Land, Sea, and Air*, London, 1927, p.205
[326] Ibid, p.205
[327] Ibid, p.210
[328] Halpern, P.G., *The Naval War in the Mediterranean 1914-1918*, London, 1987, p.280

half-a-mile of the Otranto Straits, there were plenty of gaps for enemy U-boats to sneak through.[329]

At 3.30 am on the night of 14–15 May 1917 the Battle of the Otranto Straits began when the Allied drifter line came under heavy attack by three light cruisers of the Imperial Austrian Navy – SMS *Helgoland*, SMS *Saida* and SMS *Novara*. (SMS stands for Seiner Majestät Schiff – His Majesty's Ship) Austrian commander, Linienschiffkapitan Nikolaus Horthy, later claimed his attack was prompted by the increasing difficulty faced by U-boats passing through the Otranto Barrage, although there is no evidence to show this. Rear Admiral Kerr believed it might have been due to an Austrian U-boat getting caught in the nets 36 hours earlier, but the only known success of 'the Net' occurred when the U6 was destroyed in May 1916.[330] At first the Austrians sailed parallel to the barrage and in the half-light the drifter crews thought they were Allied warships, but then the attack suddenly began when *Saida* opened fire on four drifters of 'C Division' in the centre of the line. Then the 3,500 ton *Helgoland* attacked the drifters at the western end, where 'N Division' was based. Skipper Joe Watt, of the *Gowan Lea*, fired his 'pop-gun' at the Austrian and then tried to ram the *Helgoland* before abandoning his own ship after it was riddled with shell holes; an action that led to him being awarded the Victoria Cross.[331] At 4.00 am the *Novara* attacked the drifters of 'O' and 'S' Divisions at the eastern end of the barrage. It was here that Able Seaman Harris, working the wireless on board HM Trawler *Floandi*, was killed by one of the twelve direct hits his ship received. Harris refused to leave his post in the midst of the battle and continued to send messages calling for assistance until he was killed at his desk by a piece of shrapnel. Remarkably, the *Floandi* remained afloat, but five other members of her crew were killed, accounting for six out of the total of thirteen British deaths in the whole engagement. The Austrian attack on the barrage ended at 5.37am when British light cruisers HMS *Bristol* and HMS *Dartmouth* arrived to chase the Austrians back to Cattaro in Montenegro, home port of the Austro-Hungarian Fifth Fleet. The battle continued until the early afternoon, when both fleets broke off the engagement after their ships sustained serious damage.

The Battle of the Otranto Barrage was the largest naval confrontation in the Adriatic during the Great War, and hailed as a great victory in Austria-Hungary. Their three cruisers and two destroyers sank one Allied destroyer, a munitions ship as well as fourteen of the forty-seven drifters that were manning the barrage that night. They also captured seventy-two Allied personnel. However, like the Battle of Jutland with which it has been compared, tactical success did not lead to a strategic shift in the balance of naval power in the Adriatic and the Allied blockade of Austria-Hungary continued.[332] In reality the actual result of the battle was to make: *"a not very effective barrage temporarily even less effective."*[333] However, it was still a highly embarrassing episode for the Royal Navy, which possibly explains the Admiralty's

---

[329] Snelling, S., *The Otranto Straits Affair*, in Britain at War, No.112, August 2016, pp.60-69
[330] Kerr, op. cit., p.210
[331] Snelling, S., *The Otranto Straits Affair*, in Britain at War, No.112, August 2016, pp.60-69
[332] Halpern, P.G., *The Naval War in the Mediterranean 1914-1918*, London, 1987, p.365
[333] Ibid, p.365

parsimonious response when Rear Admiral Kerr submitted a list of 119 drifter crewmen to receive exceptional bravery awards, on 21 May 1917. Rear Admiral Allan Everett, the Naval Secretary, was unimpressed and said Kerr's list had to be cut by two-thirds. The Sea Lords also argued that the largely co-opted civilian drifter crews ought to have put up much sterner resistance to the Austrian cruisers during this "rout."[334] Given that Able Seaman Harris was eventually mentioned in Despatches and Rear Admiral Kerr took particular interest in his role in the battle, he was probably one of those recommended for a Conspicuous Gallantry Medal that was axed by the Admiralty. Rear Admiral Kerr later wrote bitterly that *"fourteen drifters were sunk and several lives sacrificed on the altar of parochialism."*[335]

Bronze panel on the Harris memorial depicting his death.

Within weeks news of Harris' brave exploits received a boost when Rear Admiral Kerr proposed to submit his telegraph log, recovered from the wireless operating cabin on *Floandi*, to be *"preserved as an exhibit in the National War Museum".*[336] That institution, now called the Imperial War Museum, had just been founded by the War Cabinet, on 5 May 1917. Perhaps Kerr's decision to highlight Harris' logbook was motivated by his belief that the young Wireless Operator had been denied the medal he truly deserved, albeit posthumously. The Press reported how Harris had *"continued to send and receive messages, although the drifter was being riddled by shells, until he was killed by a piece of shrapnel whilst writing in the*

[334] Snelling, S., *The Otranto Straits Affair*, in Britain at War, No.112, August 2016, pp.60-69
[335] Kerr, op. cit., p.210
[336] *Birmingham Daily Post*, 21 July 1917

log. The piece of shell perforated the log, and the line made by his pencil when he was hit and collapsed can be seen on the page upon which he was writing. The operator was found dead in his chair, lying over the log."[337] The bravery of the young Able Seaman was admired by many people in Wolverhampton and it prompted a campaign to build a memorial in his honour. By the end of July 1917 the Harris memorial fund stood at £120.[338]

Before being placed in the National War Museum, Harris' logbook was loaned by the Admiralty to Alfred Bird, MP for Wolverhampton West, who in turn passed it on to the Town Clerk. Over the Bank Holiday weekend of 4-6 August 1917 the logbook was exhibited to public gaze in a glass case in Wolverhampton Art Gallery, alongside George Phoenix's portrait of *"the young hero."*[339] Visitors queued to file past it as if it were a medieval holy relic, left open at the page on which Harris was writing at the instant of his death. More than one thousand visitors viewed the log book on the Sunday, a further 5,732 on Bank Holiday Monday and, *"correspondingly large numbers of visitors during the remainder of the week."*[340] Then it was deposited at the National War Museum temporary exhibition at Burlington House and, in 1918, a special pass was issued to the Harris family so that they could visit it in private.[341] A few weeks later the winning design for the proposed memorial to Harris was selected by well-known sculptor Albert Toft. From a field of thirteen *"sketch models"* put forward by past and present pupils at the Wolverhampton School of Art, Toft chose the one entered by Robert Jackson Emerson, the second master at the School.[342] The design was for a plinth-mounted bronze bust of Harris, based on the photograph which appeared in the Press and was used by Phoenix to paint the sailor's portrait.[343] The front of the plinth included a rectangular bronze frieze depicting the wireless operator slumped dead over his desk, still wearing his headphones. A model and photograph of the memorial were submitted to the Council Parks and Baths Committee on 31 Dec 1917, with a proposal that it be located *"in a prominent position in the town"* showing the suggested site *"within the open space in Lichfield Street adjacent to the Art Gallery".* The mayor was concerned about the potential cost and stipulated that it had to be erected without entailing any expense upon the Corporation.[344]

In the meantime some limited national recognition of the young sailor's bravery was confirmed when, on 30 August 1917, the Press reported on the awards given to the men involved in the Battle of the Otranto Barrage: *"Ord. Teleg. Douglas Morris Harris, RNVR, ON Z9359 (Bristol) (killed in action) has been mentioned in despatches."* [345] It is interesting to compare the case of Harris with another local sailor, Ordinary Seaman John Henry Carless of Walsall. He was killed in action on

---

[337] Ibid, 21 July 1917
[338] *Birmingham Daily Gazette*, 2 August 1917
[339] *Birmingham Daily Post*, 6 August 1917
[340] *Staffordshire Advertiser*, 11 August 1917
[341] Cornish, P., *Matters of Conflict: Material, Culture, Memory and the First World War*, p.47
[342] *Birmingham Daily Post*, 22 August 1917
[343] *Midland Counties Express*, 2 June 1917
[344] Wolverhamptonswar.wordpress.com
[345] *Western Daily Press*, 30 August 1917

17 November 1917, while serving on HMS *Caledon* during the inconclusive Second Battle of Heligoland Bight. Carless was awarded the Victoria Cross for conspicuous bravery and devotion to duty; *"whilst mortally wounded in the abdomen, he still went on serving the gun at which he was acting as a rammer"*, collapsed, got up again and *"set a very inspiring and memorable example"* to his crewmates before dying.[346] Although both Harris and Carless died in action whilst doing their duty it is hard to avoid the conclusion that one earned a VC because he was loading a gun whereas the other was only mentioned in despatches because he was operating a wireless. Ironically in August 1918 the authorities in Walsall approached Emerson to produce a memorial to Carless VC based on his design for Harris. That memorial now stands in front of Walsall Art Gallery and Museum in Lichfield Street, and was unveiled in February 1920.

The unveiling of the Harris memorial in St. Peter's Gardens took place on the afternoon of Sunday 23 June 1918 and was widely reported in the Press under headlines such as *"Wolverhampton Hero Honoured"*[347] and *"Memorial To Heroic Wireless Operator."*[348] The ceremony was meant to be conducted by Admiral Lord Jellicoe, but he was unavailable and it fell to Harris's former Commander, Rear Admiral Mark Kerr, to lead the commemorations. Lichfield Street was closed to traffic for an hour before the start of proceedings, allowing a crowd of many thousands to assemble in the ornamental gardens in front of St Peter's Collegiate Church. They were joined by hundreds more who *"looked down from every window that happened to command a view of the grounds."*[349] The guard of honour was provided by the 4th Battalion Staffordshire Volunteer Regiment and the music by the Police Band. The Mayor, Councillor J.F. Myatt, told the crowd that they had *"assembled to consummate the wishes of the townspeople who had subscribed in honour of this national hero."*[350] He hoped the Harris memorial would encourage the townsfolk to support his plans for a permanent memorial, namely a memorial hall: *"bearing the names of those who had served in the war."*[351] The bronze bust and granite plinth, which until that point been covered by a huge Union Jack, was now unveiled by Rear Admiral Kerr, while the guard of honour presented arms and the Last Post was sounded.[352] In his eulogy Kerr told the crowd that *"These memorials are of great value, and this one shows that Wolverhampton is going to keep alive the memory of duty nobly done, in the hearts and minds of its children and their children's children."*[353]

The Harris memorial has now been in situ for more than a century and still provides a striking reminder of the Great War and the bravery of this young local sailor. The bronze plaque on the rear of the plinth, added by sailors of the Italian

[346] *London Gazette*, 14 May 1918, p.5857
[347] *Birmingham Daily Post*, 24 June 1918
[348] *The Scotsman*, 24 June 1918
[349] *Wolverhampton Express & Star*, 24 June 1918
[350] *Birmingham Daily Post*, 24 June 1918
[351] Ibid, 24 June 1918
[352] *Wolverhampton Express & Star*, 24 June 1918
[353] Ibid, 24 June 1918

navy in May 1919, records their gratitude and admiration – *'con riconoscenza l ammirazione'* - for the nineteen-year-old Wireless Operator. Able Seaman Douglas Morris Henry Harris was buried on 17 May 1917, in Taranto Town Cemetery Extension, Italy. As well as his monument in St. Peter's Gardens, he is also commemorated on the war memorial opposite St. Philip's Church, Penn Fields and the Wolverhampton Roll of Honour. At his alma mater, the Higher Grade School, a Harris Memorial Committee was established that paid £4-15 shillings for a high quality photograph of Douglas Harris on 9 January 1919. The following day it was shown to the pupils and an appeal was launched to raise funds to purchase a frame to mount it in.[354] By Monday 20 January the Committee had raised £2 and a shilling. On Thursday 22 May the memorial portrait was officially unveiled by Councillor Walsh, chairman of Wolverhampton Education Committee, at a ceremony which included *"school songs and band pieces"* as well as an address by the Councillor.[355] Unfortunately, like the memorial plaque to ex-pupils who died in the Great War, the whereabouts of the photograph is not known.

George Phoenix's portrait of Harris was displayed in the August Bank Holiday exhibition, 1917.
Used with the kind permission of Wolverhampton Art Gallery and Museum.

---

[354] Higher Grade School Log Book, 1919, pp.393-397
[355] Ibid, 1919, p.411

Bibliography

Published Sources – Local Newspapers

- Berrow's Worcester Journal
- Birmingham Gazette
- Birmingham Daily Post
- Birmingham Daily Mail
- Dudley Herald
- Evening Despatch
- Kidderminster Shuttle
- Smethwick Telephone
- Staffordshire Advertiser
- Walsall Advertiser (to 1915)
- Walsall Observer and South Staffordshire Chronicle
- Wolverhampton Chronicle and Staffordshire Advertiser
- Wolverhampton Express and Star

Published Sources – Collections of Original Documents

Wolverhampton Archives & Wolverhampton Teachers' Archive Group, *The First World War and Wolverhampton* (Wolverhampton: 1989)

Published Sources – Books and Articles

Anon	*A History of the Wolverhampton and Midland Counties Eye Infirmary* (Wolverhampton: Whitehead Brothers, 1931)
Anon	*Vulcan Manufacturing (Wolverhampton) Limited: Builder's Ironmongery, Boot Grindery, Cycle Accessories etc.: New Griffin Works Wolverhampton* (Wolverhampton: Vulcan Manufacturing, 1955)
Barnsby, George J.	*A History of Wolverhampton, Bilston and District Trades Union Council, 1885-1990* (1994)
Brew, Alec	*The History of Black Country Aviation* (Alan Sutton, 1993)
Brew, Alec	*Wolverhampton Voices* (Tempus, 2004)
Carter, Kathleen (ed)	*Letters from the Trenches* (Brewin Books, 2000)
Cawood, Ian	'Life after Joe: Politics and War in the West Midlands, 1914-1918', *Midland History*, 42 (1) (2007), pp. 92-117
Evans, Roy	*Wolverhampton Warriors* (Bright Pen, 2010)
Fantom, Paul	'Zeppelins over the Black Country: The Midlands' First Blitz', *Midland History*, 39 (2) (2014), pp. 236-54

Jones, Clement *et al*	*Wolverhampton Quakers, 1704-1988: A Brief History of the Religious Society of Friends and their Meeting Houses in Wolverhampton - 1704 to 1988* (Wolverhampton: Clark & Howard, 1989)
Jones, G.W.	*Borough politics: A Study of the Wolverhampton Town Council, 1888-1964* (London: Macmillan, 1969)
Lawrence, Jon	'The Complexities of English Progressivism: Wolverhampton Politics in the Early Twentieth Century', *Midland History*, 24 (1) (1999), pp.147-66
Pearson, Michael	*The Black Country in the Great War* (Pen and Sword, 2014)
Rhodes, Peter	*For A Shilling a Day* (Black Country Society, 2002)
Robinson, Eric (comp)	*Old Wolverhampton, 1860-1914: An Exhibition of Photographs* (Wolverhampton; Wolverhampton Art Gallery, 1972)
Taylor, David	*The Impact of World War One on the Smestow Vale Villages* (Youcaxton, 2017)
Upton, Chris	*A History of Wolverhampton* (Chichester: Phillimore, 1998)
Walters, Jeremy	*My Father's Wolverhampton, 1905-1931* (2015)

Unpublished Sources

Gower, S.J.L.	'The Civilian Experience of World War I: Aspects of Wolverhampton, 1914-1918, Unpublished PhD Thesis, University of Birmingham, 2000

Index